Making Meaning

ACPA Publications

Denise Collins, Indiana State University, Books and Media Editor
Paul Shang, University of Oregon, Developmental Editor

ACPA–College Student Educators International, headquartered in Washington, D.C., at the National Center for Higher Education, is the leading comprehensive student affairs association providing outreach, advocacy, research, and professional development to foster college student learning.

ACPA is committed to publishing materials that are of timely assistance to student affairs practitioners in specific functional areas or topics of concern. ACPA Publications reviews proposals for thought papers, guidance for good practice, handbooks for functional areas, and other guidebooks of demonstrated interest to student affairs practitioners. ACPA Publications welcomes submissions from authors who desire to develop a work to be issued by a national professional association with international interests. Publications are focused subjects that are of immediate and continuing use to the student affairs practitioner.

ACPA continues to be recognized for its leadership in addressing issues and trends in student affairs within higher education. One aspect of our mission is to support and foster college student learning through the generation and dissemination of knowledge, which informs policies, practices, and programs for student affairs professionals and the higher education community through publications. Manuscripts selected for publication are peer-reviewed and professionally edited.

We value feedback regarding this publication and other ACPA products. To find out more, visit www.myacpa.org, e-mail info@acpa.nche.edu, or call 1.202.835.2272.

Making Meaning

Embracing Spirituality, Faith, Religion, and Life Purpose in Student Affairs

Edited by
JENNY L. SMALL

Foreword by
CHRISTOPHER MACDONALD-DENNIS

STERLING, VIRGINIA

COPYRIGHT © 2015 BY ACPA–COLLEGE
STUDENT EDUCATORS INTERNATIONAL

Published by Stylus Publishing, LLC
22883 Quicksilver Drive
Sterling, Virginia 20166-2102

Library of Congress Cataloging-in-Publication Data

Making meaning : embracing spirituality, faith, religion, and life purpose in
student affairs / edited by Jenny L. Small. – First edition.
  pages cm
Includes bibliographical references and index.
ISBN 978-1-62036-276-1 (pbk. : alk. paper)
ISBN 978-1-62036-275-4 (cloth : alk. paper)
ISBN 978-1-62036-277-8 (library networkable e-edition)
ISBN 978-1-62036-278-5 (consumer e-edition)
1. Student affairs services–Moral and ethical aspects–United States.
2. Counseling in higher education--Moral and ethical aspects–
United States. 3. College students–Religious life–United States.
4. Universities and colleges–United States–Religion. I. Small, Jenny
L., editor of compilation.
LB2342.92.M354 2015
378.1'97--dc23

                                                                      2014035699

13-digit ISBN: 978-1-62036-275-4 (cloth)
13-digit ISBN: 978-1-62036-276-1 (paper)
13-digit ISBN: 978-1-62036-277-8 (library networkable e-edition)
13-digit ISBN: 978-1-62036-278-5 (consumer e-edition)

Printed in the United States of America

All first editions printed on acid-free paper
that meets the American National Standards Institute
Z39-48 Standard.

Bulk Purchases

Quantity discounts are available for use in workshops and for staff
development.
Call 1-800-232-0223

First Edition, 2015

10   9   8   7   6   5   4   3   2   1

Contents

Acknowledgments

THIS BOOK WOULD NOT have been written were it not for the contributions and support of a great many people. Most critically, I thank the 11 authors who brought insights, expertise, and creativity to their chapters. Going into this project, I knew I would not be able to answer all the questions I had. I clearly made the right choice in bringing in all of you to teach me what I did not know. Thank you for sharing your wisdom with the field.

Second, I would like to thank Dr. Denise Collins, the team at ACPA Books and Media, and Stylus Publishing for offering to publish our book. It is an honor to contribute to the body of literature you have produced. In particular, I am extremely grateful to Dr. Paul Shang, University of Oregon, who served as associate editor and the critical first reader of the manuscript. Paul raised the quality of our work in so many ways.

As well, I have been inspired and motivated by the scholars, practitioners, and students who demonstrate a commitment to supporting spirituality, faith, religion, and life purpose in higher education student affairs. I am grateful to ACPA for connecting me to so many of you.

On a personal note, I would like to thank my family for graciously allowing me the time I needed to make my vision for this book a reality. This is for you.

Jenny L. Small

Foreword

Faith. Belief. Meaning. Purpose.

These concepts are heady ones that often seem too difficult to handle for many student affairs professionals. We have so many tasks on our plates that it does not seem possible to tackle yet one more area of a student's life. I would argue, though, that we have been doing this work, even if we may not characterize it as such. When residence life professionals have that discussion with the first-year student who was raised in a religious tradition that "does not approve of" homosexuality yet finds herself with a queer roommate, we are talking about faith. The discussions we often have with those students who choose not to drink alcohol are often discussions of morality. Thus, I would argue that we have always been talking about these issues.

I realize, though, that I may be unique. While my mother told me as a child never to talk about religion because it only would turn out ugly, I have always clamored for these discussions. Since I first received my calling to the ministry 30 years ago (one I am only now fulfilling), I have loved talking to others about how we make meaning in the world. In many ways, I have been waiting for this book my entire professional career.

When I graduated from my master's degree program in college student development and counseling 20 years ago, I looked forward to working with students around issues of morality, faith, values, and meaning making. Since this was a major part of my college experience, I knew that students were clamoring to discuss these issues with both fellow students and student affairs professionals alike. I remembered the late nights in my residence hall talking to my floor mates about our religious journey, what we believed about a higher power, and the things that mattered most deeply to us.

Unfortunately, I entered a profession that often seemed loathe to talk about religion. We certainly talked about moral decision making but we never discussed the basis for morality.

From where did students get their morals and values? What were the spiritual traditions that undergirded their meaning making? It seemed that only in the Jewish student organization that I advised could I have this discussion with students and other staff advisors. Others on campus viewed religion as the "third rail" which we should never discuss.

Unfortunately, ACPA, my professional home, did not seem particularly open to discussing these issues. While the Association for Christians in Student Development were allowed to program for their group, the larger association did not necessarily see faith development as part of our work with students. Luckily, ACPA listened to those of us who saw faith and spirituality as a key part of our role on campus and created the Commission for Spirituality, Faith, Religion and Meaning. This group works to ensure that ACPA is a leader and voice on student spirituality and spiritual/faith/existential development in college, community college, and university communities. The commission studies best practices that promote pluralism for religion and belief in college settings. The other area of its focus has to do with research engagement, which includes the creation of the book that you are holding.

While I appreciate the work of the commission, I am particularly excited about this book. Over the years, I began to read more calls for student affairs professionals to take issues of religion and meaning making seriously but did not see one place where I could read the literature in this burgeoning field. I eagerly read many of the books and articles that Jenny Small cites in the introduction. However, I was still searching for a book that presented a good overview of where we have been, where we currently are, and where we are going as a profession around issues of religion, spirituality, and meaning making.

This book is that book.

The emphasis on both students and student affairs professionals is a particular strength of this book. As student affairs professionals, it is our role to support students regarding their faith and religious identity. However, like our students, we are people who have our own faith traditions, spiritual journeys, and ways of making meaning. How can we help our students grapple with these issues if we have not done so ourselves? Sharon Lobdell's chapter on how professional associations have supported student affairs professionals is an important reminder that those who help students also need assistance in thinking through our own faith journeys.

Moreover, the inclusion of nontheistic and secular humanist perspectives demonstrates to me the commission's commitment to inclusion. Although

I identify as a progressive Christian and have written on the experience of religiously liberal Jewish undergraduates, I know that we each seek meaning in many different ways. For me, it may be through Jesus of Nazareth and the Abrahamic God, but for others it may be through science and art.

As I read the book that you hold, I realized that I was witnessing the birth of a movement. *Making Meaning: Embracing Spirituality, Faith, Religion, and Life Purpose in Student Affairs* will rightfully be seen as the springboard for a larger movement and research agenda in student affairs. I can imagine scholars in the future perusing this volume before conducting any research into religion in the lives of college students. This book tells us where we have been, where we currently are, and where we are going as a field of inquiry. If anyone wants to know how this movement began, this is the place to start. In many ways, this book serves as a foundation for the research agenda going forward.

I look forward to seeing the field that arises from this book.

Christopher MacDonald-Dennis
December 2014

1

Introduction

Jenny L. Small

NEARLY 15 YEARS AGO, Patrick Love and Donna Talbot challenged the field of student affairs to fill the "void [that] has existed on campus and in academe related to spirituality and spiritual development" (Love & Talbot, 1999, p. 363). More recently, leaders such as Robert Nash (2001) and Eboo Patel (2007) have stated that religion and secularism are the next great bastion of pluralism work. It is time to consider whether we have responded appropriately to this call. These elements of human diversity are critical throughout the United States as a whole and also within the microcosms of our higher education institutions. Both as contributing members of a society and as leaders of social change, higher education professionals have a responsibility to engage in this discussion.

There are also demands made by the very nature of the student affairs field. At one level, our work is about serving students' total selves (ACPA–College Student Educators International, 2011), and, undoubtedly, the way students make meaning in the world is a critical element of these selves. We must consider the impact of what they value, how they make moral decisions, and from where they derive their inspiration and vocation. We need to hear their crises of faith, spiritual struggles, and questions of life purpose (Parks, 2011). And, of course, we need to be ready to get involved with both interfaith and intrafaith tensions (Small, 2011). As discussions of diversity in terms of race, ethnicity, gender, sexual orientation, and ability have become commonplace, in a sense, similar conversations about diversity in belief (among other forms) have been lagging (Pascarella, 2006). Even just a decade ago, a "paucity of attention to religion and spirituality" (Benson, Roehlkepartain, & Rude, 2003, p. 207) existed within the broader social sciences. They simply have not been a part of the way many of us know and understand our students.

Despite this situation, there are researchers and practitioners who are committed to having this conversation and helping to spread it throughout student affairs. In the past 10 to 15 years there has been a dramatic proliferation in research and best practices surrounding spirituality, faith, religion, and life purpose in the field. Even the basic act of listing out all these terms, instead of using the simpler and shorter expression "spirituality," demonstrates that we now recognize multiple paths students take toward personal meaning making. There has also been a strong trend toward working for religious and secular pluralism on college and university campuses. *Making Meaning: Embracing Spirituality, Faith, Religion, and Life Purpose in Student Affairs* examines this critical and contested element of college student diversity. This book will study the twofold questions of (a) what has enabled this topic to reach a "tipping point" (Gladwell, 2000) in student affairs research and practice, so that it has become an acceptable, even integral, aspect of the field; and (b) how scholars and practitioners can build on this success for the future.

At the broader level, it is necessary to take a step back from this dramatic change to ask ourselves how we have evolved as a field. What does this say about our shared identity? Have we come to value spirituality, faith, religion, and life purpose more than we did 15 years ago? Are we becoming more open, honest, or forthright about what matters to us? According to a 2006 study of more than 40,000 faculty nationwide, 81% consider themselves to be spiritual people, either to some extent or to a great extent (Higher Education Research Institute, 2006, p. 3), yet only 25% scored high on a measure of commitment to fostering students' personal development (p. 6). This mismatch is concerning, both for students and for faculty members' alignment between their own beliefs and practice. A study of 177 student affairs professionals found that "almost 66% of student affairs professionals reported 'consider[ing] yourself a spiritual person,' as an accurate or extremely accurate self-descriptor, and just over half (54.8%) considered the objective to 'integrate spirituality into my life' as very or extremely important" (Kiessling, 2010, p. 3). Yet an additional phenomenological study of 24 student affairs professionals found that "many student affairs professionals have not given serious consideration to the topic [of life purpose]," possibly because "the pace of student affairs work is not conducive to much reflection" (Craft & Hochella, 2010, p. 6).

These studies' findings raise several questions: Have we actually become more comfortable with sharing our innermost beliefs? Is this conversation about spirituality, faith, religion, and life purpose sweeping through higher education, or are we only hearing from the vocal few? Have practitioners been able to surpass the many significant challenges they face when encouraging these types of expression on campus? And what about the expansion of related research? Is this a straightforward case of researchers studying themselves? Or has this trend truly expanded beyond those scholars who want to advocate for their own personal beliefs to those who simply think this is an interesting, important topic? As one prominent scholar recently asked, "So, have we arrived yet, in terms of unraveling the topic of student spirituality?" (Strange, 2012, p. 207).

Undoubtedly, there are many who would respond, no, we have not yet arrived. As Eberhardt (2007) pointed out, questions of how to embrace religious diversity on college campuses can lead to "provocative dilemmas" (p. 1) and "powerful emotions" (p. 2) for the people involved. Some academics have suggested that the whole arena of meaning making is "none of our business" (Astin, Astin, & Lindholm, 2011, p. 6) and not relevant to learning in higher education settings. Others more willing to teach on this topic may struggle with where the boundaries on free speech lie (Eckes, 2012). For practitioners, multiple factors may influence keeping one's distance from religion and spirituality, such as discomfort in discussing such a personal topic, a lack of support from supervisors, or a concern with being perceived as trying to convert students to a certain worldview (Burchell, Lee, & Olson, 2010). Critically, a recent study of professionals involved in the National Association of Campus Activities also revealed that "spirituality is not embraced as a foundational concept of the [student affairs] profession," (Kiessling, 2010, p. 8), at least among members of this particular association.

Students as well may perceive that this issue is far from resolved. For example, some evangelical Christians believe that other students at public universities have "a negative perception of them" (Moran, Lang, & Oliver, 2007, p. 25). This is no small matter, as literature has noted the differential effects of attending public, secular private, or religious private institutions on religious and spiritually related activities and student development (Bowman & Small, 2013; Gonyea & Kuh, 2006). All of these are real, pressing concerns that impact the willingness of scholars and practitioners to address meaning making in higher education as well as their ability to foster positive change.

In order to begin answering our questions and addressing these controversies, we must engage in critical reflection. Reflection is a necessary element of education (Boud & Walker, 1998; Cowan, 1998). As student affairs professionals, reflecting on how student affairs has changed gives us a chance to pause, reassess, and recommit ourselves to that which we value. We can reflect on a particular research/practice area to see how far we have come and how far we still need to go. This model of reflecting on history, in order to provide direction for the future, has already been quite successful in a recent publication about multicultural student services on campus (Stewart, 2011), which reminds us as members of the student affairs field that "as we move toward the future, we must remain mindful of the lessons of the past" (p. 9).

Meaning making will not be the last topic that goes from the fringes of scholarship and practice in student affairs into the mainstream. We might hazard a guess as to the next frontier, but the "what" is potentially less critical than the "how" and "why" of making change. Some of us have already begun working to have our voices heard on a nontraditional topic. As one researcher said, "Scholars interested in religion and education can point towards a path that has not been without struggle but with a hopeful future" (Nelson, 2010, p. 84). Because we have worked to get our questions raised and addressed, we may have relevant advice on how to accomplish this and how to do it intentionally rather than accidentally or in fits and starts. Critical reflection on how we made this all happen can allow us to synthesize the concrete, applicable action steps for doing this again with another topic. This ability to serve as a model is but one purpose for the work the authors engage in with this book.

ONE INDIVIDUAL'S JOURNEY

Why are student affairs professionals engaging in the work of fostering religious and secular pluralism more than ever before on college campuses? Why has the research stream grown into a flood? Are faculty members following the leads of their students, or are professionals the ones opening the doors? Or is it a case of mutually reinforcing interests?

The authors in this book, *Making Meaning*, ask these questions, sometimes answering them in very subjective ways. Spirituality, faith, religion, life purpose: These are deeply personal elements of our identities, and they cannot be fully discussed without acknowledging that they impact the writers in this volume. Therefore, throughout the book, some contributing authors have chosen to share their own personal stories, illustrating at the individual level how our field has evolved over the recent years. This is but one way in which we have become more authentic, allowing for the opportunity to bring our own life stories into the work that we are doing. As well, this openness follows the lead of previous literature on this topic (i.e., Bryant Rockenbach, Walker, & Luzader, 2012).

I will use elements of my own personal journey as a student, scholar, and practitioner as the first example of the evolution I have observed in the field of student affairs. I have truly noticed a parallel evolution in my career and in the field of student affairs: As I have gotten more fully immersed in the work of college student religion and spirituality, the field has also become more involved with it. I like to think that it is a matter of both being in the right place at the right time and also being but one small part of the effort to move the process forward.

I entered the field of student affairs in 1999, with a nontraditional job working with Reform Jewish college students for the Union for Reform Judaism (called, at the time, the Union of American Hebrew Congregations). I worked with students on campuses across North America on skills such as recruitment, leadership, programming, fund-raising, and collaborating with professional staff. In 2000, I began studying for my MA in student personnel administration at Teachers College, Columbia University, while retaining my full-time job. The required course on college student development theory was my first introduction to the theoretical background of working with this population. Disappointing for me personally, however, was the lack of inclusion of minority religious and nonreligious voices in faith development theories, such as Fowler (1981) and Parks (1986). This was through no fault of my professor, because existing theories truly had not examined non-Christian worldviews.

In fall 2003, I enrolled full time at the University of Michigan for my PhD in higher education, ready to explore more deeply the intertwined topics of religious diversity and inclusive theories of student development. With the university having just experienced the Supreme Court cases regarding the consideration of race in admissions (Peterson, 2003), I observed that many of the faculty and students in our department were understandably focused on questions of race in higher education. Still, I had questions about religion and how it factored into students' lives and institutional contexts. I felt like a bit of an outsider. My questions were not usual. My ideas were not exactly mainstream at the University of Michigan.

In terms of my research, I admit that I wanted to see my own religious affiliation (Jewish) better represented. And so I took that desire on as a responsibility to contribute, and I wrote my first paper about the words college students use to talk about spiritual transformation (Small, 2007). I also attended conferences, including one held at the University of Vermont in 2006 (ACPA–College Student Educators International, 2006), possibly the first higher education conference organized at the national level to discuss the topic of religious diversity on the college campus.

Inspired and invigorated, I soon had the opportunity to contribute my own research to the cause of religious diversity. For my dissertation study, I recruited 21 students of varied religious and secular backgrounds and analyzed the ways they spoke about religion and spirituality, in both interfaith and intrafaith settings and through reflection documents and interview sessions with me (Small, 2008). In the end, I found qualitative evidence of four faith frames or "the lenses through which students see the world" (Small, 2009, p. 13). These were the Christian, Jewish, Muslim, and atheist frames, as I came to understand them from the students in my study. I then turned my research into a book (Small, 2011), which describes the frames and the critical influences of religious privilege and marginalization on students' identity development. I concluded my book with the following:

> In addition to simply creating a fuller picture of faith diversity at America's colleges and universities, this book is intended to motivate every type of campus professional to make changes in the environments around them, to make colleges and universities more inclusive and supportive, and to help students grow and relate with one another in positive manners. Indeed, educators have a moral imperative to improve their campus environments in these ways so that all students, regardless of religious affiliation, are justly treated. The relative positions of students' faith groups in American society indicate that we must be diligent in our efforts. The practice of working with college students incorporates the imperative to honor the unique contributions of a myriad of faith perspectives and to dismantle the continued social injustice of Christian privilege on college campuses. (p. 160)

In 2009, ACPA, my professional home, also became the host of the Task Force for Spirituality, Faith, and Religion to discuss these questions. The task force officially transitioned into being the Commission for Spirituality, Faith, Religion, and Meaning (CSFRM) in 2010, taking on all the rights, roles, and responsibilities of an ACPA commission. As well, the process used to determine the name of the CSFRM very specifically included the different terms individuals use to describe their ways of making meaning (an inclusivity I have chosen to mirror in the title of this book). The commission's initial mission was to do the following:

> Provide ACPA members an arena within which to conduct research and assessment, strengthen their professional competencies, and enrich their self-knowledge and professional knowledge about issues related to spirituality, faith, and religion in higher education. In addition, acting within the ACPA governance structure and with the ACPA International Office, [the CSFRM] will assist in positioning ACPA to be an informed voice on spirituality and faith as they relate to student development, the administration of student affairs, and the organization of governance structures within a college, community college, or university setting. (ACPA Task Force for Spirituality Faith and Religion, 2008, p. 1)

In 2012, I became the chair-elect of the CSFRM, to serve from 2013 to 2015 as chair of a group of approximately 160 members that just a few years before did not exist. I describe my personal history not for biographical purposes but as a way of showing one path into and through this work. I arrived as someone who felt sometimes like an outsider, using that feeling as motivation. I still hold on to that, even as I gain the perspective of an insider through my involvement in leadership at ACPA. The other personal anecdotes shared by contributing authors describe different paths, which taken together demonstrate a convergence. I believe there has been a certain synergy between the demands and needs of students, the research interests of scholars, and the eagerness of practitioners and members of professional associations to do the relevant work on their campuses.

ORGANIZATION OF THE BOOK

Part history of the field, part prognostication for the future, the authors in *Making Meaning* discuss how student affairs has reached this critical juncture in its relationship with religious and secular diversity and why it is poised to create lasting change on college campuses in the future. The retrospective chapters of the book tackle certain questions, namely, what were the driving forces that brought the field of student affairs to this point, and what are the fundamental transformations that have occurred throughout higher education because of these forces? How did we go about fostering change, and how has this change impacted people and institutions at a broader level?

What are the lessons and learning we can take away and apply to that next great phase of higher education's growth? The analytical tools used in these chapters include literature review, research synthesis, and examination of historical documents. Contributors were asked to tackle the *why* and *how* questions of this history, using both available evidence and their own personal reflections, which are based on expertise in the topic and/or prominence in the profession.

Other chapters constitute the forward-looking nature of the book. They cover similar topics, with experts proposing ways in which the field of student affairs can continue to make a positive impact on students' lives. Undoubtedly, there is still much work to do, with individual students to be reached and served, institutional leaders to be convinced, and research discoveries to be made. Many challenges remain, including developing a widespread understanding of the legal considerations applicable to providing guidance, as well as discussion of spiritual development within public institutions. These challenges cannot be ignored in an honest assessment of the field. Similar analytical tools as in the retrospective chapters have been used, but the contributing authors have also opened their imaginations to all that is possible in a future that explores questions of meaning making. In these chapters, as well, the authors address the broad thematic questions about sources of change and lessons learned for student affairs as a whole.

Throughout the chapters, authors refer to a shared set of demographic data about the religious affiliations of college students. Different demographers delimit their statistical analyses in varied ways. For example, the Pew Forum on Religion & Public Life (2012) provides important information comparing the "unaffiliated" with the "affiliated" (p. 33) but does not offer much information about religious minorities. The Higher Education Research Institute (HERI; Higher Education Research Institute, 2005) has provided these nuanced denominational data, but the information is not current. In order to compensate for these issues, I have created a composite demographic profile for recent first-year college students at four-year institutions, utilizing data compiled by HERI and published in the *Chronicle for Higher Education* during the years 2009–2012 ("This Year's Freshmen," 2009, 2010, 2011, 2012). According to this composite, religious affiliations of first-year college students from 2009–2012, in descending order, were Roman Catholic, 26.23%; none, 22.65%; other Christian, 12.65%; Baptist, 10.23%; Church of Christ, 4.95%; Methodist, 4.25%; Lutheran, 3.48%; Jewish, 2.68%; Presbyterian, 2.95%; other religion, 2.85%; Episcopalian, 1.38%; Buddhist, 1.23%; Muslim, 1%; Mormon, 0.8%; Hindu,

0.78%; United Church of Christ/Congregationalist, 0.78%; Eastern Ortho-
dox, 0.68%; Seventh-Day Adventist, 0.38%; Quaker, 0.2%. (Rounding of
numbers may yield a total greater than 100%.) This composite demographic
profile is but one of the many factors that tie together the next eight chapters
of this book, which have been written by a collaborative group of faculty
members, student affairs practitioners, and graduate students.

Part One of this book focuses on the research on spirituality, faith, religion, and life purpose, as well as the evolution of faith development theories.
In Chapter 2, Sam Siner provides an overview of the still-expanding theories
of faith and spiritual development. Research in this area has come very far
since James Fowler (1981) first published his major work *Stages of Faith: The
Psychology of Human Development and the Quest for Meaning*. Fowler's theory
describes a six-stage development of faith over the lifetime, a model that has
been heavily influential since its publication (Streib, 2005). Fowler's work
is not without controversy, as it has been challenged for Christian-centrism
(for example, Slee, 1996; Stamm, 2006; Tisdell, 1999). There is now a much
larger theoretical base with which to work, including theories on Muslim
faith development (Peek, 2005), Jewish faith development (Kushner, 2009;
MacDonald-Dennis, 2006), atheist and other secular worldviews (Nash,
2003), and the influence of faith frames in diverse students' daily lives
(Small, 2011). Papers from diverse perspectives and about diverse students
(such as Siner, 2011) now appear more frequently. Siner tackles these topics
and more in the examination of current faith development research avenues.

In Chapter 3, Vivienne Felix and Nicholas A. Bowman synthesize other
research foci, such as the campus climate for religion/spirituality and the
relationship between religious minority/majority status and various student
outcomes. As theory has evolved, so too have other questions about students' daily lives and the roles played by spirituality, faith, religion, and life
purpose. Felix and Bowman provide a helpful look at this research as well
as a historical perspective on religion at U.S. college campuses. As higher
education has evolved to become more inclusive and supportive of students'
varied religious, spiritual, and secular paths toward making meaning, related
research has expanded significantly.

In Chapter 4, Tricia A. Seifert contemplates the expanding research agendas around spirituality, faith, religion, and life purpose. She describes her
theory of the pendulum, in which American higher education has swung
from its historical foundation in religion to the science-focused, religion-
averse 20th century and now to a fragile middle position, in which religious
and secular diversity are being seriously considered and embraced. Seifert

highlights intertwined strands of influence that have radically altered higher education's relationship to spirituality, faith, religion, and life purpose, including the so-called quarter-life crisis phenomenon (Robbins & Wilner, 2001) and the social and political climate launched by the terrorist attacks of September 11, 2001. She analyzes these trends and then imagines the still-emerging new frontiers of research.

Part Two of *Making Meaning* takes on the role professional associations in advancing the student affairs field's commitment to these topics. In Chapter 5, Dafina-Lazarus Stewart presents the influence and leadership of professional associations, such as ACPA and NASPA–Student Affairs Administrators in Higher Education, in discussions and organization around spirituality, faith, religion, and life purpose. She closely examines how the four official journals of these associations have been instrumental in the ever-expanding research focus on these topics. Professional associations have also led in supporting new professionals, advocating at a national level, and developing professional resources for practitioners in the field, including the extremely critical competencies for fostering religious and secular pluralism on campus (Kocet & Stewart, 2011). Stewart reviews these important field-wide developments.

In Chapter 6, Sharon Lobdell considers the future of spirituality, faith, religion, and life purpose work within professional associations, including the support these groups provide for practitioners as they examine their own religious and secular identities. She looks at the support offered for graduate students, the impact of considering spirituality in the workplace, and partnerships with organizations both on and off campus. The work with associations is so new that there is room for boundless expansion into new programming, resources, networks, and other creative avenues. The work could follow the lead of other interest areas within the associations or try totally new strategies. Lobdell considers the many options available.

In Part Three, contributors discuss the changing nature of practice in higher education. In Chapter 7, Kathleen M. Goodman, Katie Wilson, and Z Nicolazzo describe the programs and services developed by practitioners and faculty members working in this area on their campuses. Theory, related research, and association guidance are all important, but it is at the level of practical application that students truly receive the benefits of our new insights and commitments. Examples of great new work include methods for best serving the needs of atheist students (Goodman & Mueller, 2009), the purposes and best practices for interfaith dialogues (Patel & Meyer, 2011), and the SEARCH community at Bowling Green State University (Strange, 2009). Webinars and guidebooks (Lindholm, Millora, Schwartz, & Spinosa,

2011) now abound. Goodman, Wilson, and Nicolazzo offer an illuminating case study of Miami University, a public institution, and synthesize these developments for an examination of where best practices stand today.

In Chapter 8, Frank Shushok Jr. and Patricia A. Perillo begin with the current context of religious and spiritual life on campus. Sharing the personal narratives of students on their campus, Virginia Tech, they describe the impact of shared tragedy on individuals' identities. They also introduce a three-pronged strategy for colleges and universities to integrate a focus on meaning making. Throughout, Shushok and Perillo take on the task of imagining the future of institutionalizing higher education's support for students' explorations of spirituality, faith, religion, and life purpose.

Finally, I conclude the book with a chapter that bridges the past and the future of student affairs' relationship with spirituality, faith, religion, and life purpose through research, professional associations, and practice. This chapter also synthesizes the discussion from the rest of the volume, reexamining the question of how student affairs has changed as a field through its struggle with, and eventual embrace of, the power of making greater meaning during the college years. Overall, *Making Meaning* provides a comprehensive resource for student affairs scholars and practitioners seeking to understand these topics and apply them in their own research and daily work.

REFERENCES

ACPA–College Student Educators International. (2006). *ACPA conference on religious and spirituality differences*. Retrieved from http://www.myacpa.org/pd/spirituality/

ACPA–College Student Educators International. (2011). *Mission*. Retrieved from http://www2.myacpa.org/about-acpa/mission

ACPA Task Force for Spirituality Faith and Religion. (2008). *Proposal to establish an ACPA Task Force for Spirituality, Faith, and Religion*. Unpublished manuscript.

Astin, A. W., Astin, H. S., & Lindholm, J. A. (2011). *Cultivating the spirit: How college can enhance students' inner lives*. San Francisco: Jossey-Bass.

Benson, P. L., Roehlkepartain, E. C., & Rude, S. P. (2003). Spiritual development in childhood and adolescence: Toward a field of inquiry. *Applied Developmental Science, 7,* 205–213.

Boud, D., & Walker, D. (1998). Promoting reflection in professional courses: The challenge of context. *Studies in Higher Education, 23,* 191–206.

Bowman, N. A., & Small, J. L. (2013). The experiences and spiritual growth of religiously privileged and religiously marginalized college students. In A. Bryant Rockenbach & M. J. Mayhew (Eds.), *Spirituality in college students' lives: Translating research into practice* (pp. 19–34). New York: Routledge.

Bryant Rockenbach, A., Walker, C. R., & Luzader, J. (2012). A phenomenological analysis of college students' spiritual struggles. *Journal of College Student Development, 53,* 55–75.

Burchell, J. A., Lee, J. J., & Olson, S. M. (2010). University student affairs staff and their spiritual discussions with students. *Religion & Education, 37,* 114–128.

Cowan, J. (1998). *On becoming an innovative university teacher.* Buckingham: SRHE and Open University Press.

Craft, C. M., & Hochella, R. (2010). Essential responsibilities of student affairs administrators: Identifying a purpose in life and helping students do the same. *Journal of College and Character, 11*(4). doi:10.2202/1940-1639.1744

Eberhardt, D. (2007). Ethical issues on campus: Respecting religious pluralism. *Journal of College and Character, 8*(3). doi: 10.2202/1940-1639.1172

Eckes, S. (2012). Faculty religious speech in class. *Religion & Education, 39,* 133–146.

Fowler, J. W. (1981). *Stages of faith: The psychology of human development and the quest for meaning.* San Francisco: HarperCollins.

Gladwell, M. (2000). *The tipping point: How little things can make a big difference.* New York: Little, Brown.

Gonyea, R. M., & Kuh, G. D. (2006). *Independent colleges and student engagement: Do religious affiliation and institutional type matter?* Bloomington, IN: Center for Postsecondary Research.

Goodman, K. M., & Mueller, J. A. (2009). Invisible, marginalized, and stigmatized: Understanding and addressing the needs of atheist students. *New Directions for Student Services, 2009*(125), 55–63.

Higher Education Research Institute. (2005). *The spiritual life of college students: A national study of college students' search for meaning and purpose.* Los Angeles: University of California, Higher Education Research Institute.

Higher Education Research Institute. (2006). *Spirituality and the professoriate: A national study of faculty beliefs, attitudes, and behaviors.* Los Angeles: University of California, Los Angeles, Higher Education Research Institute.

Kiessling, M. K. (2010). Spirituality as a component of holistic student development: Perspectives and practices of student affairs professionals. *Journal of College and Character, 11*(3). doi:10.2202/1940-1639.1721

Kocet, M. M., & Stewart, D. L. (2011). The role of student affairs in promoting religious and secular pluralism and interfaith cooperation. *Journal of College and Character, 12*(1). doi:10.2202/1940-7882.1762

Kushner, K. (2009). The journey of identity development for Jewish Millennial college students. *Journal of the Indiana University Student Personnel Association, 2009,* 29–42.

Lindholm, J. A., Millora, M. L., Schwartz, L. M., & Spinosa, H. S. (2011). *A guide-book of promising practices: Facilitating college students' spiritual development.* Los Angeles: Regents of the University of California.

Love, P., & Talbot, D. (1999). Defining spiritual development: A missing considera-tion for student affairs. *NASPA Journal, 37,* 361–376.

MacDonald-Dennis, C. (2006). Understanding anti-Semitism and its impact: A new framework for conceptualizing Jewish identity. *Equity & Excellence in Education, 39,* 267–278.

Moran, C. D., Lang, D. J., & Oliver, J. (2007). Cultural incongruity and social status ambiguity: The experiences of evangelical Christian student leaders at two Midwestern public universities. *Journal of College Student Development, 48,* 23–38.

Nash, R. J. (2001). *Religious pluralism in the academy: Opening the dialogue.* New York: Peter Lang.

Nash, R. J. (2003). Inviting atheists to the table: A modest proposal for higher education. *Religion & Education, 30*(1), 1–23.

Nelson, J. (2010). The evolving place of research on religion in the American Educational Research Association. *Religion & Education, 37,* 60–86.

Parks, S. D. (1986). *The critical years: The young adult search for a faith to live by.* New York: Harper & Row.

Parks, S. D. (2011). *Big questions, worthy dreams: Mentoring emerging adults in their search for meaning, purpose and faith* (Rev. ed.). San Francisco: Jossey-Bass.

Pascarella, E. T. (2006). How college affects students: Ten directions for future research. *Journal of College Student Development, 47,* 508–520.

Patel, E. (2007). Religious diversity and cooperation on campus. *Journal of College and Character, 9*(2). doi:10.2202/1940-1639.1120

Patel, E., & Meyer, C. (2011). The civic relevance of interfaith cooperation for col-leges and universities. *Journal of College and Character, 12*(1). doi:10.2202/1940-1639.1764

Peek, L. (2005). Becoming Muslim: The development of a religious identity. *Sociol-ogy of Religion, 66,* 215–242.

Peterson, J. (2003). U.S. Supreme Court rules on University of Michigan cases. *University of Michigan News Service.* June 23. Retrieved from http://ns.umich .edu/new/releases/20237

Pew Forum on Religion & Public Life. (2012). *"Nones" on the rise: One-in-five adults have no religious affiliation.* Washington, DC: Author.

Robbins, A., & Wilner, A. (2001). *Quarter-life crisis: The unique challenges of life in your twenties.* New York: Putnam.

Siner, S. (2011). A theory of atheist student identity development. *Journal of the Indiana University Student Personnel Association, 2011,* 14–21.

Slee, N. M. (1996). Further on from Fowler: Post-Fowler faith development research. In L. J. Francis, W. K. Kay, & W. S. Campbell (Eds.), *Research in religious education* (pp. 73–96). Leominster, UK: Gracewing.

Small, J. L. (2007). "Do you buy into the whole idea of 'God the Father'?" How college students talk about spiritual transformation. *Religion & Education, 34*(1), 1–27.

Small, J. L. (2008). *College student religious affiliation and spiritual identity: A qualitative study.* Unpublished doctoral dissertation, University of Michigan, Ann Arbor.

Small, J. L. (2009). Interfaith and intra-faith dialogue among religiously diverse college students. *About Campus, 13*(6), 12–18.

Small, J. L. (2011). *Understanding college students' spiritual identities: Different faiths, varied worldviews.* Cresskill, NJ: Hampton Press.

Stamm, L. (2006). The dynamics of spirituality and the religious experience. *Religion & Education, 33*(2), 91–113.

Stewart, D. L. (Ed.). (2011). *Multicultural student services on campus: Building bridges, re-visioning community.* Sterling, VA: Stylus and ACPA–College Student Educators International.

Strange, C. (2009). Creating communities to encourage engagement and spiritual questions: An interview with Carney Strange. *Spirituality in Higher Education Newsletter, 5*(3). Retrieved from http://www.spirituality.ucla.edu/publications/ newsletters/5/strange.php

Strange, C. C. (2012). The study of spirituality: An epilogue. Are we there yet? If so, where? In A. Bryant Rockenbach & M. J. Mayhew (Eds.), *Spirituality in college students' lives: Translating research into practice* (pp. 199–207). New York: Routledge.

Streib, H. (2005). Faith development research revisited: Accounting for diversity in structure, content, and narrativity of faith. *International Journal for the Psychology of Religion, 15,* 99–121.

This year's freshmen at 4-year colleges: A statistical profile. (2009). *Chronicle of Higher Education*. Retrieved from http://chronicle.com/weekly/v55/i21/freshmen_trends.htm

This year's freshmen at 4-year colleges: A statistical profile. (2010). *Chronicle of Higher Education*. Retrieved from http://chronicle.com/article/This-Years-Freshmen-at-4-Year/63672/

This year's freshmen at 4-year colleges: A statistical profile. (2011). *Chronicle of Higher Education*. Retrieved from http://chronicle.com/article/A-Profile-of-This-Years/126067/

This year's freshmen at 4-year colleges: A statistical profile. (2012). *Chronicle of Higher Education*. Retrieved from http://chronicle.com/article/A-Profile-of-Freshmen-at/133637/

Tisdell, E. J. (1999). The spiritual dimension of adult development. *New Directions for Adult and Continuing Education, 1999*(84), 87–95.

Part One

Research and Theories

2

The Evolution of Spiritual and Faith Development Theories

Sam Siner

S PIRITUALITY AND FAITH DEVELOPMENT are topics that pose challenges for dialogue and analysis. Although prominent thinkers going back to Plato and Aristotle have publicly pondered questions of faith, for many of us it is an intensely personal subject, generally limited to discussion in places of worship or the home. However, as professionals and scholars of higher education, we cannot ignore issues of spiritual and faith development. They affect college students in many ways—emotionally, socially, mentally—and at a time when students are undergoing crucial developmental milestones and constructing their own identities. If we value holistic student development, we neglect students' spiritual and faith development at their peril.

Education scholars have begun only in the past few decades to study how people develop their faith over the course of their lives, as both an internal process and one that involves a community of like-minded individuals. When we apply this line of thought to college students, guiding questions include the following: What are faith, spirituality, and religion? Why are they important to study? How do college students develop their faith, spirituality, or religion over time? How might this developmental process differ among the diversity of religious and spiritual paths that college students follow, and what factors have influenced the expansion of faith development theory beyond Fowler's (1981) initial conception?

This chapter begins to answer these questions by examining the progression of major theories of spiritual and faith development over the past three decades. I start with Fowler, whose studies of faith and spirituality still profoundly influence the current body of work on the topic. I move to Parks (1986, 2000), who extended Fowler's work to college students and introduced the concepts of emerging adulthood and mentoring communities. I then examine the contemporary scholarship devoted to giving a voice to students who identify with many diverse faiths, including those who lack privilege in modern-day American society. To illustrate a process of spiritual identity development, I will incorporate my own story as a young adult man navigating my way through my Jewish identity and through the field of student affairs. Finally, I take a step forward, reflecting on next steps for the field. Throughout the chapter, I also address the question of why significant changes have occurred in the direction of research on spiritual and faith development.

First, it is important to distinguish among the concepts of faith, spirituality, and religion. There is no consensus on what these terms mean, and many scholars have struggled with this distinction (Love & Talbot, 1999; Tolliver & Tisdell, 2006). *Faith* refers to a process of making meaning (Fowler, 1981), which may comprise a trust in some truth, a "dynamic, composing, multi-faceted activity" (Parks, 1986, p. 26). Spirituality and religion, by contrast, involve a belief in something larger than the self. *Spirituality* refers to the beliefs in something sacred, and *religion* refers to the actions surrounding those beliefs (Small, 2011). Spiritual growth, as a developmental process, happens as students "explore who they are and what they do as true expressions of spirit, values, and commitment" (Hindman, 2002, p. 174).

FOWLER'S UNIVERSAL THEORY OF FAITH DEVELOPMENT

In 1981, James Fowler, a Christian minister and professor of theology, published his groundbreaking book, *Stages of Faith: The Psychology of Human Development and the Quest for Meaning*. His father was a Methodist minister, and his mother came from a Quaker tradition (Fowler, 2004). He grew up with a deep sense of connection to a Christian God and earned his doctorate in theology at Harvard University. While at Harvard during the civil rights movement, he wanted to find a way to "honor the dynamics of doubt" (Fowler, 2004, p. 409) and describe faith in a practical way.

Fowler (1981) began by reflecting on the nature of faith. Rather than trying to rigidly define this complex term, he drew on philosophy to attempt to illustrate it. Fowler said that *faith* is "the ways we go about making and maintaining meaning in life" (p. xii). He described faith as our experiences of emotions such as love, fear, and hope, as well as "a search for an overarching, integrating and grounding trust in a center of value and power sufficiently worthy to give our lives unity and meaning" (p. 5), whether that power is religious or not.

Fowler (1981) then posited that faith is a universal human trait, and as such, its development over time can be studied just like any other human trait. He was influenced by Piaget and Kohlberg, important theorists who believed that development is an interaction between people and their environment, that people develop new ways of knowing and new behaviors over the life span, and that later stages of development are more "adequate" than earlier stages (Fowler, 1981, p. 101). However, unlike Piaget and Kohlberg, Fowler (1981) determined that faith development must take both emotions and imagination into account.

In addition, Erikson's stages of psychosocial development played a significant role in Fowler's thinking. Erikson postulated a set of age-based stages throughout the life span, each one with a crisis that a person must overcome in order to live a more mature life. Fowler (1981) employed a similar approach to his work, proposing that people undergo a set of "structural stages" (p. 108). In each of these stages, people's faiths develop as they make meaning of the underlying changes happening throughout the life span (developing identity, intimacy, and so forth).

Stages of Faith

Fowler (1981) carried out his own structured interviews and identified a set of structural stages of faith development that correspond with eras of the life span. Similar to the work of Erikson, each stage has an emergent strength that results from successful navigation of a crisis as well as a deficiency that can result from failure to adapt to the crisis. The first stage post-infancy, *Intuitive-Projective Faith*, happens during childhood, where the child learns imagination and images (or, negatively speaking, becomes preoccupied with terror and taboos). The second stage, *Mythic-Literal Faith*, occurs during the school years, where young students learn about their communities' stories and beliefs. The third stage, *Synthetic-Conventional Faith*, arises during adolescence. During this phase, a person will have an *ideology*, or a "clustering of values and beliefs" (p. 173), that has not been critically examined. If this goes unchecked, a person may become too reliant on others' value systems.

As adolescents become young adults, they may move into the fourth stage, *Individuative-Reflective Faith*, where young adults differentiate their conceptions of faith from those of other people. The fifth stage, *Conjunctive Faith*, may happen during midlife or later, if at all. It refers to a process of maintaining one's own faith while recognizing its inherent relativity among many conceptions of faith. Finally, the *Universalizing Faith* stage is an idealized state of embracing love and justice, beyond the scope of one particular faith. Inspirational figures such as Martin Luther King Jr. and Mother Teresa would fit into this category.

Criticism and Application

Fowler's theory of faith development has been tremendously influential for scholars and practitioners alike, but several criticisms have been leveled at it (Slee, 1996; Streib, 2003). One criticism is that Fowler's stages are too prescriptive and normative, implying that a later stage is objectively better than an earlier stage (Stamm, 2006). This may reflect a value judgment of what level of faith complexity is "better," which is a potentially unwise judgment to make (Courtenay, 1994). Another is the tension between universality and pluralism—in other words, whether Fowler's theory can really claim to hold true for all people while still accounting for religious diversity outside a Judeo-Christian perspective (Tisdell, 1999). Snarey (1991) found evidence for universality among several different religions, but overall the evidence is mixed. As students attending college have become even more incredibly diverse in their religious identities (Higher Education Research Institute [HERI], 2005), it has become more important for faith and spiritual development theories to represent as many students as possible. Toward this goal, newer research has studied various non-Christian religions in more depth, which will be explored later in this chapter.

Slee (1996) summarized other criticisms against Fowler's work. One such criticism is that his theory is biased toward a "Western, white, liberal, and masculinist world-view, and to the disadvantage of any who stand outside this experience" (Slee, 1996, p. 92). Other scholars have explored Fowler's framework with respect to gender, finding that a faith development theory should take into account a much more relational perspective in order to fully represent women (Devor, 1989). Further studies found a high correlation between faith stage and socioeconomic status, implying that Fowler's theory may be biased toward individuals of a higher status (Slee, 1996).

However, despite these criticisms, Fowler's (1981) theory remains highly influential, and it can be helpful when working with college students on issues of faith. As the first two stages of this model of development occur in childhood, presumably most college students would find themselves around the third or fourth stage. When working with students who seem to have a strong sense of faith but have not reflected on it, practitioners can help them reflect on what their faith means to them, especially as they encounter other students with differing faith perspectives. Alternatively, students may be deeply conflicted between the faith they grew up with and their experiences in college. Perhaps they are even considering adopting a completely different belief system. Practitioners can help these students to understand that this is a normal process and support them in their efforts toward greater self-understanding.

PARKS: MENTORING STUDENTS THROUGH THEIR FAITH JOURNEYS

A fuller understanding of faith development as it relates to college students must include the writings of Sharon Daloz Parks (1986, 2000). While serving in various roles, including student affairs administrator, professor, religious chaplain, and scholar, she talked with many students and observed how they went about the process of making meaning in their lives. She drew on Fowler's theory of faith development, as well as foundational developmental theories by Piaget, Erikson, Perry, Gilligan, and others, but she noticed that these theories were missing an important aspect of what college students were experiencing. These theories had made young adulthood seem like a transitional phase, rather than an ongoing and critically important developmental stage. In 1986, Parks published a pivotal book, *The Critical Years: The Young Adult Search for a Faith to Live By*, outlining her new theory of how college students make meaning of their lives. She then updated her theory in 2000 in her book *Big Questions, Worthy Dreams: Mentoring Young Adults in Their Search for Meaning, Purpose, and Faith*.

Parks (2000) described faith as a canopy, or "the deep ground, the loom on which the rest of the particular threads of life's tapestry find their place" (p. 34). Rather than finding meaning merely in one part of life, such as a career, a relationship, or a religious text, Parks suggested that a monumental task of emerging adulthood is coming to terms with what consistently and dependably unites all the disparate parts of one's life. This task, in essence, involves learning how to feel at home in a complicated and sometimes alienating world.

Parks's Stages of Emerging Adult Faith Development

Successfully accomplishing this daunting task, Parks (2000) suggested, takes multiple developmental stages and a certain type of nurturing environment. Parks proposed a four-stage model of emerging adult faith development, with a distinct form of knowing, form of dependence, and form of community associated with each stage. The first stage is *Adolescent/Conventional*. During this stage, a person makes meaning by relying on an authority figure, such as a parent, teacher, or religious doctrine. A person in this stage tends to think in dualistic terms and to be dependent on external authority figures for meaning making. The second and third stages generally represent the progression that people go through during the college years and beyond. The second stage, *Emerging Adult*, consists of probing commitment, where people realize that meaning is relative and start to tentatively assert their own voices. This is a process called fragile inner-dependence, or increasing dependence on one's own voice. The third stage, *Tested Adult*, occurs when people have lived through various experiences with probing commitment and have developed strong faith and trust in their ways of seeing the world. This is called confident inner-dependence. Some college students approach this stage, although they may cycle back through to the Emerging Adult stage as they prepare to leave college and face a completely new set of challenges. Finally, the last stage, *Mature Adult*, represents another level of confidence that typically does not happen until middle age or later.

Mentoring Communities

Parks (2000) also recognized that this process does not happen in a vacuum but involves interplay between a person's need for autonomy and need for belonging. Therefore, each stage also is associated with a type of community that a person would seek out. In the Adolescent/Conventional stage, a person seeks out a conventional community, in which members conform to norms without examining them. This can include high school cliques, rigid ethnic or religious groups, or groups with inflexible gender roles. The Emerging Adult stage, by contrast, is marked by mentoring communities. As people realize there are a lot of different directions that life can take, they may look for a community of mentors to help provide confidence and perspective during the process of finding their own voices. At a university, these communities can include student organizations, living–learning communities, involvement with faculty, and so on (Love, 2001). However, as people move into the Tested Adult stage, they look for a self-selected group of people who match their newly cemented core values. Finally, Mature Adults will be open to other people in a much more organic way, while holding on to their beliefs.

Imagination and mentoring are at the core of Parks's theory. Mentoring is the mechanism that carries people to new levels of meaning making, and imagination is the catalyst for this process. Applying this theory to our work as student affairs professionals and faculty, we can create communities that foster mentorship and imagination to help our students enrich the way they make meaning in their lives. First, we need to create mentoring communities on campus, such as living–learning communities, community service organizations, or religious groups (Hartley, 2004). Our communities also need to stimulate students to ask "big-enough questions" such as "Who am I?" and "Who do I want to become?" (Parks, 2000, p. 177). We can do this through conversations with students, with meaningful programming, and by cultivating an educational and philosophical culture on our campuses.

Communities also need to expose students to people unlike themselves in order to disrupt assumptions and lead to critical thinking and reflection. This is one reason why diversity and social justice programs are so important; ideally, they encourage dialogue and commitment to the common good, which can assist students with weaving an ever-widening canopy of meaning, as well as with figuring out their own identities with respect to faith and spirituality (Hartley, 2004). Student affairs professionals can take other steps to promote faith development and making meaning, such as encouraging students to journal, incorporating conversations about faith and spirituality into staff training, affirming students' extracurricular activities as they relate to their spiritual journeys, and focusing on the role of community standards in campus judicial systems (Love, 2001). In addition, faculty in the classroom can create an environment that inspires students to explore many forms of knowledge: cognitive, affective, relational, spiritual, and cultural (Tolliver & Tisdell, 2006).

MY PERSONAL JOURNEY

A personal anecdote may serve to illustrate the benefits of diverse, intellectually stimulating mentoring communities for student meaning making. During my undergraduate years at the University of Illinois at Urbana-Champaign, I was fortunate to find a dynamic mentoring community, Unit One Living–Learning Community. Unit One, housed in Allen Hall, had an artistically, socially, and intellectually stimulating culture. We had dozens of academic courses offered in the hall, as well as guests-in-residence who stayed in the hall for a week at a time, presenting on topics as diverse as gender and sexuality, peace in the Middle East, open source instrument making, and sustainability. Living and then working as a live-in program advisor in this community, I participated in frequent conversations with peers, faculty, and staff about what life meant, who I was, and where I wanted to go. Just as Parks (1986) described the process of finding one's own voice with the help of a community of supporters, I was able to begin to find my own voice. Because of my experience in Unit One—and more specifically, because of the mentors I found in my friends and supervisors—I decided to serve others and go into student affairs. To this day, I continue to seek out mentors who will continue to support me in developing my inner voice and redefining my commitment to helping others.

In addition, the development of my Jewish identity can serve as an example of a minority faith development journey, which I discuss in the next section. According to Love and Talbot (1999), student affairs professionals must reflect on their own spiritual development before they can help students. I grew up in a Reform Jewish family that was active in the Jewish community in the Chicago area. I attended Jewish camp for many summers, went to synagogue almost every Friday night during middle school, and learned to play guitar so I could lead Jewish music when I was in high school. I grew up in a primarily Christian town, but because I was involved with other Jewish activities, I felt a sense of pride in my Jewish identity.

At the same time, though, I was always aware that this identity made me different from, and sometimes isolated from my peers. While other students were going to social events, I was attending synagogue. While other students were celebrating Christmas with a huge tree, I was celebrating Chanukah with a small menorah. And although I wore a Jewish star necklace and was proud of my identity, I was aware that some potential romantic partners (or their families) might reject me after finding out I was Jewish.

During my freshman year of college at Harvard, I realized that I did not know whether I was identifying as Jewish for myself or for my family. I decided that I needed space to figure that out, and so I skipped High Holiday services for the first time in my life. I did not do anything Jewish for about two years, during which my life and worldview went through a massive upheaval and I decided to transfer to the University of Illinois at Urbana-Champaign. At Illinois, as I made my first group of close Jewish friends, became involved with Hillel, and even got into a long-term relationship with a Jewish woman, I began to challenge internalized stereotypes about myself and other Jews.

As a result, I left college with a new sense of pride in my Jewish identity, this time formulated on my own terms. Since then, I have used my skills in community building and strategic planning to create new dynamic Jewish young adult engagement opportunities in Bloomington, Indiana, and Austin, Texas. I also use my Jewish music skills to enrich my own and other people's spiritual experiences at various synagogues. I still struggle with both internal and external oppression, such as figuring out how to embrace my masculinity as a Jewish man (especially when the stereotype of the emasculated, neurotic Jewish man still exists in American culture) and how to carve out time and space for my Jewish identity in a busy world with many competing demands. But it is a worthwhile struggle.

SPIRITUAL AND FAITH DEVELOPMENT FOR NON-CHRISTIAN COLLEGE STUDENTS

Although Fowler's and Parks's theories provide a meaningful framework to ground an exploration of college student spiritual and faith development, these theories have been criticized for employing a primarily Christian theology based on a limited sample of students (Stamm, 2006; Tisdell, 1999). Indeed, at four-year colleges, nearly 9% of students identify with a non-Christian religion, and 22% of students do not identify with any religion (Small, 2011; see Chapter 1 of this volume for more information on demographics). Together, almost a third of students are not affiliated with the dominant Christian religion in the United States. Because of these diverse student demographics, faith development theory is rapidly diversifying, as well. Scholarship in the field is beginning to examine the unique developmental paths that students of many different belief systems may experience.

Faith Frames

As one recent example of this new, more diverse direction of faith development theory, Small (2011) carried out an interfaith study on the way college students of various belief systems approach meaning making. Small interviewed 21 American college students, affiliating with Christianity, Judaism, Islam, and atheism, and identified a set of perspectives, or faith frames, associated with each belief system.

In all the faith frames studied, students differentiated between religion as an institutional entity and spirituality as a focus on something greater than one specific religious belief. However, there were major differences among the faith frames. The Christian faith frame involved several common understandings among students: a focus on Jesus Christ and the Bible, an emphasis on religion as an institution, a recognition of diverse perspectives within Christianity, and a reluctance to impose Christianity on other religions in the United States.

By contrast, the faith frames of minority religions differed significantly, partly as a result of a lack of religious privilege in the United States. The Jewish faith frame focused on the choices surrounding religious rituals as well as the lack of security that Jews face in the world as a result of their religion. The Muslim faith frame focused on upholding rituals in a secular world and dialoguing with other religions. The atheist faith frame focused on a lack of belief in God and a "deep insecurity over atheists' position in society, which is actualized by conflicted interactions with religious others" (Small, 2011, p. 68).

Understanding these faith frames may help student affairs professionals and faculty approach developmental conversations in a more effective way. Christian students may be focused on the theological aspects of their religion, but are also aware of their privilege in the United States, exploring how to work toward understanding other religious beliefs without compromising their own. Jewish students may struggle with the tension between wanting to make their own choices about ritual practice and feeling that they may be going against the solidarity of the Jewish people as an oppressed group. Muslim students may experience difficulties including figuring out how to balance ritual practice with secular culture as well as perceived pressure to dialogue with other religions in order to cope with oppression. Atheist students may struggle with clarifying what it means not to believe in God in a primarily religious society, experiencing marginalization and feeling resentment as a result.

Recent research has explored the experiences of college students in each of these minority belief systems. I will now expand on some of the current literature relating to faith development within Judaism, Islam, and atheism, recognizing that this review is missing a wide variety of other religions, faiths, and belief systems. This is because there is limited research on the experiences of college students identifying with other religious beliefs. In fact, one of the recommendations proposed is to encourage further research into college students' experiences of other diverse belief systems.

Jewish Students   As an identity, Judaism can be seen as a religion and an ethnicity and possibly even a nation and/or a race (MacDonald-Dennis, 2006). Because of the uniquely ethno-religious nature of Judaism, Jewish student identity development can be viewed in multiple ways: in terms of ethnic identity, racial identity, and social identity. MacDonald-Dennis (2006) proposed a theory of Jewish ethno-religious identity development in five stages, based on the stages of Phinney's model of ethnic identity development. The first stage, *Ethno-religious Awareness*, is when students realize that they are Jewish and that this makes them different from other people. The second stage, *Acceptance/Minimization*, is when students "come into contact with anti-Semitism and begin to believe what they hear" (MacDonald-Dennis, 2006, p. 272). In the third stage, *Awakening to Historic and Political Consciousness to Anti-Semitism*, Jewish students realize that anti-Semitic stereotypes and prejudices are part of a pervasive system of oppression, and they recognize internalized anti-Semitism. The fourth stage, *Rejection of Christian Hegemony*, is when Jewish students begin to challenge others who make privileged statements about Christianity or who put down other religions. The last stage, *Redefinition*, is when students integrate their newly reexamined Jewish identity into their larger senses of self.

When working with Jewish students, educators can take several actions. We can incorporate Judaism into more social justice, antiracist, and diversity programs. Unfortunately, Judaism is rarely discussed in these types of programs, partly because of lack of knowledge and partly because Jews are seen as a privileged, religious, White, assimilated group (Langman, 1999). This can send a message to Jewish students that their perceptions of anti-Semitism and oppression are less true, or less important, than oppression faced by other groups (MacDonald-Dennis, 2006). Blumenfeld and Klein (2009) offered other ways to support Jewish students on campus: Our campuses can offer kosher food, our libraries can stock books and videos on Jewish topics, and our departments can sponsor speakers and events that cater to Jewish interests.

In addition, Kushner (2009) explained that many American Jewish college students see their identities as primarily cultural, leading them to seek out networks of friends in Jewish communities, which helps fulfill their need for belonging. These Jewish communities can serve as mentoring communities, providing a place for students to explore their interests and reflect on their religious and ethnic identities. Therefore, we can encourage students to seek out Jewish organizations (such as Hillel and Chabad) or Jewish fraternities and sororities (such as Alpha Epsilon Pi and Alpha Epsilon Phi) and participate in social experiential education opportunities (such as immersion trips to Israel; see Kushner, 2009). Relating to the identity theory that MacDonald-Dennis (2006) proposed, these steps can help Jewish students embrace their Jewish identity and find ways to reject anti-Semitism.

Muslim Students   Islam is the fastest-growing religion in the United States as well as the soon-to-be second largest American religious group behind Christianity (Ali & Bagheri, 2009). Muslim college students face a unique set of challenges. The most significant challenge is that many students constantly feel that others are judging them in terms of stereotypes such as "Muslim terrorist" or "oppressed Muslim women" (Nasir & Al-Amin, 2006, p. 25), whether they experience acts of overt discrimination or not. This self-consciousness was exacerbated for many Muslim students after September 11, 2001, as fear of Muslims increased in the United States on college campuses. Unfortunately, Muslim students face not only stereotypes and discrimination but also anti-Islamic speech and hate crimes, both inside and outside the classroom (Ali & Bagheri, 2009). Furthermore, Muslim students face institutional challenges, such as a lack of halal food on campus, dining hall schedules that do not align with Ramadan, a campus culture of alcohol consumption that goes against Islamic values, and stigma against female Muslim students who wear a hijab, or veil (Ali & Bagheri, 2009). As a result, many Muslim students find themselves distancing emotionally from a hostile campus environment and suffering from stereotype threat, sometimes leading to poorer academic performance (Nasir & Al-Amin, 2006).

Peek (2005) interviewed 127 Muslim university students and proposed a model of Muslim religious identity development. In the first stage, *Religion as Ascribed Identity*, Muslim students view their religion without critical examination, as a natural extension of how they were raised. Pressure to assimilate into mainstream American culture leads many Muslim students to the second stage, *Religion as Chosen Identity*, where they reflect on the values and beliefs of their upbringing, seek out peer groups as mentoring communities to support them in this process, and decide which aspects of Islam they find meaningful. The third stage, *Religion as Declared Identity*, is when Muslim students more openly and publicly affirm their religious identities. They may choose to proactively teach others about their religion in order to correct public misconceptions about their identity.

As student affairs professionals and faculty, we can support Muslim students in many ways. We can encourage Muslim students to seek out Muslim groups on campus, encourage departments to hire professors who are knowledgeable about Islam, plan events and speakers related to Islam, provide Muslim students with access to physical spaces to pray, provide halal meals in the dining halls, and adjust dining hall schedules during Ramadan to allow students to eat (Nasir & Al-Amin, 2006). Other helpful steps to foster a campus culture that embraces and accepts Islam include putting Islamic religious holidays on the academic calendar, creating more alcohol-free social experiences on campus, assessing the Muslim student experience through surveys and focus groups, creating safe spaces for dialogue, and training professors to speak with respect about Islamic issues in classes (Ali & Bagheri, 2009). Relating to Peek's (2005) theory, these steps may help Muslim students navigate the challenges of a secular society and develop their religious identities with support from others in their communities.

Atheist Students There is even less scholarship on atheist students than there is on Jewish or Muslim students. Atheist students (defined by Goodman and Mueller [2009] and others as the lack of belief in a god or gods) lack both the dominant Christian privilege in the United States and the relative privilege of being associated with any religious group. Therefore, these students face their own distinctive set of challenges. Of college students polled, 21% say they do not believe in God (HERI, 2005), but these students are "invisible, stigmatized, and marginalized" (Goodman & Mueller, 2009, p. 57). In fact, other students refer to them in ways such as "bitter, mean-spirited, Satanic, immoral . . . empty . . . [and] ignorant" (Nash, 2003, p. 6).

Oser and his colleagues (Oser, Reich, & Bucher, 1994) posited a theory of the "religious" development of atheists, drawing a distinction between temporary and worked-through atheists (p. 44). Little research or theory about atheists has occurred since then. In 2011, I aimed to create a theory to describe the experience of one of my best friends, who identifies as atheist but feels that he cannot tell many people for fear of being ostracized. By listening to his struggle, I recognized that atheist students may be members of a marginalized, invisible minority identity group. Based on that conceptualization, I adapted theories by Fassinger (1998) and Small (2011) to create a theory of how atheist students develop their social identities. I proposed that atheist students undergo a process of awareness, exploration, deepening/commitment, and internalization/synthesis (Siner, 2011). Within each of those four stages, there is an individual component, in which students become more aware of their lack of belief in God and reflective of what that means for them. There is also a group component, in which students become aware of and begin to participate in mentoring groups of students who share their beliefs (Siner, 2011). Future scholarship may validate or amend this model.

Nash (2003) issued a declaration for student affairs professionals and faculty to begin to pay attention to the needs of students who share this highly invisible and marginalized identity. According to Nash (2003) and Goodman and Mueller (2009), we can take several steps to create a more supportive environment for atheist students. We can foster a more religiously pluralistic environment, consisting of open and honest dialogue between students of different faiths. This can help break down misconceptions and stereotypes between believers and nonbelievers. To do this, we can do our own work as professionals to learn more about atheism, and we can encourage students to read books and listen to speakers who talk about atheist topics. We can include atheist students in programming and in interfaith efforts and help atheist students to find staff and faculty who share their identity. We can also encourage atheist students to join mentoring communities. If they do not exist on campus, there are online communities that could serve that role too, such as Reddit, which claims to have the world's largest atheist forum (Reddit, 2013). Relating to my theory on social identity development, these steps can help atheist students to deepen their commitment to and pride in their atheist identity in the context of a supportive community.

Furthermore, we need to be careful about the way we approach the topic of spirituality, faith, religion, and life purpose, so as to not further marginalize those in our community who identify as atheist. It is important for us to validate their lived experiences. In 2012, I presented my theory of atheist student identity development at the NASPA–Student Affairs Administrators in Higher Education and ACPA–College Student Educators International national conferences. These presentations sparked engaging and vibrant dialogue about supporting atheist students, faculty, and staff on our campuses. However, several participants stated that they felt uncomfortable or offended by the use of the terms *faith* or *spirituality* in conjunction with atheism. Atheism, they suggested (and as defined by scholars such as Smith, 1979), is a lack of a faith in God, and therefore does not fit well with a traditional faith-oriented framework.

Christian Privilege and Religious Oppression

As previously mentioned, faith development theories have diversified considerably since Fowler and Parks proposed their theories, in large part because colleges have become increasingly diverse in their student populations.

However, in reference to diversity, it is essential to acknowledge the role of religious power and privilege in the United States. In her interviews, Small (2011) found that students perceived three levels of religious privilege in American society:

> At the top of the structure are the Christians, who hold the mainstream world-view in this country. In the middle are the other religious groups, who fit in with a religious society but differ from the dominant ideology. At the bottom are the atheists, who do not concur with the highest value of those religions, God belief, and generally do not participate in organized religious institutions. (p. 112)

Other scholars have discussed this phenomenon, as well, calling it Christian privilege, or the unearned advantages that Christians experience in the United States (Clark, Vargas, Schlosser, & Alimo, 2002). Fairchild (2009) talked about how the Christian faith is normalized while other faiths are marginalized. Schlosser (2003) listed 28 benefits of Christian privilege, including the following:

- I can be sure to hear music on the radio and watch specials on television that celebrate the holidays of my religion.
- I can assume that I will not have to work or go to school on my . . . religious holidays.
- I can be financially successful and not have people attribute that to the greed of my religious group.
- I do not need to educate my children to be aware of religious persecution for their own daily physical and emotional protection (p. 48).

Reflecting back to Fowler and Parks, these theorists carried out their research primarily through a Christian lens, even though they intended to have their theories apply universally (Stamm, 2006; Tisdell, 1999). Fowler was a Christian minister, for example, and Parks (2000) referred to *God* in her work, even though she defined that as something broader than a particular religion's conception. As a result of their particular faith lenses, Fowler's and Parks's theories may not be able to adequately represent the experience of someone of a minority faith. This is why more specific research into various faiths, including students' experiences of religious oppression, continues to be valuable.

For example, Small (2011) noted that with respect to religious oppression, Jewish students may have a difficult time recognizing how marginalization plays out in society, even if they feel it. They may also be reluctant to engage in authentic interfaith dialogue, so as not to damage the perceived standing of their oppressed religion. Muslim students, especially after September 11, 2001, tended to feel marginalization much more strongly, and so they also tended to take action more often, sometimes through political activity or study. Atheist/agnostic students tended to have a strong sense of marginalization, as well, seeing religion as something that negatively affected their lives. Because they may feel shunned by religion as an entity, they may keep even more silent about their true feelings, especially in interfaith settings.

WHAT'S NEXT?

The field of higher education and student affairs is undergoing its own journey with respect to spirituality, faith, religion, and life purpose on college campuses. Student affairs professionals and faculty still lack some basic ways to talk about this topic. For example, the most recent American Psychological Association (2010) *Publication Manual* provides guidelines for writing about identity in terms of race, ethnicity, sexual orientation, disability, and age, but it offers no guidance for religion. However, the state of research on this topic is progressing from infancy—broad, general theories of faith development—to adolescence, where we are beginning to examine a diverse and wide range of student experiences in the realms of spirituality, faith, religion, and life purpose. This is a work in progress, and yet another reason why books such as *Making Meaning* are important in student affairs research.

I suggest a few directions for future research to move developmental theory forward. One such direction is to study how religious identity intersects with race, culture, sexual orientation, and other identities (Stewart & Lozano, 2009). Another direction is to study how students at different types of colleges (public, private secular, private religious, etc.) experience faith identity development (Bowman & Small, 2010). In addition, more research should be performed on the developmental experiences of students of each religious group: religions previously studied, such as Christianity, Judaism, and Islam; religions not previously studied, such as Hinduism, Buddhism, and Baha'i; other worldviews, such as agnosticism; and differences within each religion, such as Reform versus Conservative Jews. It would also be useful to validate and/or amend theories such as my (Siner, 2011) atheist student identity development theory. In addition, further research should study the relationship between students' spiritual and faith identities and student outcomes. Mayrl and Oeur (2009) explored this relationship, finding mixed results on how religiosity affects academic success but also finding that religiosity seems to have a positive effect on students' satisfaction with college as well as a mitigating effect on drinking and drug use. This area of research is ripe for additional inquiry into student outcomes such as sense of belonging, retention, and engagement.

It is clear that issues of spirituality, faith, religion, and life purpose affect students developmentally in many important ways. Students deal with these kinds of developmental challenges on a daily basis, but their journeys are often invisible to others. The next chapter in this book will provide additional perspective, painting a broad picture of the history of religion on college campuses, campus climate toward religion and spirituality, and student outcomes relating to religious identification.

REFERENCES

Ali, S. R., & Bagheri, E. (2009). Practical suggestions to accommodate the needs of Muslim students on campus. *New Directions for Student Services, 2009*(125), 47–54.

American Psychological Association. (2010). *Publication manual of the American Psychological Association* (6th ed.). Washington, DC: Author.

Blumenfeld, W. J., & Klein, J. R. (2009). Working with Jewish undergraduates. *New Directions for Student Services, 2009*(125), 33–38.

Bowman, N. A., & Small, J. L. (2010). Do college students who identify with a privileged religion experience greater spiritual development? Exploring individual and institutional dynamics. *Research in Higher Education, 51,* 595–614.

Clark, C., Vargas, M. B., Schlosser, L., & Alimo, C. (2002). It's not just "secret Santa" in December: Addressing educational and workplace climate issues linked to Christian privilege. *Multicultural Education, 10*(2), 52–57.

Courtenay, B. C. (1994). Are psychological models of adult development still important for the practice of adult education? *Adult Education Quarterly, 44*(3), 145–153.

Devor, N. G. (1989). *Toward a relational voice of faith: Contributions of James Fowler's faith development theory, psychological research on women's development, relational feminist theology, and a qualitative analysis of women ministers' faith descriptions.* Unpublished doctoral dissertation, Boston University, Boston.

Fairchild, E. E. (2009). Christian privilege, history, and trends in U.S. religion. *New Directions for Student Services, 2009*(125), 5–11.

Fassinger, R. E. (1998). Lesbian, gay, and bisexual identity and student development theory. In R. L. Sanlo (Ed.), *Working with lesbian, gay, bisexual, and transgender college students: A handbook for faculty and administrators* (pp. 13–22). Westport, CT: Greenwood Press.

Fowler, J. W. (1981). *Stages of faith: The psychology of human development and the quest for meaning.* San Francisco: HarperCollins.

Fowler, J. W. (2004). Faith development at 30: Naming the challenges of faith in a new millennium. *Religious Education, 99,* 405–421.

Goodman, K. M., & Mueller, J. A. (2009). Invisible, marginalized, and stigmatized: Understanding and addressing the needs of atheist students. *New Directions for Student Services, 2009*(125), 55–63.

Hartley, H. V. (2004). How college affects students' religious faith and practice: A review of research. *College Student Affairs Journal, 23,* 111–129.

Higher Education Research Institute. (2005). *The spiritual life of college students: A national study of college students' search for meaning and purpose.* Los Angeles: University of California, Higher Education Research Institute.

Hindman, D. M. (2002). From splintered lives to whole persons: Facilitating spiritual development in college students. *Religious Education, 97,* 165–182.

Kushner, K. (2009). The journey of identity development for Jewish Millennial college students. *Journal of the Indiana University Student Personnel Association, 2009,* 29–42.

Langman, P. F. (1999). *Jewish issues in multiculturalism: A handbook for educators and clinicians.* Northvale, NJ: Jason Aronson.

Love, P. G. (2001). Spirituality and student development: Theoretical connections. *New Directions for Student Services, 2001*(95), 7–16.

Love, P., & Talbot, D. (1999). Defining spiritual development: A missing consideration for student affairs. *NASPA Journal, 37,* 361–376.

MacDonald-Dennis, C. (2006). Understanding anti-Semitism and its impact: A new framework for conceptualizing Jewish identity. *Equity & Excellence in Education, 39,* 267–278.

Mayrl, D., & Oeur, F. (2009). Religion and higher education: Current knowledge and directions for future research. *Journal for the Scientific Study of Religion, 48,* 260–275.

Nash, R. J. (2003). Inviting atheists to the table: A modest proposal for higher education. *Religion & Education, 30*(1), 1–23.

Nasir, N. S., & Al-Amin, J. (2006). Creating identity-safe spaces on college campuses for Muslim students. *Change, 38*(2), 22–27.

Oser, F. K., Reich, K. H., & Bucher, A. A. (1994). Development of belief and unbelief in childhood and adolescence. In J. Corveleyn & D. Hutsebaut

(Eds.), *Belief and unbelief: Psychological perspectives* (pp. 39–62). Amsterdam: Rodopi.

Parks, S. D. (1986). *The critical years: The young adult search for a faith to live by.* New York: Harper & Row.

Parks, S. D. (2000). *Big questions, worthy dreams: Mentoring young adults in their search for meaning, purpose and faith.* San Francisco: Jossey-Bass.

Peek, L. (2005). Becoming Muslim: The development of a religious identity. *Sociology of Religion, 66,* 215–242.

Reddit. (2013). *R/atheism.* Retrieved from http://www.reddit.com/r/atheism/

Schlosser, L. Z. (2003). Christian privilege: Breaking a sacred taboo. *Journal of Multicultural Counseling and Development, 31,* 44–51.

Siner, S. (2011). A theory of atheist student identity development. *Journal of the Indiana University Student Personnel Association, 2011,* 14–21.

Slee, N. M. (1996). Further on from Fowler: Post-Fowler faith development research. In L. J. Francis, W. K. Kay, & W. S. Campbell (Eds.), *Research in religious education* (pp. 73–96). Leominster, UK: Gracewing.

Small, J. L. (2011). *Understanding college students' spiritual identities: Different faiths, varied worldviews.* Cresskill, NJ: Hampton Press.

Smith, G. H. (1979). *Atheism: The case against God.* Buffalo, NY: Prometheus.

Snarey, J. (1991). Faith development, moral development, and nontheistic Judaism: A construct validity study. In W. M. Kurtines & J. L. Gewirtz (Eds.), *Handbook of moral behavior and development* (Vol. 2: *Research*, pp. 279–305). Hillsdale, NJ: Lawrence Erlbaum.

Stamm, L. (2006). The dynamics of spirituality and the religious experience. In A. W. Chickering, J. C. Dalton, & L. Stamm (Eds.), *Encouraging authenticity & spirituality in higher education* (pp. 37–65). San Francisco: Jossey-Bass.

Stewart, D. L., & Lozano, A. (2009). Difficult dialogues at the intersections of race, culture, and religion. *New Directions for Student Services, 2009*(125), 23–31.

Streib, H. (2003). Faith development research at twenty years. In R. R. Osmer & F. L. Schweitzer (Eds.), *Developing a public faith: New directions in practical theology* (pp. 15–42). Saint Louis, MO: Chalice Press.

Tisdell, E. J. (1999). The spiritual dimension of adult development. *New Directions for Adult and Continuing Education, 1999*(84), 87–95.

Tolliver, D. E., & Tisdell, E. J. (2006). Engaging spirituality in the transformative higher education classroom. *New Directions for Adult and Continuing Education, 2006*(109), 37–47.

3

A Historical and Research Overview of Religious/Worldview Identification in Higher Education

Vivienne Felix and Nicholas A. Bowman

IT MIGHT SEEM ODD that Muslim students would want to attend a Christian-affiliated college or university. In 2010, only 12 undergraduate students at the Catholic-affiliated University of Notre Dame—out of approximately 8,000—identified as Muslim (Mervosh, 2010). However, this choice of enrollment is becoming increasingly common. At the University of Dayton (also a Catholic institution), the number of international students from predominantly Muslim countries has increased sixfold in the past decade (Pérez-Peña, 2012). Although many Muslim students are initially startled by the prevalence of crosses and other Christian imagery, they generally appreciate the overall emphasis on religion and moral behavior (Mervosh, 2010; Pérez-Peña, 2012). Two single-campus studies have examined the experiences of Muslim women who wear a headscarf, or hijab; interestingly, the study that interviewed students at a Christian-affiliated university (Seggie & Sanford, 2010) found a more welcoming campus climate than the one that occurred at a nonsectarian university (Cole & Ahmadi, 2003). These patterns illustrate the complexity of the experiences and challenges that religious minorities may face on college campuses.

This chapter provides an overview of issues pertaining to students' religious/worldview identification at colleges and universities. By "religious/

worldview identification," we are referring to students' self-identification with a particular religious affiliation (e.g., Buddhist, Methodist) or with no religious affiliation at all. In the first section of this chapter, we provide a brief historical overview of religion and religious pluralism in American higher education. Next, we discuss research on the experiences of campus climate for students with different religious/worldview identifications. Finally, we review the literature on the link between religious/worldview identification and various student outcomes, including religiosity, spirituality, college satisfaction, well-being, academic achievement, and retention. We also point out the extent to which the research findings seem consistent with the historical role of religion and attempt to explain the results that seem contrary to expectations.

HISTORICAL CONTEXT OF HIGHER EDUCATION IN THE UNITED STATES

It would be impossible to understand the role of religion in higher education without first acknowledging its historical context. Although the United States is a relatively young country, the tradition of postsecondary education has deep roots. America's colleges and universities developed prior to the implementation of an organized system of schools and even before the idea of mandatory school attendance had gained a foothold in everyday conversation (Tozer, Senese & Violas, 2009) and legal practice (Hutt, 2012). Through the 19th century, the movement from voluntary to mandatory schooling gained momentum. Twenty-five states opted to enact compulsory attendance laws during 1870–1890 (Hutt, 2012). Although attitudes about schools reflected a shift in societal views on the role of parents in their children's education, the evolution of American higher education reflected society's changing attitudes on the purpose of education and its intended audience.

Most people would agree that higher education in the United States has a culture of its own. Given its history, a significant part of that culture is religion. To understand how religion became so intertwined with the culture of the academy, it is important to consider the way in which America's colleges and universities were founded. A distinctly European mind-set was transplanted to the United States. It viewed learning, particularly higher education, as an extended experience of privilege. England, Scotland, France, and Germany were the primary countries of influence (Levine & Nidiffer,

1997). According to Turner (2003), Germany provided higher education in the United States with "the characteristic concepts and institutions of graduate education" (p. 71). Specifically, the German educational model drew a distinction between preparatory studies and the type of rigorous study facilitated by a university education (Turner, 2003). This educational model emphasized original research and seminar-based learning (Lucas, 1994). French collegiate instruction focused on the sciences and offered the polytechnic university to the United States (Angulo, 2012). Colonial college founders rejected the autonomy common to British higher education and instead chose to model their educational structures after Scottish education, which favored leadership from an external board over faculty control (Thelin, 2011). According to Thelin (2011), the external board gave "legal definition to the college as an incorporated institution" (p. 11). England left what might be considered to be one of the most significant imprints on the undergraduate experience: the physical campus. The college and university system was fashioned after Queen's College in Oxford and Emmanuel College in Cambridge (Lucas, 1994; Thelin, 2011). Inspired by Oxford and Cambridge, colonial college founders imitated quadrangle architecture. Thelin noted, however, that total transplantation of this physical feature was never realized fully.

The history of American higher education is noteworthy for more than its organization or physical features. Religion—Christianity, in particular—was central to the establishment of colleges and universities. Nine colleges were founded prior to 1770, and each institution asserted some interest in the spiritual development of students. Often called the colonial colleges, the first colleges and universities in the United States were Harvard College, Dartmouth College, the College of William and Mary, Yale College, the University of Pennsylvania, Princeton University, Columbia University, Brown University, and Rutgers College (Thelin, 2011). Spiritual development was typically framed from a Christian perspective, in part because many of the nation's earliest colleges were founded with the support of the Protestant Church (McKinney, 1997). In describing the cultural context of colleges established during the colonial period, Thelin (2011) reported, "The colonies were a Christian world, and more accurately, a Protestant world" (p. 13). For example, Yale was founded by Congregationalists, and masters and scholars of the College of William and Mary were required to pledge their loyalty to the Church of England (Thelin, 2011).

Harvard University, founded in October 1636, was the first institution of higher education to open its doors in the United States; a primary goal espoused in its doctrine was to promote Christianity (Lucas, 1994). One of its founding documents explained the purpose of the institution in this way: "Every one shall consider the main end of his life and studies to know God and Jesus Christ, which is eternal life . . . and therefore to lay Christ in the bottom, as the only foundation of all sound knowledge and learning" (Lucas, 1994, p. 104). Similarly, in a 1945 newspaper interview regarding quotas limiting Jewish student admission, President Hopkins of Dartmouth College declared, "Dartmouth is a Christian college, founded for the Christianization of its students" (Buchsbaum, 1987, p. 82).

For a very long time, higher education in the United States catered to the Christian worldview. Turner (2003) commented that, more often than not, the educational mind-set of the 18th century "did assume, almost subliminally, the unity of knowledge: all truth flowing, as was supposed, from God" (p. 51). Before the mid-19th century, most colleges followed similar curricula, as the valued knowledge bases of the colonial college system included rhetoric and elocution, mathematics, logic, divinity, and natural philosophy. Moral philosophy was often a common capstone course in the institutions present during the Revolution and the Civil War (Turner, 2003). However, after the Civil War, the influence of Christianity in higher education significantly declined as science and technology grew in importance (McKinney, 1997).

CHRISTIAN INFLUENCES IN EDUCATION AND DISCRIMINATION AGAINST JEWISH STUDENTS

Two important facts frame the roots of higher education in the colonial United States. First, religion has underpinned the philosophical and curricular aspirations of American higher education since the system's inception (Thelin, 2011). This was particularly true for the colonial colleges. According to Thelin (2011), "Religion occupied a central but confined place in the colonial colleges. . . . The colonies were a Christian world, and more accurately a Protestant world" (p. 11). Second, higher education was never created in the spirit of inclusion, as access was initially limited, in practice, to upper-class White men (Lucas, 1994; Thelin, 2011).

In its earliest stages, many men admitted to colleges and universities in the United States were interested in joining the clergy (Thelin, 2011). Before 1700, nearly half of all Harvard College (now Harvard University) graduates were employed in ministry work (McKinney, 1997). This commitment to the work of the clergy may have contributed, in tandem with the high expenses of an 18th century university education (Lucas, 1994), to low levels of college enrollment overall. Although colonial colleges did not offer programs that culminated in divinity degrees, the colleges did support the idea that the institutions should produce a class of men who were educated, of high character, and able to adhere to largely Protestant Christian values. According to Lucas (1994), the founders of the College of New Jersey (now Princeton University) declared:

> Though our great intention was to erect a seminary for educating ministers of the gospel, yet we hope it will be a means of raising up men that will be useful in other learned professions—ornaments of the state as well as the church. (p. 105)

Overall, alliances between the church and higher education persisted for years, which contributed to the highly gendered and religiously oriented nature of higher education rhetoric. As a result of this focus on the clergy, the curriculum emphasized piety and character formation (Lucas, 1994).

The development of higher education in the United States echoes the sociopolitical developments of each era and reflects the overt biases of American society. Embedded in the cultural heritage of colleges and universities were the deeply held prejudices prevalent in society as a whole. Essentially, higher education was used as a tool of societal stratification. Education made it possible to operationalize, through institutions, a system of inclusion and exclusion grounded in biases related to race, ethnicity, class, and religion. Butchart (1988), for example, found that education was deeply influenced by society in his exploration of the intersection of racism, politics, and the ability of African Americans to access higher education. To bolster the assertion that history and educational practice always serve a political purpose, Butchart (1988) referenced Horace Mann Bond, a man who "grounded his studies in a firm sense of education's social embeddedness" (p. 341). Bond theorized that education relied on external factors and argued that education was "capable neither of developing autonomy nor of reforming its economic or political contexts" (Butchart, 1988, pp. 341–342).

Resistance to difference is embedded within the history of American higher education, and religion and ethnicity have emerged as especially sensitive topics. In the colonial era, the earliest colleges were founded within a largely Protestant Christian tradition. Many Protestant denominations were upheld as part of the "accepted learned Protestant denominations" (Thelin, 2011, p. 13). Even though there were many Protestant denominations in existence at the time, Thelin (2011) noted, "Religion occupied a central but confined place in the colonial colleges. Although the New World provided some opportunities for religious freedom not found in England or Europe, it does not follow that the colonies were hospitable to religious tolerance" (p. 13). Although attempts were made to encourage religious tolerance across denominations, by the mid-18th century tolerance for interdenominational cooperation had deteriorated. Thelin (2011) found that "this practice broke down when the dominant denomination at a particular college clashed with the varied mix of Methodists, Baptists, and Quakers among students and their parents" (p. 15). Eventually, this led to the establishment of colleges founded by other denominations, a trend that grew significantly in the 19th century. Within the academy, few colleges held a deliberate system of exclusion on the basis of religion, ethnicity, or social class. However, during 1890–1910, high school students often attended institutions "that made sense in terms of proximity, affordability, and homogeneity" (Thelin, 2011, p. 172). In spite of the process of self-selection, the diversity of the academy did slowly shift.

Many Jewish families, for example, immigrated to the United States from 1881–1924 (Turk, 2009). Not coincidentally, changing attitudes toward immigration grew alongside the growing rate of immigration (Thelin, 2011). Jewish people, in particular, faced a unique set of challenges within the postsecondary environment. Brodkin (1998) commented, "Racism in general, and anti-Semitism in particular, flourished in higher education" (p. 30). Prior to 1900, official anti-Semitic admissions policies were rare. However, by the 20th century, negative attitudes toward Jewish students swelled with the growth of the Jewish college student population. Not coincidentally, Jewish students were perceived as a social threat because of their difference in religion from the Christian majority.

It is unquestionable that the Jewish college student experience has been shaped, both directly and indirectly, by the unfolding of American history. Halperin (2001) provided a specific example of the exponential growth of Jewish students in the college environment and the way it intersected with societal attitudes:

> Overt anti-Jewish prejudice in the academic community in the United States reached its zenith when the children of these eastern European Jewish immigrants began to enter college in large numbers. By 1902, for example, 90% of the undergraduates at City College of New York were Jewish. (p. 141)

Pollak (1983) wrote about the population spike, stating that "the American Jewish population had increased by 90 per cent in the ten-year period between 1907 and 1918, from 1,777,185 to 3,390,301" (p. 114). Despite rapid growth, what is even more fascinating is that both Jewish men and women accessed higher education at a time when women were systematically discouraged from the educational environment. Turk (2009) wrote about Amelia D. Alpiner, who was the first Jewish female collegian to be identified based on religion and was a member of the class of 1896 at the University of Illinois at Urbana-Champaign.

Jewish students were routinely disqualified from college enrollment through prejudiced admissions policies (Thelin, 2011; Wechsler, 1977). Exclusionary tactics included requirements to attend chapel services, preferences for children of alumni, class size restrictions, intelligence tests, and detailed application forms that requested photo identification in addition to information about religion, father's name, and father's birthplace (Brodkin, 1998). At Dartmouth College, one admissions officer disclosed that the photo requirement allowed staff to eliminate applicants who "strongly demonstrated Hebrew physiognomy [physical features]" (Freedman, 2000, para. 25). At a 1918 meeting for the Association of New England Deans, a handful of college leaders expressed concern that their institutions "might be overrun by Jews" (Brodkin, 1998, p. 31).

Exclusion through admissions processes was not limited to the undergraduate environment. Jewish students were frequently denied admission to medical schools and law schools, as well (Buchsbaum, 1987; Halperin, 2001). Quotas were implemented to limit the number of Jewish students who could enroll at an institution, and these attitudes were widely supported by college presidents. Abbott Lawrence Lowell, who served as president of Harvard during 1909–1933, said, "[If] every college in the country would take a limited proportion of Jews, I suspect we should go a long way toward eliminating race feeling among the students" (Freedman, 2000, para. 12). From this statement, it can be inferred that his resolution to the challenge of anti-Semitic attitudes was to limit or possibly spread out the very presence of this population. At the Dental School of Emory University, Dean John E. Buhler impeded the academic progress of Jewish students; reports show that approximately 65% of Jewish students enrolled at Emory during his tenure failed or needed to repeat one or more years of course instruction (Mytelka, 2012). Buhler had also implemented an application process that classified prospective students as "Caucasian, Jew, or Other" (Mytelka, 2012, para. 1).

Yet, in spite of prevailing and vocalized sentiments, Thelin (2011) commented, "prior to 1900, official anti-Semitism in admissions was far less than the discrimination a Jewish student would face from fellow students within the campus culture" (p. 173). If and when Jewish students did arrive on America's college campuses, they were often barred from extracurricular activities, such as joining fraternities. Most fraternities were founded at a time when higher education was only an option for upper-class White Protestant men; in the early 20th century, a number of fraternities adopted clauses that expressly required Whiteness and Christianity as membership criteria (James, 2000). In response to this atmosphere of exclusion, Jewish communities, like African Americans, chose to create their own social organizations. When the National Inter-Fraternity Council was created in 1910, Jewish and African American fraternities were not invited to participate. According to James (2000), "From 1945 to 1949, fraternity life became one testing ground for how Blacks, Whites, Protestants, Catholics, and Jews would relate on the postwar campus" (p. 303).

CAMPUS CLIMATE FOR RELIGION AND SPIRITUALITY

In short, U.S. higher education has historically privileged the beliefs and practices of Christian students, particularly in the era we have described (before 1950). These dynamics are quite similar to those that occurred within American society more generally. We presented this overview, in part, to set the scene for understanding religious pluralism in higher education today (Chapter 4 of this book discusses some recent events and dynamics that are quite noteworthy). Given this historical context, it is reasonable to expect that non-Christian students would perceive a more hostile campus religious/worldview climate and fare more poorly on a number of outcomes than Christian students would.

When describing the research findings, we often distinguish among three broad groups: religious majority, religious minority, and religiously unaffiliated students. We define religious minority students as those who identify with either a non-Christian religion (e.g., Islam, Judaism) or a marginalized Christian religion (e.g., Mormonism). Because Mormons and Seventh-Day Adventists are marginalized by other Christian groups (Schlosser, 2003), we feel it is appropriate to classify them as religious minorities (for a more detailed justification, see Bowman & Small, 2010). Religious majority students are those who identify with a mainline or evangelical Protestant denomination or with Catholicism. Religiously unaffiliated students do not identify with any organized religion. The number of Americans who do not identify with a particular religion has increased substantially over the past 20 years; they now compose about 22% of American undergraduates at four-year institutions (see Chapter 1 for more information on demographics) and almost a third of American adults under 30 years old (Pew Forum on Religion & Public Life, 2012). This group is also surprisingly heterogeneous; among young adults who are religiously unaffiliated, about half believe in God, about a third are unsure of their beliefs, and only about a sixth are atheists (Smith & Snell, 2009). We use the term *religious/worldview identification* to be inclusive of these religiously unaffiliated students.

Religious minority students' identities are occasionally made salient to strangers, acquaintances, and friends through their wearing a yarmulke, hijab, or other markers of religious observance. However, religious minority status is often invisible to others unless—or until—it is somehow revealed. Many people are aware of the prejudice, stereotyping, and discrimination that people of color and women face; possessing an invisible stigma or minority social status can also lead to considerable stressors and challenges (Clair, Beatty, & MacLean, 2005; Pachankis, 2007). Many of these concerns are associated with concealing this minority status and deciding whether, when, how, and to whom to disclose that status. The adverse psychological consequences of concealment or disclosure are greater when the stigmatized status is viewed more negatively and when the potential consequences of revealing that status are more severe. As a result, some religious affiliations are riskier to identify with than others are. Within a national sample of American adults, Jews were actually viewed as favorably as mainline Protestants and Catholics, whereas Mormons and Muslims were viewed much more poorly (Putnam & Campbell, 2010). This perception stands in stark contrast to earlier perceptions and treatment of Jews, because Jews in the United States are now broadly viewed as "White folks" who are not from a different ethnic group (Brodkin, 1998). The risk and stress involved with this (non-)self-disclosure is also a function of the environment, as students' acceptance of and interest in religious difference differ considerably across colleges and universities (Mayhew, 2012).

Given these dynamics and the historical legacy of religious prejudice, one might expect that students who identify with minority religions would report the most hostile campus climate for religious and spiritual inclusivity. Some small-scale qualitative studies support this view. For example, Cole and Ahmadi (2003) found that Muslim women who wore the hijab (headscarf) at one nonsectarian university faced considerable discrimination for their religious beliefs and practices, and some students even discontinued this practice as a result. Seggie and Sanford (2010) also found that Muslim female students at a religiously affiliated campus faced misunderstandings and occasional outright prejudice and discrimination. Moreover, in interviews with Christian, Jewish, Muslim, and atheist students at a public university, Small (2011) found that students from all belief systems agreed on the presence of a three-tier status hierarchy in which Christians were at the top, non-Christians were in the middle, and atheists were at the bottom. Others have focused on the practices that contribute to Christian privilege on college campuses, such as the scheduling of the academic year around Christian holidays, the presence of Christian-related symbols and practices (even when these are framed as nondenominational or sectarian), and the difficulty accommodating the religious observances of non-Christian students (Clark, Vargas, Schlosser, & Alimo, 2002; Seifert, 2007). Atheists may also face substantial challenges; for instance, even the recent dialogue about religious and spiritual inclusivity on college campuses can overlook or denigrate the meaning-making systems of these students (Goodman & Mueller, 2009; Nash, 2003). Consistent with this view, atheist students report a more hostile climate for nonreligious acceptance than any other group (Bryant Rockenbach, Mayhew, & Bowman, in press).

Perhaps surprisingly, some religious majority students report encountering substantial difficulties on college campuses as well. Many evangelical Christians feel that the campus culture is inconsistent with—and sometimes directly hostile toward—their beliefs, values, and behaviors (Bryant, 2005; Hulett, 2004; Magolda & Gross, 2009; Moran, Lang, & Oliver, 2007). Specifically, these students have reported that their views are misunderstood and/or stereotyped, instructors and students make derogatory comments about Christianity in classroom settings, the hedonism on college campuses is inconsistent with Christian values, and they are themselves a marginalized minority group. A multi-institutional study showed that religious majority students actually perceive the most negative campus religious/spiritual climate, whereas religiously unaffiliated students perceive the most positive campus climate, and students who identify with minority religions are generally in the middle (Mayhew, Bowman & Bryant Rockenbach, 2014). Furthermore, Protestants and Catholics who are strongly committed to their religions feel that the campus climate is especially hostile, as these students may perceive the largest disparity between their own worldviews and the prevailing norms at nonsectarian institutions.

Given the historical legacy of discrimination toward religious minority students, why do religious majority students feel that the campus environment is now unwelcoming toward them? Multiple factors may have contributed to this dynamic. First, over the last 40–50 years, colleges and universities have become more secular and religiously diverse, so Christianity now plays a less central role on nonsectarian campuses (Waggoner, 2011). This shift has been codified in a number of ways, such as the renaming of "Christmas Break" to "Winter Break." In this example, the renaming serves to diminish the centrality of Christianity (which may upset Christian students), but this break still occurs every year during Christmas (which allows many Christian students, but not other students, to celebrate their primary religious holiday with their families). Colleges and universities have a difficult task in simultaneously attending to the needs and interests of religious majority, religious minority, and religiously unaffiliated students, because actions that are intended to welcome one group run the risk of alienating another group.

Second, people are surprisingly unlikely to think that other groups are encountering a hostile climate, so students from numerous religious/worldview identifications can feel that they are marginalized without recognizing the challenges that others face. For instance, female students have long dealt with a hostile campus climate, particularly in sciences, technology, engineering, and mathematics fields (e.g., Hill, Corbett, & St. Rose, 2010), so one might assume that they would be more sensitive to campus climate issues for other marginalized groups. However, women and men do not differ systematically in their perceptions of campus racial climate, regardless of whether they are asked about the current climate on their campuses (Hurtado, 1994; Locks, Hurtado, Bowman, & Oseguera, 2008; Mayhew, Grunwald & Dey, 2005) or they are provided hypothetical scenarios and asked whether discrimination may have played a role (Suarez-Balcazar, Orellana-Damacela, Portillo, Rowan, & Andrews-Guillen, 2003).

Third, students from majority groups are often defensive or resistant when their privilege is discussed and challenged (e.g., Blumenfeld & Jaekel, 2012; E. L. Brown, 2004; Vaccaro, 2010), so Christian students may perceive explicit efforts to decentralize Christian perspectives and include non-Christian perspectives as promoting a hostile environment. Moreover, many institutions' commitment to objectivity and the scientific method could be framed as inherently at odds with religious perspectives. Within a large national undergraduate sample, Scheitle (2011) found that more than two-thirds of students did not perceive conflict between religion and science; instead, they viewed these two domains as collaborative or independent of each other. However, these perspectives varied considerably across groups: Students who identified as Protestant and as religiously committed were particularly likely to perceive a conflict in which they are "on the side of religion" (Scheitle, 2011, p. 177).

RELIGIOUS/WORLDVIEW IDENTIFICATION AND COLLEGE STUDENT OUTCOMES

Religious/worldview identification is associated with a variety of outcomes during the college years. Perhaps not surprisingly, religiously unaffiliated students have greater declines in religious commitment and growth, along with greater increases in religious skepticism, than students who identify with a religious organization (Bryant, 2008; Small & Bowman, 2011). Students who identify with minority religions also exhibit greater increases in religious skepticism than do mainline Protestant students (Small & Bowman, 2011). The findings for religious/spiritual struggle are mixed; some studies suggest that religiously unaffiliated and religious minority students experience somewhat greater struggle than religious majority students do (Bryant, 2011; Bryant & Astin, 2008), whereas evidence from other research suggests the opposite pattern (Small & Bowman, 2011). In general, religious majority students are most committed to their religions/worldviews, religiously unaffiliated students are the least committed, and religious minorities are in the middle (Mayhew & Bryant Rockenbach, 2013).

The results for spiritual outcomes overlap with these findings to some extent. Religiously unaffiliated students tend to have greater decreases in spirituality than students who identify with a specific religious group, but students from religious minority and majority groups do not differ in their spiritual growth (Bowman & Small, 2010, 2012; Bryant & Astin, 2008; Bryant, Choi, & Yasuno, 2003). Changes in students' spiritual quests are actually unrelated to religious/worldview identification (Bowman & Small, 2010, 2012). Consistent with that finding, students from various religious and nonreligious backgrounds all ask a variety of spiritual questions (M. S. Brown, 2012; Cherry, DeBerg, & Porterfield, 2001), and students' definitions of spirituality are reasonably consistent regardless of their religious/worldview identifications (Mayhew, 2004; Zabriskie, 2005). In short, although substantial group disparities exist in terms of students' engagement and commitment with their religions/worldviews, the search for meaning and spiritual questioning is prevalent across religious/worldview identifications.

Therefore, research and practice that focus exclusively on religious activities and perspectives may overlook an important domain of spiritual query and growth that is prevalent among nonreligious and religious minority students.

Some additional studies have examined the development of an ecumenical worldview, which describes one's openness to and interest in diverse religious traditions. Religious minority students tend to have greater increases in ecumenical worldview than both religious majority and religiously unaffiliated students do (Bryant Rockenbach & Mayhew, 2013a; Mayhew, 2012). For almost all the research on student outcomes described in this section, the differences in growth serve to accentuate precollege differences (Feldman & Newcomb, 1969). In other words, religious/worldview identification is related to students' entering levels of religiosity, spirituality, and ecumenical worldview (Higher Education Research Institute [HERI], 2005), and these disparities actually increase during the college years.

Religious/worldview identification is also related to many outcomes and experiences that do not directly pertain to religion, spirituality, or faith. For instance, students who are religiously unaffiliated or religiously disengaged tend to have lower college satisfaction (Bowman, Felix, & Ortis, 2014; Bowman & Toms Smedley, 2013; Mooney, 2010), are less satisfied with their lives overall (Smith & Snell, 2009), and have reduced well-being (Bowman & Small, 2012) than other students. Moreover, religious minorities tend to have the greatest increases in psychological distress, whereas Protestants tend to have the most improved physical health during college (Bryant & Astin, 2008). In sum, religious majority students fare better than other students do both psychologically and physically at American colleges and universities, which is consistent with the historical privilege that these students have enjoyed.

Furthermore, religious/worldview identification is sometimes associated with college experiences. Religious minority students engage in more frequent cross-racial interaction than Protestant students do (Park & Bowman, 2014), and Muslims engage in more curricular and cocurricular diversity experiences than Protestants and Jews do (Cole & Ahmadi, 2010; Park, 2012). Given many religious minorities' frequent engagement across religious difference, they may be more willing and interested in interacting across other forms of difference. In contrast, religious/worldview identification is generally unrelated to engaging in challenging experiences outside the classroom (Bryant, 2011) as well as academic and nonacademic experiences (Bowman, Mayhew, & Bryant Rockenbach, 2013).

Finally, some differences in academic outcomes are also evident. For instance, Jews tend to have higher college GPAs than students who identify with other worldviews (Bowman et al., 2014; Mooney, 2010), and Jews also have higher graduation rates than Protestants (Bowman et al., 2014). Such findings are consistent with historical patterns, as discriminatory admissions practices toward Jews were sometimes enacted because administrators at elite universities thought that Jews were too prevalent and successful within the student population (Wechsler, 1977). Furthermore, this finding also illustrates important patterns among different groups of religious minorities (also see Bryant, 2006; Cole & Ahmadi, 2010). At a religiously affiliated university, students whose religious identification matched their institution's affiliation had higher retention rates than did other students (Patten & Rice, 2009), which suggests that religious aspects of student–institution fit may also contribute to adjustment and persistence (see also Morris, Beck, & Mattis, 2007). Religious/worldview identification is rarely considered in higher education research and assessment, so the link between this form of identity and students' engagement, achievement, and retention is noteworthy.

CONCLUSION

Research on college students' religious/worldview identification has benefitted greatly from the availability of large-scale datasets. In particular, the Spirituality in Higher Education project at the HERI at UCLA has provided an exceptional data source that contains a diverse sample of students and institutions (see Astin, Astin, & Lindholm, 2011; Bryant Rockenbach & Mayhew, 2013b). As a result, scholars have offered an improved understanding of whether and how religious/worldview identification is related to the development of religiosity, spirituality, and ecumenical worldview among college students. The large number of colleges and universities in this study has also permitted the examination of institutional attributes associated with student experiences and outcomes as well as how student and institutional characteristics may interact to predict student outcomes. This focus on religion, spirituality, and worldview is important to scholars, higher education practitioners, religious leaders, and others who wish to understand and promote student growth, development, and success.

However, some limitations and gaps in knowledge need to be addressed. Various studies have found that the campus religious/spiritual climate is hostile toward Christians (e.g., Hulett, 2010; Moran et al., 2007), Jews (Small, 2011), Muslims (e.g., Cole & Ahmadi, 2003; Speck, 1997), and atheists (Bryant Rockenbach et al., in press). Some of the findings appear to be directly contradictory; for instance, it is unclear whether faculty are hostile toward Christianity and assume that students are generally non-Christian (Moran et al., 2007) or whether faculty are generally hostile toward non-Christian perspectives (Speck, 1997). Given that much of this research is qualitative and/or uses small samples, it is difficult to know whether the findings from any study might generalize to other students or institutions. Do students from each of these religions/worldviews face similar challenges at all schools? Or do these dynamics vary considerably across campuses? To what extent and how do faculty promote discussion of religiosity and spirituality in the academic environment? Perhaps students who identify with different religions/worldviews experience the same environment in very different ways? Multi-institutional studies that provide a nuanced understanding of campus religious/spiritual climate would be ideal to answer these questions.

In general, research has faced a tension between exploring a specific religious or nonreligious group in detail (as qualitative studies have generally done) versus aggregating students from various religious and/or nonreligious traditions into a single group. For instance, much of the quantitative research cited examined religiously unaffiliated students, but this heterogeneous group consists of atheists, agnostics, and those who believe in God. Moreover, religious minority students may be an even more diverse group that could include dozens or even hundreds of religions and faiths. This grouping is likely the result of both sample size considerations (there often are not enough Seventh-Day Adventists, for example, to examine them as a separate group) and an expectation that religious minority groups will have similar outcomes to one another (given their shared minority status in the past and present). However, is this combination a reasonable practice? To what extent do student experiences and outcomes differ among religious minorities, among religious majorities, and among the religiously unaffiliated? The sort of multi-institutional research project described above could provide an understanding of both the breadth and depth of religious/worldview identifications. In Chapter 4 of this book, Tricia Seifert continues this line of discussion about the future of research on religion and spirituality in higher education.

REFERENCES

Angulo, A. J. (2012). The polytechnic comes to America: How French approaches to science instruction influenced mid-nineteenth century American higher education. *History of Science, 50,* 315–338.

Astin, A. W., Astin, H. S., & Lindholm, J. A. (2011). *Cultivating the spirit: How college can enhance students' inner lives.* San Francisco: Jossey-Bass.

Blumenfeld, W. J., & Jaekel, K. (2012). Exploring levels of Christian privilege awareness among preservice teachers. *Journal of Social Issues, 68,* 128–144.

Bowman, N. A., Felix, V., & Ortis, L. (2014). Religious/worldview identification and college student success. *Religion & Education, 41,* 117–133.

Bowman, N. A., Mayhew, M. J., & Bryant Rockenbach, A. N. (2013, April). *Students' religious affiliation, institutional characteristics, and college experiences.* Paper presented at the annual meeting of the American Educational Research Association, San Francisco.

Bowman, N. A., & Small, J. L. (2010). Do college students who identify with a privileged religion experience greater spiritual development? Exploring individual and institutional dynamics. *Research in Higher Education, 51,* 595–614.

Bowman, N. A., & Small, J. L. (2012). Exploring a hidden form of minority status: College students' religious affiliation and well-being. *Journal of College Student Development, 53,* 491–509.

Bowman, N. A., & Toms Smedley, C. (2013). The forgotten minority: Examining religious affiliation and university satisfaction. *Higher Education, 65,* 745–760.

Brodkin, K. (1998). *How Jews became White folks and what that says about race in America.* New Brunswick, NJ: Rutgers University Press.

Brown, E. L. (2004). What precipitates change in cultural diversity awareness during a multicultural course: The message or the method? *Journal of Teacher Education, 55,* 325–340.

Brown, M. S. (2012). *The nature of spiritual questioning among select undergraduates at a Midwestern university: Constructions, conditions, and consequences.* Unpublished doctoral dissertation, Bowling Green State University, Bowling Green, OH.

Bryant, A. N. (2005). Evangelicals on campus: An exploration of culture, faith, and college life. *Religion & Education, 32*(2), 1–30.

Bryant, A. N. (2006). Exploring religious pluralism in higher education: Non-majority religious perspectives among entering first-year college students. *Religion & Education, 33*(1), 1–25.

Bryant, A. N. (2008). The spiritual struggles of college students: Illuminating a critical developmental phenomenon. *Spirituality and Higher Education Newsletter, 4*(4), 1–8.

Bryant, A. N. (2011). The impact of campus context, college encounters, and religious/spiritual struggle on ecumenical worldview development. *Research in Higher Education, 52,* 441–459.

Bryant, A. N., & Astin, H. S. (2008). The correlates of spiritual struggle during the college years. *Journal of Higher Education, 79,* 1–28.

Bryant, A. N., Choi, J. Y., & Yasuno, M. (2003). Understanding the religious and spiritual dimensions of students' lives in the first year of college. *Journal of College Student Development, 44,* 723–746.

Bryant Rockenbach, A., & Mayhew, M. J. (2013a). How institutional contexts and college experiences shape ecumenical worldview development. In A. Bryant Rockenbach & M. J. Mayhew (Eds.), *Spirituality in college students' lives: Translating research into practice* (pp. 88–104). New York: Routledge.

Bryant Rockenbach, A., & Mayhew, M. J. (Eds.). (2013b). *Spirituality in college students' lives: Translating research into practice.* New York: Routledge.

Bryant Rockenbach, A., Mayhew, M. J., & Bowman, N. A. (in press). Perceptions of the campus climate for non-religious students. *Journal of College Student Development.*

Buchsbaum, T. (1987). A note on Antisemitism in admissions at Dartmouth. *Jewish Social Studies, 49,* 79–84.

Butchart, R. E. (1988). "Outthinking and outflanking the owners of the world": A historiography of the African American struggle for education. *History of Education Quarterly, 28,* 333–366.

Cherry, C., DeBerg, B. A., & Porterfield, A. (2001). *Religion on campus.* Chapel Hill: University of North Carolina Press.

Clair, J. A., Beatty, J. E., & MacLean, T. L. (2005). Out of sight but not out of mind: Managing invisible social identities in the workplace. *Academy of Management Review, 30,* 78–95.

Clark, C., Vargas, M. B., Schlosser, L., & Alimo, C. (2002). It's not just "secret Santa" in December: Addressing educational and workplace climate issues linked to Christian privilege. *Multicultural Education, 10*(2), 52–57.

Cole, D., & Ahmadi, S. (2003). Perspectives and experiences of Muslim women who veil on college campuses. *Journal of College Student Development, 44,* 47–66.

Cole, D., & Ahmadi, S. (2010). Reconsidering campus diversity: An examination of Muslim students' experiences. *Journal of Higher Education, 81,* 121–139.

Feldman, K., & Newcomb, T. (1969). *The impact of college on students.* San Francisco: Jossey-Bass.

Freedman, J. O. (2000). Ghosts of the past: Anti-Semitism at elite colleges. *Chronicle of Higher Education, 47*(14), B7.

Goodman, K. M., & Mueller, J. A. (2009). Invisible, marginalized, and stigmatized: Understanding and addressing the needs of atheist students. *New Directions for Student Services, 2009*(125), 55–63.

Halperin, E. C. (2001). The Jewish problem in U.S. medical education: 1920–1955. *Journal of the History of Medicine and Allied Sciences, 56,* 140–167.

Higher Education Research Institute. (2005). *The spiritual life of college students: A national study of college students' search for meaning and purpose.* Los Angeles: University of California, Higher Education Research Institute.

Hill, C., Corbett, C., & St. Rose, A. (2010). *Why so few? Women in science, technology, engineering, and mathematics.* Washington, DC: American Association of University Women.

Hulett, L. S. (2004). Being religious at Knox College: Attitudes toward religion, Christian expression, and conservative values on campus. *Religion & Education, 31*(2), 41–61.

Hulett, L. S. (2010). Exploring spiritual engagement at secular Knox College. *Religion & Education, 37,* 245–268.

Hurtado, S. (1994). The institutional climate for talented Latino students. *Research in Higher Education, 35,* 21–41.

Hutt, E. L. (2012). Formalism over function: Compulsion, courts, and the rise of educational formalism in America, 1870–1930. *Teachers College Record, 114*(1), 1–27.

James, A. W. (2000). The college social fraternity antidiscrimination debate, 1945–1949. *Historian, 62,* 303–324.

Levine, A., & Nidiffer, J. (1997). Key turning points in the evolving curriculum? In J. G. Gaff, J. L. Ratcliff, & Associates (Eds.), *Handbook of the undergraduate curriculum* (pp. 53–85). San Francisco: Jossey-Bass.

Locks, A. M., Hurtado, S., Bowman, N. A., & Oseguera, L. (2008). Extending notions of campus climate and diversity to students' transition to college. *Review of Higher Education, 31,* 257–285.

Lucas, C. J. (1994). *American higher education: A history.* New York: St. Martin's Press.

Magolda, P., & Gross, K. E. (2009). *It's all about Jesus! Faith as an oppositional subculture.* Sterling, VA: Stylus.

Mayhew, M. J. (2004). Exploring the essence of spirituality: A phenomenological study of eight students with eight different worldviews. *NASPA Journal, 41,* 647–674.

Mayhew, M. J. (2012). A multi-level examination of college and its influence on ecumenical worldview development. *Research in Higher Education, 53,* 282–310.

Mayhew, M. J., Bowman, N. A., & Bryant Rockenbach, A. N. (2014). Silencing whom? Linking campus climates for religious, spiritual, and worldview diversity to student worldviews. *Journal of Higher Education, 85,* 219–245.

Mayhew, M. J., & Bryant Rockenbach, A. N. (2013). Achievement or arrest? The influence of campus religious and spiritual climate on students' worldview commitment. *Research in Higher Education, 54,* 63–84.

Mayhew, M. J., Grunwald, H. E., & Dey, E. L. (2005). Curriculum matters: Creating a positive climate for diversity from the student perspective. *Research in Higher Education, 46,* 389–412.

McKinney, L. J. (1997). *Equipping for service: A historical account of the Bible college movement in North America.* Fayetteville, AR: Accrediting Association of Bible Colleges.

Mervosh, S. (2010, October 5). Muslim students fit into life at Notre Dame. *Notre Dame-Saint Mary's Observer.* Retrieved from http://www.ndsmcobserver.com/news/muslim-students-fit-into-life-at-notre-dame-1.1665041

Mooney, M. (2010). Religion, college grades, and satisfaction among students at elite colleges and universities. *Sociology of Religion, 71,* 197–215.

Moran, C. D., Lang, D. J., & Oliver, J. (2007). Cultural incongruity and social status ambiguity: The experiences of evangelical Christian student leaders at two Midwestern public universities. *Journal of College Student Development, 48,* 23–38.

Morris, J., Beck, R., & Mattis, C. (2007). Examining worldview fit and first-year retention at a private, religiously affiliated institution. *Journal of the First-Year Experience and Students in Transition, 19,* 75–88.

Mytelka, A. (2012, October 6). Emory U. dental school faces up to anti-Semitic past. *Chronicle of Higher Education.* Retrieved from http://chronicle.com/blogs/ticker/jp/emory-u-dental-school-faces-up-to-anti-semitic-past

Nash, R. J. (2003). Inviting atheists to the table: A modest proposal for higher education. *Religion & Education, 30*(1), 1–23.

Pachankis, J. E. (2007). The psychological implications of concealing a stigma: A cognitive-affective-behavioral model. *Psychological Bulletin, 133,* 328–345.

Park, J. J. (2012). When race and religion collide: The effect of religion on interracial friendship during college. *Journal of Diversity in Higher Education, 5,* 8–21.

Park, J. J., & Bowman, N. A. (2014, November). *Race and religion in college: Exploring the relationship between religion and cross-racial interaction.* Paper presented at the annual meeting of the Association for the Study of Higher Education.

Patten, T. A., & Rice, N. D. (2009). Religious minorities and persistence at a systemic religiously-affiliated university. *Christian Higher Education, 8,* 42–53.

Pérez-Peña, R. (2012, September 2). Muslims from abroad are thriving in Catholic colleges. *New York Times.* Retrieved from http://www.nytimes.com/2012/09/03/education/muslims-enroll-at-catholic-colleges-in-growing-numbers.html

Pew Forum on Religion & Public Life. (2012). *"Nones" on the rise: One-in-five adults have no religious affiliation.* Washington, DC: Author.

Pollak, O. B. (1983). Antisemitism, the Harvard Plan, and the roots of reverse discrimination. *Jewish Social Studies, 45,* 113–122.

Putnam, R. D., & Campbell, D. E. (2010). *American grace: How religion divides and unites us.* New York: Simon & Schuster.

Scheitle, C. P. (2011). U.S. college students' perception of religion and science: Conflict, collaboration, or independence? A research note. *Journal for the Scientific Study of Religion, 50,* 175–186.

Schlosser, L. Z. (2003). Christian privilege: Breaking a sacred taboo. *Journal of Multicultural Counseling and Development, 31,* 44–51.

Seggie, F. N., & Sanford, G. (2010). Perceptions of female Muslim students who veil: Campus religious climate. *Race, Ethnicity, and Education, 13,* 59–82.

Seifert, T. (2007). Understanding Christian privilege: Managing the tensions of spiritual plurality. *About Campus, 12*(2), 10–17.

Small, J. L. (2011). *Understanding college students' spiritual identities: Different faiths, varied worldviews.* Cresskill, NJ: Hampton Press.

Small, J. L., & Bowman, N. A. (2011). Religious commitment, skepticism, and struggle among college students: The impact of majority/minority religious affiliation and institutional type. *Journal for the Scientific Study of Religion, 50,* 154–174.

Smith, C., & Snell, P. (2009). *Souls in transition: The religious & spiritual lives of emerging young adults.* New York: Oxford University Press.

Speck, B. W. (1997). Respect for religious differences: The case of Muslim students. *New Directions for Teaching and Learning, 1997*(70), 39–46.

Suarez-Balcazar, Y., Orellana-Damacela, L., Portillo, N., Rowan, J. M., & Andrews-Guillen, C. (2003). Experiences of differential treatment among college students of color. *Journal of Higher Education, 74*(4), 428–444.

Thelin, J. R. (2011). *A history of American higher education* (2nd ed.). Baltimore, MD: Johns Hopkins University Press.

Tozer, S., Senese, G., & Violas, P. (2009). *School and society: Historical and contemporary perspectives* (6th ed.). New York: McGraw-Hill.

Turk, D. B. (2009). College students in the United States. In Jewish Women's Archive, *Jewish women: A comprehensive historical encyclopedia.* Retrieved from http://jwa.org/encyclopedia/article/college-students-in-united-states

Turner, J. (2003). *Language, religion, knowledge: Past and present.* Notre Dame, IN: University of Notre Dame Press.

Vaccaro, A. (2010). What lies beneath seemingly positive campus climate results: Institutional sexism, racism, and male hostility toward equity initiatives and liberal bias. *Equity & Excellence in Education, 43*(2), 202–215.

Waggoner, M. D. (2011). Sacred and secular tensions in contemporary higher education. In M. D. Waggoner (Ed.), *Sacred and secular tensions in contemporary higher education: Connecting parallel universities* (pp. 1–17). New York: Routledge.

Wechsler, H. S. (1977). *The qualified student: A history of selective college admissions in America.* New York: Wiley.

Zabriskie, M. (2005). *College student definitions of religiosity and spirituality.* Unpublished doctoral dissertation, University of Michigan, Ann Arbor.

4

What's So Funny About Peace, Love, and Understanding?

Or, Why Higher Education Is Finally Talking About Faith, Belief, Meaning, and Purpose

Tricia A. Seifert

EW ISSUES IN U.S. higher education have experienced more of a pendulum swing in terms of their focus in the academy than issues related to faith, belief, meaning, and purpose. Vivienne Felix and Nicholas Bowman, in this volume, traced the historical context of higher education in the United States and the decidedly Christian orientation of early American colleges. In this chapter, I consider the pendulum shift higher education administrators and faculty have taken, moving from an educational approach that was originally sectarian in nature to one that was firmly secular. Increasingly, a number of higher education administrators and faculty appear to seek to negotiate the middle ground of providing students with a place to explore their faith and beliefs. I also consider how this influences students' search for meaning, and purpose, in relation to the individual and the collective. From the historical context of a swinging pendulum to the current middle ground, in this chapter I posit that the direction of future research will focus on two domains of inquiry. One domain will emphasize individuals' quests and journeys to articulate and own their sense of meaning and purpose, particularly as individuals' religious, spiritual, and/or worldview identities intersect with other axes of identity. The other domain will examine the collective, describing how people understand different worldviews, faiths, and religions and how institutions create places and spaces to recognize and celebrate the plurality of ways of being in this world. In discussing these two strands, I interweave my personal journey toward understanding faith, belief, meaning, and purpose.

THE PENDULUM SWINGS

Colleges in the United States served a critical purpose at their founding in the 17th century. They educated men to serve in civic roles in their fledgling communities in the New World, not incidentally educating them to meet the religious needs of their fellow colonists. Marsden (1992) commented that higher education "was thought of as a religious enterprise as well as a public service" (p. 10), educating future clergy and fortifying the religious convictions of all students. The culminating course (what might be called a senior capstone today) in moral philosophy reaffirmed Christian truths. Frederick Rudolph (1962/1990), in his influential volume *The American College and University: A History*, quoted a student as describing the course as one that embraced "man in his unity, and God in his sovereignty" (p. 141). Concretizing students' Christian values was a cornerstone of a college education. Throughout the 19th century, although faculty may have disagreed with one another on a number of areas related to the curriculum (perhaps none so vigorously as with the introduction of the elective system), the commitment to the senior moral philosophy capstone course was maintained (Rudolph, 1962/1990). It may be argued that such courses were an entrenched component of the curriculum at this point in postsecondary education's historical evolution. This perspective is perhaps best exemplified by a quote from the president of Trinity College in North Carolina in 1868: "Without religion a college is a curse to society" (Rudolph, 1962/1990, p. 139).

With the introduction of the German university model, the faculty role shifted from one of mentor and tutor to one of researcher and lecturer (Rudolph, 1962/1990; Thelin, 2011). The new university focused on creating and disseminating knowledge, largely supplanting the college's earlier focus of educating students for roles in their communities as clergy or lay civic leaders. Outside those fields of study where ethics, morals, and belief were consonant to the disciplines' discourses (for example, philosophy and the social sciences), the new university model was the educational manifestation of rationalism, privileging intellectual development and displacing much of the emphasis on students' character (mainly religious) development. As Longfield (1992) noted, at this point higher education "would abandon their earlier efforts to serve God and simply pursue a mission of service to the nation" (pp. 65–66).

This is not to say that character development was without champions within U.S. higher education in the early 20th century. Motivated by Dewey's philosophy to attend to the whole person, *The Student Personnel Point of View* guided the emerging field of student personnel workers (student affairs practitioners, in today's language) to "reach his [*sic*] maximum effectiveness through clarification of his purposes . . . and through progression in religious, emotional and social development" (American Council on Education, 1937, p. 4). The 1937 and subsequent 1949 (American Council on Education, 1949) versions of *The Student Personnel Point of View* provided philosophical guidance to the field of professionals who worked in tandem with faculty to create learning environments for holistic student development. Building on the liberal focus of educating students to live an examined life and to know themselves, until the early 1960s it was not uncommon for some student affairs staff to have religious or theological training to facilitate this type of personal exploration (Chickering, Dalton, & Stamm, 2006).

Between the onset of professionalization of the field of student affairs and treading the line between church and state at public institutions, navigating the contours of supporting holistic student development with regard to students' religious, spiritual, and/or worldview development has been a difficult task for student affairs practitioners. At ACPA–College Student Educators International's 2013 International Colloquium, which focused in part on supporting students in their religious, spiritual, and/or worldview development from various international perspectives, Denny Roberts, past president of ACPA, shared his hesitation during the 1970s and 1980s of initiating conversations with students that concerned issues of faith, belief, meaning, and purpose. With the "unspoken rule that separation of church and state limits our ability to see religion/spirituality as part of the holistic development of students" (Talbot & Anderson, 2013, p. 194) firmly entrenched during that time (and arguably to the present day), few higher education administrators and faculty members employed in public institutions formally attended to students' religious, spiritual, and/or worldview development.

College student trend data collected from the Cooperative Institutional Research Program at UCLA provide an empirical perspective of how the increasing secularization of the academy, particularly after the tumult of the

1960s, relates to students' goals for their education. Asking first-year students to rate the importance of various goals, the "Me Generation" (Lasch, 1979) illustrated their interest in the material rewards of postsecondary education. Compared with students from the 1960s, fewer students in the following decades identified developing a meaningful philosophy of life as an important or essential goal of higher education while being very well-off financially and getting a good job gained in importance (Pryor, Hurtado, Saenz, Santos, & Korn, 2007). In stark contrast to the early days when Christian values were central to a college education, the pendulum had swung to the far side, where the intellectualism of the modern research university met the consumerism and commodification of higher education.

Although the focus on extrinsic rewards has fueled students through college in recent decades, such a singular focus has seemed also to power existential uncertainty a few years or a decade after college completion (Baxter Magolda, 2001, 2009), with some calling this period of time the "quarterlife crisis" (Robbins & Wilner, 2001). The quarterlife is most frequently associated with emerging adulthood, the evolution from the teenage years to the early 30s (Robbins, 2004; Robbins & Wilner, 2001; Smith & Snell, 2009), replete with transitions and questions at the center of each transition. These questions are often referred to as the "Big Questions" (Dalton, Eberhardt, Bracken, & Echols, 2006; Parks, 2000) and include asking, "Who am I? What do I believe? What is the good life?" In response to the existential questions and crises of the quarterlife, the last 15 years has seen a reemergence of the concepts of "faith, spirituality, religious commitment, character, and vocation" being considered in the literature on college student development (Trautvetter, 2007, p. 239).

It would be nice to think that higher education administrators and faculty came to recognize their part in students' holistic development, particularly as it pertains to religious, spiritual, and/or worldview development, simply as a manifestation of easing students through their quarterlives. But the events that took place one September morning seem to have pushed higher education administrator and faculty actions in a way that may have been previously unimaginable. In the same way that my parents can tell me where they were when John F. Kennedy was shot, I can say where I was when I first heard about the attacks on September 11, 2001. September 11th forever changed how U.S. postsecondary educators viewed issues related to religion, spirituality, and worldview. The separation between church and state at public postsecondary institutions was exposed as the tragedy heightened the recognition that faith/belief/worldview is (and has always been) an important facet of people's identity. What may have simply been viewed as differences among Protestants, Catholics, and Jews took on new dimensions that included Muslims, Sikhs, Hindus, atheists, and secular humanists among many other faith and worldview communities (Nash, 2001). Consistent with Nash's (2001) assertion that religious pluralism is the defining dimension of the diversity dialogue in the 21st century, it was as if this dimension of pluralism reared its head and refused to be summarily dismissed.

With one's faith/belief/worldview as a central dimension in the discussion of identity, the pendulum has swung back—perhaps to a place in the middle—where administrators and faculty in higher education institutions, sectarian and secular, are beginning to facilitate conversations centered on the search for meaning and purpose as a means to understand students' religious, spiritual, and/or worldview identities (Astin, Astin, & Lindholm, 2011; Braskamp, Trautvetter, & Ward, 2006; Chickering et al., 2006; Connor, 2008; Nash, Bradley, & Chickering, 2008; Nash & Murray, 2010).

In tracing how the pendulum has swung, one might ask, "Why does the higher education community need to care?" In a time of fiscal constraint with persistent cries for postsecondary education to do more with less (Wellman, Desrochers, & Lenihan, 2008) and to educate students for the workforce (Carnevale & Desrochers, 2002), how can higher education administrators and faculty possibly take on another task?

There are a couple of reasons why the higher education community can no longer take a hands-off approach to religious, spiritual, and worldview development as they did for the last quarter of the 20th century. First, many higher education institutions' mission statements claim a commitment to values-based outcomes like character, social responsibility, and citizenship, (Astin et al., 2011) and thus the administrators and faculty at these institutions are accountable to students' development in these areas. Second, the global society faces intransigent geopolitical social environmental problems: war (largely as a response to religious/worldview conflicts), famine, poverty, and climate change, to name but a few. Technical knowledge will be wholly inadequate as a response to these problems as they call for graduates with self-awareness, empathy, and a genuine concern for others (Astin et al., 2011). The age of reason and objective rational science was a charade; one simply cannot separate one's head from one's heart—the cognitive from the affective—and claim anything but an absolution of authenticity (Palmer, 2007). If American higher education administrators and faculty are to realize their institutions' missions of public service to the nation, they must recognize that values-based outcomes are rooted in developing students' hearts as well as their minds. To be sure, this is (and will be) an uncomfortable role for some of our faculty and staff, but it is one that is borne out of necessity in the 21st century.

Bob Dylan (1964/2004) warned, "the times, they are a-changin'," and they have. The American higher education community's emphasis has been on a pendulum, swinging from educating clergy to nearly disavowing any role in facilitating students' contemplation of Big Questions, aside from those asked in the confines of a lecture hall, to large-scale national surveys of students and faculty perceptions of spirituality (see Astin et al., 2011). In the current climate, students' existential uncertainty—their search for meaning and purpose—coupled with the new angle of diversity that religious/spiritual/worldview pluralism has brought to college campuses, makes apparent that higher education administrators and faculty have found themselves faced with seriously addressing the lament sung so poignantly by Elvis Costello, "What's so funny 'bout peace, love and understanding?" (Lowe, 1974). After decades of privileging the intellect, it seems U.S. higher education administrators and faculty are faced with taking seriously issues related to faith, belief, meaning, and purpose. The question is are they up to the task?

As noted in the introduction of this chapter, I believe future research and actions taken by the higher education community aimed at fostering students' religious, spiritual, and worldview development will span across the individual and collective domains. In the following sections, I interweave my personal story as an individual searching for a sense of meaning and purpose and how this search was facilitated by a mentoring community of the collective. I tell my story to exemplify how researchers and the higher education community have operated in these contexts and suggest directions they may consider in the future.

UNDERSTANDING THE INDIVIDUAL WITHIN THE COLLECTIVE

I attended a small religiously affiliated liberal arts college. It was the kind of college that at one time had a clear religious focus but over the years had become more secular. There was a beautiful chapel on campus, and there was a dedicated group of students from various faith communities who hosted a series of religious and ecumenical events. I was not a regular chapel-goer, but I enjoyed the variety of speakers hosted in that space. I recall the commitment of the student group to both meet the spiritual needs of Christian students on campus (it was a Methodist college, after all) and educate students to the beliefs held by other faith traditions. Tibetan monks came to campus, prayed, and created the most beautiful sand mandala as a focal point of meditation. It was the first time I heard of the whirling dervishes, a sect of Sufis.

As much as I enjoyed learning about the beliefs of others, attending chapel was only the beginning of my journey to understand my beliefs, vocation, and purpose in life. I learned these things (and continue to learn them more deeply) in conversation and communion with others. Early in my first year, a group of friends and I would sit up until the wee hours of the morning on the university lawn talking. We talked about hopes, dreams, issues of the day, and what we could do to make the world a better place. They were late-night conversations exploring what we believed and why. What meaning did we hold for our actions?

What was powerful about these conversations was they weren't a free-for-all; there was a recognized and respected structure. Only the person with the talking stick could speak. For that moment in time, with the talking stick in hand, you had the floor. Those who wanted to comment would signal, and when you were done, you passed the stick. I remember this as a place where I could really be heard. There was nothing planned about these conversations. They were simply a place to go, sit, listen to others, think about what others said in light of my own meaning making and understanding, and share my perspective. I remember a few times campus security would come by and ask what we were doing. But as we were sitting in an orderly circle, just talking, they left us alone. In fact, sometimes they stood close enough to listen. It was as if they, too, were interested in being part of this dialogue.

Together, this group of friends and acquaintances was on a collective quest. We were asking Big Questions. We may have been seeking big answers, as well, but my memory was that we were mostly trying out our individual responses to the Big Questions. I don't think I knew then, but I have come to realize that in my first year at college, I was trying to follow the instructions of the Bohemian-Austrian poet and novelist Rainer Maria Rilke (1903) to "live the questions now" (para. 2) so that we may someday "gradually, without even noticing it, live our way into the answer" (para. 2). I can't underscore what a profound experience this was as a first-year college student. It opened the door for me to question and ponder for a lifetime.

Likening a student's faith development to preparing a boat for white water, Dalton and Crosby (2010) suggested that "faith provides the capacity to sustain purpose and meaning in the midst of conflict and change" (p. 1).

Recognizing the great potential for white water in my own life, I was on a quest to build my boat—to secure the keel, to craft the hull. I was trying to establish my own sense of faith. Fowler (1981) defined *faith* as "the ways we go about making and maintaining meaning in life" (p. xii). Similarly Parks (2000) defined *faith* as the "act of composing and being composed by meaning" (p. 20) and indicated that meaning making "is the activity of composing a sense of the connections among things: a sense of pattern, order, form, and significance" (p. 19). In trying to see the relationship between parts of the hull and the keel, I was simply being human. As Parks shared: "To be human is to desire relationship among the disparate elements of existence" (p. 19). So as I went about building my boat, I was engaged in the act of "faithing," which Parks stated is "putting one's heart upon that which one trusts as true" (p. 24). In these many long nights on the lawn talking with friends, I was trying to discern what it was that I could trust as true. How did I know that my keel would withstand the waves? That my hull was secure?

Individual Intersecting Identities

My questioning came from my social position as a White woman from a small rural town, raised in a middle-class family, who attended a Methodist church and was involved in youth worship and community outreach. These various identities intersected as I tried to distill what I believed in, who I was, and how I saw myself in relationship to others. Current research has seized on the notion of intersectionality as a way to understand how students negotiate the fluid saliency of different identity dimensions in developing an authentic self (Jones, Kim, & Skendall, 2012). Other research has examined students' racialized ethnic identities (Patton & McClure, 2009; Stewart, 2002; Watt, 2003) and gendered and sexual expressions of identity (Gold & Stewart, 2011) as they intersect with students' religious, spiritual, and worldview identities (Tisdell, 2003).

Tisdell (2003) reminded us that spiritual development happens in a historical, cultural, and gendered context. Tisdell drew on Hays's (2001) ADDRESSING (Age and generational influences, Developmental and acquired Disabilities, Religion and spiritual orientation, Ethnicity, Socioeconomic status, Sexual orientation, Indigenous heritage, National origin, and Gender) framework to describe the complexity of the sociocultural context in which people live. Spiritual journeys, according to Tisdell, are deeply situated within a sociocultural context in which reclaiming and remembering (the process of spiraling back to elements of earlier religious and spiritual traditions) often occur simultaneously with unlearning and confronting culturally oppressive ideology.

The notion of confrontation runs consistently through the research examining the intersections of religious, spiritual, and worldview and other identities (Gold & Stewart, 2011; Rahman, 2010; Stewart & Lozano, 2009; Tisdell, 2003; Watt, 2003). For example, queer Muslims are at the intersection of two subordinated identities within the North American context (where Muslim is subordinate in terms of religion, national identity, ethnicity, and often class hierarchies, and sexual identity is subordinate in the heterosexual, heteronormative matrix; Rahman, 2010). Rahman (2010) asserted that gay Muslims are more than just a hybrid of these two intersecting identities and that the dominant identity categories are "ontologically incomplete" (p. 953) precisely because of their exclusion of "others." Exclusion of the other within any identity dimension is often at the center of such confrontation.

Stewart and Lozano (2009) highlighted how the intersections of identity are fraught with dynamics related to power and oppression. For example, people of color who are Christian "may understand their religious identity within the Christian community not as a source or location of privilege but as aligned with the struggle against racial and ethnic oppression" (p. 26). This idea was advanced by Watt's "Come to the River" (2003), in which African American women use spirituality to "cope, resist and develop identity" (p. 29). Stewart and Lozano suggested people draw on the capacities of spirituality as a means to cope and resist through their assertion that "Christian privilege is, in the experiences of people of color, actually white privilege and racism, which are elements that define 'cultural Christianity'" (p. 27).

Jones and colleagues (2012) noted the challenge of developing an authentic and consistent identity given their respondents' multiple identities and how different identity dimensions move to the foreground or recede to the background depending on the context. Although they wrestled with the extent to which an "internally defined sense of self" (Jones et al., 2012, p. 715) is an appropriate developmental goal, the weight of the research strongly asserts the need for the higher education community of faculty, staff, and other administrators to provide places and spaces where students can wrestle with multiple dimensions of identity in their search for their unique sense of meaning and purpose. This desire was captured by Stewart (2002), who commented the participants in her study craved spaces on campuses that "acknowledged and welcomed" (p. 594) their multiple identities, particularly related to faith and the search for meaning.

Mentoring Communities

Students are faced with a host of questions and challenges as they negotiate their way through the quarterlife. Student affairs professionals and faculty have the opportunity to be more than a background presence and provide an active community in which students can wrestle with Big Questions at the multiple intersections of their identities. Although authors use different terms and phrases, the literature unreservedly suggests the importance of providing places and spaces—a community—as a means to facilitate students' search for meaning and purpose and in so doing develop in terms of their religious, spiritual, and worldview understanding (Braskamp et al., 2006; Nash & Murray, 2010; Palmer, 2007; Parks, 2000). Mentoring communities or communities of truth are places where learners come together in a "network of belonging" (Parks, 2000, p. 135) "to engage in a mutually accountable and transforming relationship . . . forged of trust and faith in the face of unknowable risks" (Palmer, 1983, p. 31). They are safe places to ask "big enough questions" (Parks, 2000, p. 137), to encounter otherness, to dream "worthy dreams" (Parks, 2000, p. 146), and to develop habits of mind (Parks, 2000) that allow for moral conversations grounded in humility and charity (Nash et al., 2008).

In what I know now was an early example of service-learning, I volunteered 40 hours at a homeless shelter, food pantry, and soup kitchen for women and families—Clare House—as part of my social problems course in my first year at college. I would not have had the language during my undergraduate education to call Clare House my mentoring community but it was, without a doubt, the place where I journeyed to understand what I believed, who I wanted to be, and how I wanted to be in relation to others. The questions that I asked and pondered on the college lawn came to life in my work at the Clare House: What is the good life? How do I serve my community? If God is just, why is there poverty? It was sometimes hard to work "the door," the place in the food bag line where we interacted person-to-person with the poor people we were serving. Questions about systemic poverty and society's inadequate responses were lived as I handed out a free bag of groceries, diapers, and formula to a young mother my age. Clare House was a Catholic Worker house built on the philosophy of Dorothy Day and Peter Maurin that advocated nonviolence, voluntary poverty, and the "works of mercy" (Day, 1940, para. 2). This philosophy was steeped in the physical artifacts of the house and the actions of the people who volunteered there. To this day, I remember walking through the hallway and seeing the framed prints of Jesus in a bread line with the caption, "What you have done for the least of us, you have done for me." What a powerful reminder of the foundation for the work we were doing.

I am not sure if my friend Tina (the Clare House director) had been educated in constructivist pedagogy, but she and the other volunteers certainly lived the propositions advanced by Nash and Murray (2010) and were "good company" (Baxter Magolda, 2002, p. 2) on my journey. Together, they encouraged me to take initiative in my learning (Nash & Murray, 2010). There was a huge library in the house, and I was encouraged to read and peruse at my leisure. It was the first time that I read Saint Thomas Aquinas or about Native American spirituality with its express honoring of the earth. Tina, in particular, seemed to recognize that there were "many valid ways to teach and learn" (Nash & Murray, 2010, p. 95). I learned to quiet my mind and engage in focal practices (Boers, 2012) like baking bread and working in the garden. Conversation was "the key element in all types of meaning-making" (Nash & Murray, 2010, p. 106). Tina, Father Joe, and many other volunteers were all members of this community, and we talked a lot. Meals were long and luxurious; it was the hearth and it is where we came together. They spoke of their faith openly and told stories of struggle. Around the table, we were all teachers and learners. And there were "silent spaces" (Nash & Murray, 2010, p. 109): places for prayer, meditation, and reflection. I will never forget how difficult it was the first time I tried to focus on my breath and let go of the million thoughts racing through my mind. Through all of these practices and experiences, I was journeying to better understand my beliefs, myself, and my purpose in life. At Clare House, I found a wonderful community of fellow sojourners to share my walk.

As I look back, now 20 years later, I feel fortunate that I found Clare House. I had my group of friends at college, and they were important in my formation. But as an emerging adult, it was my relationships with older adults as role models and mentors who embodied my mentoring community. My personal experience exemplifies what Christian Smith (director of the Center for the Study of Religion and Society at the University of Notre Dame) and his colleague Patricia Snell found in their research following a cohort of emerging adults over five years (Smith & Snell, 2009). They specifically highlighted the important role of parents and other adults in emerging adults' religious outcomes. When parents and others believe the old adage "my teenager doesn't listen to a thing I say" and leave emerging adults to find their own way, the emerging adults tend to be less religiously committed and practicing. Although Smith and Snell's work was not aimed at the extent to which parents and other adults in a mentoring community considered broader existential questions, one may infer from these data that again, when left to traverse this landscape alone—lacking the good company of a mentoring community—emerging adults are less likely to ask, question, and ponder these existential questions and thus may be missing the keel that keeps them afloat.

In the largest study of spirituality in American higher education, Astin, Astin, and Lindholm (2011) and their colleagues empirically demonstrated the relationship between learning in community and students' development on a host of measures of spirituality and religiousness. Acknowledging the constellation of religious outcomes are not relevant to all students and setting aside the appropriateness of the term *spirituality* to describe the other constellation of outcomes, the study defined two outcomes specifically related to students' search for meaning and purpose not associated with a higher power. *Spiritual quest* was defined as the "seeking in us that can lead to a better understanding of who we are, why we are here, and how we can live a meaningful life" (Astin et al., 2011, p. 28). *Equanimity* was defined as the sense of peacefulness, centeredness, and self-transcendence—a state of grace that allows one "to rise above or move beyond the limits of personal experience" (Astin et al., 2011, p. 50). Time spent purposefully engaged (both in terms of academic engagement as well as critically contemplating one's perceptions, experiences, and values through reading and discussing spiritual and religious matters and texts) was associated with greater gains in students' spiritual questing, as was engaging in course-based community service, helping friends with personal problems, and donating money to charity. Overall, activities (both solitary but especially in groups) with purposeful and constructive ends and that call students to be more self-reflective were positively associated with these areas of development.

Campuses from around the country have engaged in curricular and cocurricular conversations contemplating Big Questions (see the Big Questions working group sponsored by the Teagle Foundation [n.d.] and other programs described by Astin et al. [2011]). Other campuses have focused on notions of vocation (one's calling, often but not exclusively, related to theological work; see Gregg, 2005; Lilly Endowment, 2013). These programs vary in their structure and mandate but often are collaborations among interested faculty, student affairs staff, and students engaging as a mentoring community. As such, the communities may use the principles of constructivist pedagogy (Nash & Murray, 2010), engaged pedagogy (hooks, 1994), a pedagogy of engagement (Braskamp et al., 2006), or subject-centered education

(Palmer, 2007) to wrestle with Big Questions. The higher education community is doing important work in this area, stepping up to the task of developing students holistically. But several important questions beg to be asked: Are these efforts largely limited to private institutions where the separation between church and state is not an issue? To what extent do these institutional efforts recognize the intersecting identities of their students? Is the language used to promote these opportunities inclusive of the plural nature of our student bodies? In other words, is there room at the table for everyone?

A Place for All at the Table

As a first-year undergraduate student from a rural town, I had few opportunities to engage with anyone who was not Christian. Having space at the table meant including Catholics, Lutherans, Seventh-Day Adventists, and Mennonites—and this alone could cause quite the ecumenical stirring at local functions. Although there were images of Jesus and Christian icons throughout Clare House, it was in my mentoring community where I first came in contact with readings and practices from a host of faiths. Such multifaith perspectives made sense when I saw a slogan in the house that read, "God is too big to fit into one religion." I was introduced to *Tricycle*, a nonsectarian Buddhist quarterly, and to *Commonweal*, a progressive journal of religion, politics, and culture published by a lay Catholic board unaffiliated with the Roman Catholic Church. I learned to practice contemplative mindful living by reading Thich Nhat Hanh. As I learned about the beliefs of other faith traditions, I found myself less committed to my own Methodism and Christianity. I respected the ritual of religious observance and the commitment of believers, but the slogan that I read years ago at Clare House stuck with me: "God is too big to fit into one religion."

Over the years, I have begun to think of myself—like so many others do—as "spiritual not religious." Focusing on the spirit of a higher power and not the actual doctrine of a specific religion made me feel free to embrace the notion of spirituality. In fact, I got so comfortable with the term *spirituality* that I developed blinders. I failed to see how the term brings with it its own assumptions, namely, the existence of a higher power. Nowhere were those blinders more evident than in an article I published in *About Campus* about Christian privilege (Seifert, 2007). Thankfully, learning is an ongoing journey. Again, in my graduate school mentoring community, I came to understand how what I referred to as Christian privilege could be further extended to spiritual privilege.

Spiritual privilege exists when the term *spirituality* is given license to include all things associated with inner exploration, including "seeking personal authenticity, genuineness, and wholeness . . . deriving meaning, purpose and direction in life; being open to exploring a relationship with a higher power that transcends human existence and human knowing; and valuing the sacred" (Astin et al., 2011, p. 4). This definition is fairly consistent with those given by Love and Talbot (1999) and Dalton and colleagues (2006). However, Smith and Snell (2009) asserted spirituality "is not some free-floating experience of individualistic interiority and self-exploration—rather, it concerns specific practices, meanings, and experiences that are fairly closely tied to traditional religious faiths" (p. 295). This notion of spirituality is more aligned with Ellison's (1983) conception of spiritual well-being, which has as its precursor some belief in the divine (a transcendent God realized in one's religious well-being) in concert with one's existential well-being. Nash (2001) noted that the term *spirituality* can be confusing and ill-defined, and, for many, it is synonymous with *religion*. To call all things related to one's interest in the subjective inner life *spirituality* seems to give that term an extraordinary wide berth.

I now see my work in very different ways. Ever trying to be a good host, I scan the banquet room for overt, covert, and simply unintended instances when higher education administrators and faculty make a lavish spread but fail to have enough chairs for all their guests to sit at the table. Along with others (Goodman & Mueller, 2009; Goodman & Teraguchi, 2008), I have been forthright in asserting higher education must reconceptualize its role as one that facilitates students' inner development (whether that development derives out of meaning making that is religious, spiritual, and/or worldview-based [Seifert & Holman-Harmon, 2009]).

In Chapter 3, Felix and Bowman described the historical underpinnings of not just the spiritual and religious privilege present on American higher education campuses but how this privilege has been largely Christian. Yet, in the last 50 years, our campuses have become increasingly plural in terms of students' religions, spiritualities, and worldviews. The passage of the Immigration Act of 1965 brought the largest number of non-European immigrants to live, work, and study in the United States (Stamm, 2006). Couple this influx of immigrants and their children with the determined recruitment of international students, and it should come as no surprise that students at American higher education institutions today hold the most plural religious, spiritual, and worldview perspectives than at any point in history.

Given the religious, spiritual, and worldview pluralism on our campuses and students whose meaning making occurs at the intersections of multiple identity dimensions, how is the American higher education community rising to the task of being good company on students' journeys in a way that recognizes and values this pluralism? In addition to the mentoring communities mentioned previously, many campuses have made religious, spiritual, and worldview pluralism the central topic of conversation around the table. Crosby (2010) described the facilitated dinner discussion focusing on spirituality, morality, and religion as part of the "Dialogues on Diversity" series at the University of Michigan. Also drawing on the power of the hearth and food to bring people together, Goldbaum (2012) shared how the "Freedom Seder" bridges ethnic and cultural and religious, spiritual, and worldview dimensions to bring students together for dialogue. Two special issues of the *Journal of College and Character* have focused on interfaith dialogue (February 2011: see Kocet & Stewart, 2011; Patel & Meyer, 2011) and pluralist religious, spiritual, and worldview expressions on campus (May 2013: see Chander, 2013; Lohr Sapp, 2013). Many campuses have partnered with Interfaith Youth Core to bring students from various religious, spiritual, and worldview perspectives together in "common action for the common good" (Interfaith Youth Core, n.d.a, para. 2). These and similar programs draw on research by Putnam that suggests constructive relationships with those different from oneself increases knowledge about different perspectives, which leads to more positive attitudes (Patel & Meyer, 2011).

In addition to the curricular and cocurricular programs that campuses have developed to intentionally bring students from diverse perspectives together in dialogue (detailed further in Part Three of this volume), recent research has examined the broader notion of religious and spiritual campus climate with regard to student outcomes. In general, a more positive religious and spiritual campus climate is associated with increases in spiritual identification and quest (Bowman & Small, 2013), psychological well-being (Bowman & Small, 2012), and development of an ecumenical worldview (Mayhew, 2012). The Campus Religious and Spiritual Climate Survey (Interfaith Youth Core, n.d.b) has the potential to be instrumental in assisting campus leaders to better understand the opportunities and challenges facing their campuses in realizing the possibilities of supporting students' religious, spiritual, and/or worldview development. Both at the program and research levels, there appears to be a commitment to recognize and value the pluralist reality of students' lives and to examine how this level of pluralism translates into a climate supportive of intersectional self-expression.

A STABILIZING PENDULUM

If our goal as educators is to create places at the table for all to ask, share, question, and ponder, one must focus on the commonality of questions that all who seek may ask, "What do I believe? Who am I? What is a good life? What is my life's purpose?" It is through these common questions, asked in communion, that we might live into individual answers. As noted throughout the chapter, these are questions asked at the individual level and with the individual engaging with the collective. Given the surge of interest in this topic in the last 15 years, I am confident that actions taken by higher education administrators, faculty, and researchers will continue to support and examine each domain. I envision future research will continue to examine the intersectionality of identity as it relates to students' religious, spiritual, and/or worldview development. Future research may focus on identifying the sociocultural contexts that foreground the dimension of religious, spiritual, and/or worldview identity and how this foregrounding impacts the resonance of other identities. With the explosion of Interfaith Youth Core's service-learning programs on many college campuses, I envision future research will examine the confluence of the individual and the individual engaging with the collective. For example, how do students' religious, spiritual, and worldview identities and the intersections of this identity dimension with others differ for those who participate in these programs from those who do not participate? Additionally, I foresee more research examining the efficacy of Interfaith Youth Core and similar programs in terms of students' gains in self-awareness, knowledge of other worldviews, empathy, and concern for others. If these attitudes and dispositions are necessary to meet local and global needs, it is imperative to understand the extent to which and how such programs facilitate student development. Finally, I expect future research to investigate the relationships between the degree to which institutions provide mentoring communities (through Interfaith Youth Core or other programs) and participation in such programs with positive campus climates for religious, spiritual, and worldview expression.

Although I expect research will continue at pace, the bigger question is will it be enough? Can gravity hold the pendulum in the middle, where pluralism is valued and where students' intersectional identities in all their complexity are able to be brought to bear in responding to the needs of our time, which call for the union of the cognitive and the affective, head and heart? What level of institutional action needs to exist to maintain the pendulum's position? I am hopeful institutional action will step up to the challenge, but I am also a realist. There are serious obstacles to overcome if our higher education institutions are truly to educate students holistically.

First, facilitating students' holistic student development, particularly as it relates to the intersections of religious, spiritual, and worldview identity and other identities, is not viewed as central to the educational mandate at the nation's largest institutions. Although public institutions participated en masse in the Spirituality in Higher Education study, I contend that such large-scale participation was buttressed by the fact the spirituality items were appended to a well-known survey instrument of first-year students that the Cooperative Institutional Research Program has conducted for more than 40 years. Not to say that mentoring communities, as I and others have described them, do not exist at public institutions, but it is worth noting that many of the examples of such communities or Big Questions programs highlighted in various publications are located at private institutions.

Given that meaning making is linked to several definitions of faith (Fowler, 1981; Parks, 2000), stakeholders at public higher education institutions, where the largest percentage of students are educated, largely hold a position that issues related to religious, spiritual, and/or worldview development are bound by the separation between church and state and thus, it is "not our place" to educate in this arena (Talbot & Anderson, 2013). From this angle, it may be beneficial to reframe this construct as one of self-authorship. Baxter Magolda (2004) has argued poignantly that self-authorship (in which students negotiate their internal and external voices in discerning what they believe to be true, who they want to be, and how they want to be in relationship with others—key Big Questions) is the common goal of 21st-century education. Until public higher education institutions embrace the mission of holistic student development as central to students' self-authorship, institutional action focusing on facilitating students' search for meaning and purpose at the intersection of their lived identities will benefit the few, not the many.

Second, irrespective of sector (public or private), higher education institutions are being pushed to do more with less, to move students through to completion, and to prepare them for the workforce. There appears to be little room for holistic student development when fiscal constraint provides the context for policies that focus on return on investment, degree completion, and career readiness. I agree wholeheartedly with Astin, Astin, and Lindholm (2011) that the work of the future requires much more than technical skill; it demands self-awareness and an understanding of people's intersecting identities in order to make sense of and address issues contributing to war, corruption, and systemic poverty. Given that return on investment and economic/workforce development seem to drive American higher education policy, I think it will take corporate America to demand holistically developed graduates, whose self-awareness and intercultural competence are recognized as assets both to the bottom line and the company's social responsibility agenda, in order for holistic student development to be systemically adopted by higher education institutions. With the changing higher education landscape in which massive open online courses (MOOCs), badges, and other means of knowledge and skill credentialing are en vogue, it seems unlikely that higher education administrators and faculty will independently choose to invest the time and energy necessary to be good company on students' holistic developmental journeys.

Even if public institutions get on board, even if higher education leaders craft a narrative that situates holistic student development as central to their mission, Nash and Murray (2010) have suggested faculty and student affairs practitioners may feel unprepared to have such conversations with students, essentially to educate for students' holistic development. Being a part of a mentoring community requires members to reflect personally and engage respectfully with others' reflections. This kind of reflection may push faculty and staff firmly out of their comfort zones. Without deviation, the literature holds that in order to be good company for students, faculty and staff must do their own homework, their own reflective housekeeping (Allen & Kellom, 2001; Seifert & Holman-Harmon, 2009; Trautvetter, 2007). Reflection may run counter to faculty members' disciplines, which value objective detachment; not to mention, doing so takes time, a scarce resource for everyone in the academy. Taking the time to reflect means time away from doing something else, working on a research project or planning for next year's orientation. Yet self-reflection and the awareness and knowledge of intersecting identities as they influence students' searches for meaning and purpose are central spiritual competencies for student affairs practitioners (Kocet & Stewart, 2011) and necessary if campuses are to truly engage as a multicultural campus for spiritual engagement (Stewart, Kocet, & Lobdell, 2011). If there is a true desire for systemic institutional action toward educating students holistically, then time for reflection and professional development that teaches faculty and staff how to have what Nash et al. (2008) called "moral conversations" (p. 8), as being members of mentoring communities, will need to be the norm and not the exception. This is certainly not insurmountable but likely requires institutions to do some of their own meaning making as to what they believe, who they want to be, and how they want to be in relationship with their students and stakeholders. Doing so requires higher education administrators and faculty to ask their own series of Big Questions, to inspect the keels of their own boats such that they are seaworthy for the inevitable white water.

Recognizing the religious, spiritual, and worldview pluralism of today's campuses, it would be clearly misguided for the pendulum to swing back to the far end where Christian principles were the foundation of a college education. However, given that considerable international efforts both in terms of waging war and reconciling conflict center on understanding different religious, spiritual, and worldview perspectives, it seems U.S. higher education institutions cannot afford for the pendulum to swing back to a place of rational objectivity. In order to live up to its duty to serve the nation, the U.S. higher education community (boards of trustees, senior administrators, student affairs professionals, and faculty) must rise to the task of educating students holistically so they may unite heart with head to solve the intransigent problems that plague our world. The pendulum must be held firmly in the middle, where understanding one's personal search for meaning and purpose connects to a broader understanding of entire communities' faiths, beliefs, and worldviews.

REFERENCES

Allen, K. E., & Kellom, G. E. (2001). The role of spirituality in student affairs and staff development. *New Directions for Student Services, 2001*(95), 47–55.

American Council on Education. (1937). *The student personnel point of view.* Washington, DC: Author.

American Council on Education. (1949). *The student personnel point of view.* Washington, DC: Author.

Astin, A. W., Astin, H. S., & Lindholm, J. A. (2011). *Cultivating the spirit: How college can enhance students' inner lives.* San Francisco: Jossey-Bass.

Baxter Magolda, M. B. (2001). *Making their own way: Narratives for transforming higher education to promote self-development.* Sterling, VA: Stylus.

Baxter Magolda, M. B. (2002). Helping students make their way to adulthood: Good company for the journey. *About Campus, 6*(6), 2–9.

Baxter Magolda, M. B. (2004). Self-authorship as the common goal of 21st century education. In M. B. Baxter Magolda & P. M. King (Eds.), *Learning partnerships: Theory and models of practice to educate for self-authorship* (pp. 1–36). Sterling, VA: Stylus.

Baxter Magolda, M. B. (2009). *Authoring your life: Developing an internal voice to meet life's challenges.* Sterling, VA: Stylus.

Boers, A. (2012). *Living into focus: Choosing what matters in an age of distractions.* Grand Rapids, MI: Brazos Press.

Bowman, N. A., & Small, J. L. (2012). Exploring a hidden form of minority status: College students' religious affiliation and well-being. *Journal of College Student Development, 53,* 491–509.

Bowman, N. A., & Small, J. L. (2013). The experiences and spiritual growth of religiously privileged and religiously marginalized college students. In A. Bryant Rockenbach & M. J. Mayhew (Eds.), *Spirituality in college students' lives: Translating research into practice* (pp. 19–34). New York: Routledge.

Braskamp, L. A., Trautvetter, L. C., & Ward, K. (2006). *Putting students first: How colleges develop students purposefully.* Bolton, MA: Anker.

Carnevale, A. P., & Desrochers, D. M. (2002). *The missing middle: Aligning education and the knowledge economy. (Office of Vocational and Adult Education No. ED465 092.)* Washington, DC: U.S. Government Printing Office.

Chander, V. (2013). A room with a view: Accommodating Hindu religious practice on a college campus. *Journal of College and Character, 14*(2), doi: 10.1515/jcc-2013-0015

Chickering, A. W., Dalton, J. C., & Stamm, L. (2006). *Encouraging authenticity and spirituality in higher education.* San Francisco: Jossey-Bass.

Connor, W. R. (2008). A second adolescence: Two big questions and where they belong. *Journal of College and Character, 9*(4). doi:10.2202/1940-1639.1136

Crosby, D. A. (2010). Approaches to religious differences. *Journal of College and Character, 11*(1). doi:10.2202/1940-1639.1007

Dalton, J. C., & Crosby, P. C. (2010). When faith fails: Why nurturing purpose and meaning are so critical to student learning and development in college. *Journal of College and Character, 11*(3). doi:10.2202/1940-1639.1720

Dalton, J. C., Eberhardt, D., Bracken, J., & Echols, K. (2006). Inward journeys: Forms and patterns of college student spirituality. *Journal of College and Character, 7*(8). doi:10.2202/1940-1639.1219

Day, D. (1940, February). Aims and purposes. *The Catholic Worker.* Retrieved from http://dorothyday.catholicworker.org/articles/182.html

Dylan, B. (2004). The times, they are a-changin'. In *Lyrics: 1962–2001* (p. 79). London: Simon & Schuster. (Song recorded in 1964, Warner Bros. Records).

Ellison, C. W. (1983). Spiritual well-being: Conceptualization and measurement. *Journal of Psychology and Theology, 11,* 330–340.

Fowler, J. W. (1981). *Stages of faith: The psychology of human development and the quest for meaning.* San Francisco: HarperCollins.

Gold, S. P., & Stewart, D. L. (2011). Lesbian, gay and bisexual students coming out at the intersection of spirituality and sexual identity. *Journal of LGBT Issues in Counseling, 5,* 237–258.

Goldbaum, L. (2012). The freedom Seder: A bridge across ethnic, cultural, and religious divides. *Journal of College and Character, 13*(2). doi:10.1515/jcc-2012-1825

Goodman, K. M., & Mueller, J. A. (2009). Invisible, marginalized, and stigmatized: Understanding and addressing the needs of atheist students. *New Directions for Student Services, 2009*(125), 55–63.

Goodman, K. M., & Teraguchi, D. H. (2008). Beyond spirituality: A new framework for educators. *Diversity & Democracy, 11*(1), 10–11.

Gregg, C. M. (2005). Discover "vocation": An essay on the concept of vocation. *Journal of College and Character, 6*(1). doi:10.2202/1940-1639.1411

Hays, P. A. (2001). *Addressing cultural complexities in practice: A framework for clinicians and counselors.* Washington, DC: American Psychological Association Press.

hooks, b. (1994). *Teaching to transgress: Education as the practice of freedom.* New York: Routledge.

Interfaith Youth Core. (n.d.a). *About the movement.* Retrieved from http://www.ifyc .org/about

Interfaith Youth Core. (n.d.b). *Measuring interfaith.* Retrieved from http://www .ifyc.org/survey

Jones, S. R., Kim, Y. C., & Skendall, K. C. (2012). (Re-)framing authenticity: Considering multiple social identities using autoethnographic and intersectional approaches. *Journal of Higher Education, 8,* 698–724.

Kocet, M. M., & Stewart, D. L. (2011). The role of student affairs in promoting religious and secular pluralism and interfaith cooperation. *Journal of College and Character, 12*(1). doi:10.2202/1940-7882.1762

Lasch, C. (1979). *The culture of narcissism: American life in the age of diminishing expectations.* New York: Norton.

Lilly Endowment. (2013). *Programs for the theological exploration of vocation.* Retrieved from http://www.lillyendowment.org/religion_ptev.html

Lohr Sapp, C. (2013). A great and towering compromise: Religious practice and space at Duke University. *Journal of College and Character, 14*(2). doi: 10.1515/ jcc-2013-0016

Longfield, B. J. (1992). From evangelicalism to liberalism: Public Midwestern universities in nineteenth-century America. In G. M. Marsden & B. J. Longfield (Eds.), *The secularization of the academy* (pp. 46–73). New York: Oxford University Press.

Love, P., & Talbot, D. (1999). Defining spiritual development: A missing consideration for student affairs. *NASPA Journal, 37,* 361–376.

Lowe, N. (1974). (What's so funny 'bout) peace, love and understanding? 1978 recording on *Armed Forces* [EP] by Elvis Costello & The Attractions. London: Eden Studios.

Marsden, G. M. (1992). The soul of the American university: A historical overview. In G. M. Marsden & B. J. Longfield (Eds.), *The secularization of the academy* (pp. 9–45). New York: Oxford University Press.

Mayhew, M. J. (2012). A multi-level examination of college and its influence on ecumenical worldview development. *Research in Higher Education, 53,* 282–310.

Nash, R. J. (2001). *Religious pluralism in the academy: Opening the dialogue.* New York: Peter Lang.

Nash, R. J., Bradley, D. L., & Chickering, A. W. (Eds.). (2008). *How to talk about hot topics on campus: From polarization to moral conversation.* San Francisco: Jossey-Bass.

Nash, R. J., & Murray, M. C. (2010). *Helping college students find purpose: The campus guide to meaning-making.* San Francisco: Jossey-Bass.

Palmer, P. (1983). *To know as we are known: Education as a spiritual journey.* San Francisco: Harper & Row.

Palmer, P. (2007). *The courage to teach: Exploring the inner landscape of a teacher's life* (10th anniversary ed.). San Francisco: Jossey-Bass.

Parks, S. D. (2000). *Big questions, worthy dreams: Mentoring young adults in their search for meaning, purpose and faith.* San Francisco: Jossey-Bass.

Patel, E., & Meyer, C. (2011). The civic relevance of interfaith cooperation for colleges and universities. *Journal of College and Character, 12*(1). doi:10.2202/1940-1639.1764

Patton, L. D., & McClure, M. L. (2009). Strength in the spirit: A qualitative examination of African American college women and the role of spirituality during college. *Journal of Negro Education, 78,* 42–54.

Pryor, J. H., Hurtado, S., Saenz, V. B., Santos, J. L., & Korn, W. S. (2007). *The American freshman: Forty year trends, 1966–2006.* Los Angeles: Higher Education Research Institute.

Rahman, M. (2010). Queer as intersectionality: Theorizing gay and Muslim identities. *Sociology, 44,* 944–961.

Rilke, R. M. (1903). *Letters to a young poet, #4.* Retrieved from http://www.carrothers.com/rilke4.htm

Robbins, A. (2004). *Conquering your quarterlife crisis: Advice from twentysomethings who have been there and survived.* New York: Penguin.

Robbins, A., & Wilner, A. (2001). *Quarterlife crisis: The unique challenges of life in your twenties.* New York: Jeremy P. Tarcher/Putnam.

Rudolph, F. (1962/1990). *The American college and university: A history.* New York: A. Knopf. Repr. Athens: University of Georgia Press.

Seifert, T. (2007). Understanding Christian privilege: Managing the tensions of spiritual plurality. *About Campus, 12*(2), 10–17.

Seifert, T. A., & Holman-Harmon, N. (2009). Practical implications for student affairs professionals' work in facilitating students' inner development. *New Directions for Student Services, 2009*(125), 13–21.

Smith, C., & Snell, P. (2009). *Souls in transition: The religious and spiritual lives of emerging young adults.* New York: Oxford University Press.

Stamm, L. (2006). The influence of religion and spirituality in shaping American higher education. In A. W. Chickering, J. C. Dalton & L. Stamm (Eds.), *Encouraging authenticity and spirituality in higher education* (pp. 66–91). San Francisco: Jossey-Bass.

Stewart, D. L. (2002). The role of faith in the development of an integrated identity: A qualitative study of Black students at a White college. *Journal of College Student Development, 43,* 579–596.

Stewart, D. L., Kocet, M. M., & Lobdell, S. (2011). The multifaith campus: Transforming colleges and universities for spiritual engagement. *About Campus, 16*(1), 10–18.

Stewart, D. L., & Lozano, A. (2009). Difficult dialogues at the intersections of race, culture, and religion. *New Directions for Student Services, 2009*(125), 23–31.

Talbot, D. M., & Anderson, D. K. (2013). Questions of spirituality on college campuses: To engage or not to engage? In A. Bryant Rockenbach & M. J. Mayhew (Eds.), *Spirituality in college students' lives: Translating research into practice* (pp. 194–198). New York: Routledge.

Teagle Foundation. (n.d.). *Grantees' publications.* Retrieved from http://www.teaglefoundation.org/Resources/Grantees-Publications

Thelin, J. R. (2011). *A history of American higher education* (2nd ed.). Baltimore, MD: Johns Hopkins University Press.

Tisdell, E. J. (2003). *Exploring spirituality and culture in adult and higher education.* San Francisco: Jossey-Bass.

Trautvetter, L. C. (2007). Developing students' search for meaning and purpose. In G. L. Kramer (Ed.), *Fostering student success in the campus community* (pp. 236–261). San Francisco: Jossey-Bass.

Watt, S. K. (2003). Come to the river: Using spirituality to cope, resist, and develop identity. *New Directions for Student Services, 2003*(104), 29–40.

Part Two

Professional Associations

5

The Role of Professional Associations in Advancing Spirituality, Faith, Religion, and Life Purpose in Student Affairs

Dafina-Lazarus Stewart

SINCE TEMKIN AND EVANS (1998) first argued for the incorporation of spiritual development as a relevant aspect of holistic student development theory, the student affairs profession has taken notice. In the 15 years since their article was published, an explosion of publications, conference presentations, and themed institutes have featured the interrelated concepts of spirituality, religion, faith, and life purpose in higher education. Moreover, student affairs professional associations have played a key role in efforts to advance the breadth and depth of focus related to these topics. In this chapter, I document and discuss those efforts to illustrate the centrality of student affairs professional associations in this movement. I also postulate as to what lay behind these efforts. I conclude the chapter by providing recommendations for ways in which student affairs professional associations can continue to exercise leadership in the dissemination of research and scholarship; preparation of new professionals and continued professional development; and national advocacy regarding spirituality, faith, religion, and life purpose in student affairs and higher education. In particular, there is a need for greater focus on the inner lives of student affairs professionals, incorporation of competencies for this work in graduate preparation, and unified and coordinated efforts among student affairs associations.

STUDENT AFFAIRS PROFESSIONAL ASSOCIATIONS

First organized in the early 20th century, student affairs professional associations provided a valuable space for college administrators working with students outside the formal, academic curriculum to share ideas, resources, and strategies (Dungy & Gordon, 2010; Nuss, 2003). Although not a professional association solely focused on student affairs, the American Council on Education (1937, 1949) produced arguably the most definitive document on the nature, purpose, and role of student affairs as a profession, *The Student Personnel Point of View*, initially published in 1937 and then revised in 1949. NASPA–Student Affairs Administrators in Higher Education, founded in 1917 as the National Association of Student Personnel Administrators, and ACPA–College Student Educators International, founded in 1924 as the American College Personnel Association, later published a number of the most significant philosophical statements that laid the foundation for student affairs practice in the United States (Evans & Reason, 2001).

These two national umbrella student affairs professional associations (ACPA and NASPA) serve three general purposes that have evolved since the founding of these organizations nearly a century ago:

1. To provide a space for student affairs professionals and others invested in that work to collaborate on research and scholarship initiatives,
2. To share experiences and resources, and
3. To develop the guiding values and central tenets of the field.

These purposes have been galvanized to produce significant contributions to higher education administrators' and policy makers' understanding of college students' learning and development (Evans & Reason, 2001). Over the last quindecennial period (beginning in 1997), both ACPA and NASPA have applied these purposes to advance the development of scholarship and practice related to spirituality, faith, religion, and life purpose in higher education.

ROLE OF STUDENT AFFAIRS PROFESSIONAL
ASSOCIATIONS

Although *The Student Personnel Point of View* included attention to character
and moral development in 1949, the field of student affairs has been slow to
fully embrace this aspect of its role. As Kocet and Stewart (2011) asserted,
also discussed in Chapters 3 and 4 of this book, the presumed split between
mind and spirit introduced by scientific rationalism moved higher education
as a whole, including student affairs, away from attending to topics defy-
ing empirical observation, such as spirituality. Moreover, as higher education became increasingly secularized, religion and faith seemed opposed to
the academic pursuit of knowledge and ill-suited for the campus commons.
Even Fowler's (1981) theoretical model of faith development was largely
ignored initially in student development theorizing.

Nevertheless, toward the end of the 20th century, the climate shifted, and
the national conversation about religion and spirituality became much more
pronounced. As Eck (2001) has discussed, religion became a much more
central aspect of public conversation in part because of increasing sectarian
violence in the Middle East, Northern Ireland, and Bosnia, and terrorism by
radical militant Islamists. Additionally, and perhaps of greater consequence,
Eck cited the rise in immigration from countries where Christianity is not
the dominant religion and the resulting creation of ethnic-religious enclaves
in the midst of previously homo-Christian environments. Because of these
factors and the increasing presence of Christian fundamentalism in U.S.
politics (for how this worked in Catholicism, see McDonough, 2013) and
critiques of it from secular humanists and progressive theologians, the general public found itself more greatly engaged in conversations about spirituality, faith, religion, and life purpose, as well as the diversity of perspectives
regarding them.

This increased engagement in general public life also shaped the interests
and perspectives of the nation's young adults. As evidenced in the research
findings from the Pew Forum on Religion & Public Life and the Higher
Education Research Institute (HERI) cited elsewhere in this volume, matric-
ulating college students have expressed increasing interest in matters of spirituality, faith, religion, and life purpose over the last 15 years. In response
to a need to effectively and appropriately facilitate students' exploration of
these ideas both intrapersonally and interpersonally, higher education scholars and student affairs practitioners began to call on the field to reincorporate
spirituality as part of a holistic understanding of students and the college

environment. As I will discuss throughout the chapter, student affairs professional associations have been fundamental to advancing the conversation about spirituality, religion, faith, and life purpose in higher education.

The three general purposes of the national generalist student affairs professional associations identified earlier in this chapter have produced three ways that they particularly have led and influenced the incorporation of greater attention to issues of spirituality, faith, religion, and life purpose in the field. First has been through the dissemination of research and scholarship. Both ACPA and NASPA produce a variety of publications that reach full-time researchers and faculty, student affairs professionals, other higher education administrators and policy makers, and graduate students in the field. Second, each association sponsors numerous professional development opportunities that apply theory to practice, promote emerging best practices, and bring student affairs professionals into conversation with researchers and policymakers. The graduate-level preparation of student affairs professionals is also discussed in the context of professional development. Through the organizing of faculty teaching in graduate preparation programs, professional associations have provided space for faculty to trade ideas and discuss emerging trends in professional competencies that may have a bearing on graduate preparation. Third, professional associations are in the position to influence broader conversations and collaborate with other entities (e.g., other professional associations both within and beyond higher education and student affairs) to engage in national advocacy regarding these topics.

Research and Scholarship

Despite the existence of publications in other venues and earlier (for instance, Schafer [1997] cited several publications with a focus on religiosity and its correlates with wellness from the *Journal for the Scientific Study of Religion* and other religious humanities-based journals as well as an article he published with King [Schafer & King, 1990] in ACPA's *Journal of College Student Development*), from the late 1990s to the present there has been a dramatic increase in the visibility of spirituality, religion, and faith in the journals sponsored by ACPA and NASPA. This section is not meant to be a review of the literature published in that time frame; rather it serves to examine the increasing visibility of this discussion over the past 15 years within the particular profession of student affairs.

Although both ACPA and NASPA publish additional materials accessible only to the members of their specific organizations, this review focuses only on those publications that are accessible to both members and nonmembers via subscription. These journals include the *Journal of College Student Development* (*JCSD*) and *About Campus* (*AC*), published by ACPA, and the *Journal of Student Affairs Research and Practice* (*JSARP*; formerly the *NASPA Journal*) and the *Journal of College and Character* (*JCC*), published by NASPA. This review begins in 1997 to coincide with this chapter's focus on the dramatic increase in attention to topics related to spirituality, faith, religion, and life purpose in the last 15 years in student affairs contexts. The 15 years are broken up into 4- to 5-year increments: 1998–2003, 2004–2008, and 2009–2013. I searched for articles in the journals' databases where accessible and Google Scholar using any of the following keywords: *spirituality, religion, faith, meaning making.*

Love and Talbot's (1999) scholarly essay identifying spiritual development as a "missing consideration" (p. 361) for student affairs published in the *NASPA Journal* has often been cited as the initial call for student affairs' incorporation of spirituality in student affairs practice and remains a significant publication in this discussion. However, the earliest article in a student affairs journal about spirituality and college students was actually published in 1997 by *JCSD,* one of the premier journals in student affairs and higher education dedicated to research on issues related to student development theory and practice. Therefore, Schafer's (1997) report of his empirical findings correlating religiosity to wellness issues as a relevant concern for student affairs scholars and practitioners is a noteworthy landmark in this discussion. Schafer's findings explore not only a theoretical issue but also a practical one for educators invested in promoting holistic health and development among college students. Love and Talbot (1999) asserted the relevance of spirituality and religiosity to student affairs practice, but it could be said that Schafer assumed that relevance and incorporated it in his research question.

Schafer's (1997) study, "Religiosity, Spirituality, and Personal Distress Among College Students," was one of the few articles published on these topics up to that point in student affairs journals. In four- to five-year increments, the rate of publication skyrocketed for articles that directly address spirituality, religion, or faith as an element of student development, diversity, or institutional environment; review a text about these topics; or include any of these as factors related to student learning and development outcome variables. From 1997 until 2003, 26 articles related to or including spirituality, faith, or religion were published in *JCSD*. That number increased threefold for the next four-year period, 2004 through 2008, to 76 articles and held steady at 70 articles for the next four years, 2009 through the present (April

2013). A total of 172 research studies and reviews have been published in *JCSD* related to spirituality, faith, and religion. I do not point out Schafer's article in 1997 to assert that it triggered the following increase in publication in *JCSD* but rather to describe the nature of it as an antecedent to what followed.

ACPA's other subscription publication, *AC*, is not peer-reviewed, and its format is meant to appeal to a broader range of readers, including policy makers and higher education administrators, as well as student affairs professionals, faculty, and graduate students. Research findings are included among the articles published in *AC*; however, scholarly essays, applications of theory to practice, and emerging best practices dominate. In 1999, Laurence asked the provocative question, "Can religion and spirituality find a place in higher education?" (p. 11) and then concluded by suggesting that higher education adopt a religious pluralism approach. In the period of time following this article, *AC* published 10 articles through 2003 that were also scholarly essays, like Laurence's, which mostly asserted the necessity of adopting religious pluralism in higher education and student affairs work. This number quadrupled from 2004 to 2008 to 40. The final four years have seen 30 articles published so far, for a total of 80 between 1999 and 2013.

NASPA's peer-reviewed research journal, first coined the *NASPA Journal*, changed its name and its focus in 2010 to the *Journal of Student Affairs Research and Practice*. *JSARP* seeks to publish innovative and cutting-edge research, scholarly essays, and reports of applied research and emerging best practices. Before the 1999 Love and Talbot article in this journal, Temkin and Evans (1998) published a scholarly essay asserting that spiritual development should be a part of a holistic approach to student development but noting that it was too often ignored. They also wrote about the need to improve the collaboration between student affairs and religious personnel (e.g., college chaplains, religious advisers) on campus.

It is not evident that student affairs professionals were responsive to this piece in light of the fact that it is Love and Talbot's 1999 essay that has been cited far more often in later publications. Further, it is unclear what difference that one year made to breaching the dam regarding the field's attention to issues of spirituality, faith, religion, and life purpose. Temkin and Evans's (1998) call for greater collaboration between student affairs professionals and religious personnel has continued to receive less focus in publications and presentations since then. This is perhaps a result of the complex relationships between public institutions and religion and the already seamless integration of religion in most sectarian private institutions. On the one hand, such collaborations are uneasy or contentious; on the other, they are assumed and perhaps conflated.

Since the publication of Temkin and Evans's article in 1998 until 2003, the *NASPA Journal* published 12 articles related to spirituality, religion, or faith. Then, breaking with the pattern seen in *JCSD* and *AC*, the next four years (2004–2008) the journal had only three published articles on these topics. However, the final four years, under the *JSARP* masthead, the publication rate of spirituality-related articles jumped to 23, nearly double the number published in the first five years included in this review. A total of 38 publications related to spirituality, religion, and faith have appeared in NASPA's research journal.

The latest journal to join NASPA's family of publications is *JCC*. Although NASPA assumed primary responsibility for the journal's production in 2007, *JCC* was founded in 1999 as an initiative of the Hardee Center for Leadership and Ethics at Florida State University. As its name implies, the primary focus of the journal is on topics related to character and ethics in higher education. Relatedly, topics concerning religion and spirituality are also covered. Concurrent with its incorporation into NASPA, *JCC* became an online journal and added a peer-reviewed research section to complement its other featured articles, which were mostly very accessible scholarly essays and book reviews. In 2000, four articles were published in *JCC* related to spirituality, religion, or faith. By 2003, 44 such articles and reviews had been published. Between 2004 and 2008, there were 187 related articles, more than four times as many. Since 2009, there have been 117, for a total of 348 articles in *JCC* in the last 13 years.

Across all four publications, there have been 638 articles, essays, and reviews written about spirituality, religion, or faith in student affairs journals since 1997 (see Table 5.1). With the exception of *JSARP*, the 2004 to 2008 period saw the most dramatic increase in the rate of publication about these topics in the field's association-sponsored publication outlets. This dramatic rise is not unique to student affairs. Nelson (2010) documented a similar rise in related publications and conference presentations within the American Educational Research Association.

As suggested earlier, the increase in attention and focus on these issues among college students and the need for educators to effectively address these issues and facilitate conversations about them is likely a reason this expansion has taken place. However, I think that is only one part of the story. I incorporated spirituality and faith from the outset in my research regarding identity and development (see Stewart, 2002, 2008, 2009) mainly

Table 5.1
STUDENT AFFAIRS JOURNAL PUBLICATIONS ABOUT SPIRITUALITY, FAITH,
RELIGION, AND LIFE PURPOSE, 1997–2013

	JCSD	*AC*	*JSARP**	*JCC*	*Total*
1997–2003	26	10	12	44**	92
2004–2008	76	40	3	187	306
2009–2013	70	30	23	117	240
Total	172	80	38	348	638

Notes: **JSARP* was first published as the *NASPA Journal.* ***JCC* did not begin publication until 1999.

as a reflection of my personal faith journey and the centrality of faith in the lives of college students with whom I had worked as a professional before becoming faculty. I would assert that as more people in the general public have become more comfortable with discussing spirituality, faith, religion, and life purpose in the public square, the same has happened for individual scholars in the academy. Researchers explore the topics that reflect the questions with which they most deeply wrestle (Jones, Torres, & Arminio, 2013), and, as Lee Knefelkamp explicitly commented, "all theory is autobiographical" (cited in Jones & Abes, 2010, p. 151). Moreover, the increasing use of constructivist and critical research methodologies has allowed for the emergence of themes in data that are non-unitary, intangible, and ethereal. This has opened up space for the inclusion of findings related to spirituality, faith, religion, and life purpose as the products of valid research, not just anecdotal speculation. Consequently, spirituality, faith, religion, and life purpose became acceptable foci for empirical inquiry across the academy as well as in higher education and student affairs.

Professional Development and Graduate Preparation

The next area in which student affairs professional associations have contributed to the increased visibility of spirituality, faith, religion, and life purpose is through professional development opportunities. Through member involvement in special-focus committees, national conferences, regional and state conferences, and themed institutes, ACPA and NASPA have expanded opportunities for student affairs practitioners to receive professional development about spirituality among college students, religious and secular pluralism, and faith diversity.

One opportunity for student affairs professionals who work in similar functional areas or share common interests is to create affinity groups in their professional associations. As Greg Roberts, ACPA's executive director, has explained, these groups provide the curriculum for professional development in the association (G. Roberts, personal communication). Called either *commissions* (ACPA) or *knowledge communities* (NASPA), these groups organize efforts to enhance professional development opportunities and promote research and scholarship.

As commissions and knowledge communities are often developed around demographic groups or functional areas, and there is no one demographic group or definable functional area for this topic that is present across institutional contexts, issues related to spirituality, faith, religion, and life purpose can be easily overlooked. Despite these challenges, student affairs professionals began to organize communities to share resources, support, and knowledge related to these issues. The impetus for these activities was likely similar to what spurred greater research and scholarship reflected in higher rates of publication discussed above. For example, as one of the individuals most closely involved in the development of what became ACPA's Commission for Spirituality, Faith, Religion, and Meaning (CSFRM), I clearly remember our early conversations centering on the trends we were seeing among students on our campuses and deep desires to have professional lives where our faith and beliefs converged with our career motivations. Moreover, there was a consistently expressed recognition of the need for spaces where people could practice and role-model interfaith dialogue, particularly in ways that were inclusive of atheist and secular humanist pathways to meaning and life purpose.

In 2003, NASPA formed the Spirituality and Religion in Higher Education knowledge community (SRHE KC). In 2008, conversations began in ACPA to explore the possibilities of forming a commission focused on spirituality. By 2009, the CSFRM had been approved, and it immediately became active in writing and publishing, professional development, and advocacy. Bringing together professionals and researchers from a diverse array of convictional belief systems and faith traditions, these interest-group communities have provided spaces for dialogue as well as centers for action.

Both NASPA's knowledge community and ACPA's commission have sponsored meetings and professional development sessions at their respective national conferences, as well as conducted webinars and coordinated publications in association journals (e.g., Stewart, Kocet, & Lobdell, 2011).

Through the efforts of the CSFRM and the SRHE KC, professional development sessions have consistently been featured in the ACPA and NASPA national conference programs and as stand-alone institutes. For example, in 2006, ACPA sponsored an institute focused on spirituality hosted at the University of Vermont that has been regarded as an influential experience and turning point in the field's engagement with these topics as a central component of student affairs practice. At the national conferences for both associations, recent data from 2013 found that 16 sessions were presented at NASPA's conference and 10 were presented at ACPA (searching by the same keywords used to conduct the publication search above). In previous years, ACPA's annual convention featured 17 sessions related to spirituality, faith, religion, and life purpose in 2012, and 6 appeared in the 2011 convention program (information was only accessible for ACPA).

In addition to lists of resources, conference sessions, and webinars sponsored by both groups, ACPA's CSFRM has continued to advance discussion about the role of student affairs professionals related to spirituality, faith, religion, and life purpose. CSFRM began by exploring with its members what awareness, knowledge, and skills were needed to effectively promote spiritual development among college students and to create and sustain interfaith dialogue and religious and secular pluralism on college campuses. One outcome of this internal discussion was the publication of an article by Kocet and Stewart (2011) in *JCC* that suggested a set of professional competencies that are necessary for student affairs professionals to effectively navigate the complex terrain of spirituality, religion, faith, and life purpose in higher education. Kocet and Stewart's recommendations for student affairs professionals include attending to their own inner lives, enhancing their knowledge of religious minority groups, and understanding the influence of institutional context. These also echo the findings reported by Seifert and Holman-Harmon (2009) regarding student affairs professionals' work with students' inner lives. A point made in both publications is the need for student affairs educators to attend to their own inner lives as they prepare to engage in these discussions with their students.

Although much had been written about college students' inner lives, there was little that focused on the professional competencies needed to effectively facilitate such growth and development in students. Student affairs is an applied field requiring attention to both theory and practice. Therefore, it is a natural evolution in the larger discussion about spirituality, faith, religion, and life purpose in student affairs that attention has turned to how professionals can engage this work with students. Moreover, as student affairs professionals at public institutions have entered the conversation, there remain considerable concerns whether this is an appropriate role for student affairs professionals and about the legitimacy of educators having these kinds of conversations with students. What was previously regarded as purely private domain, one's inner life, is now part of the terrain in the public square. Articles such as those by Kocet and Stewart (2011) as well as Seifert and Holman-Harmon (2009) push for both the relevance and legitimacy of student affairs professionals being involved in these kinds of conversations with college students as mentors and guides, not as clerics and proselytizers.

This emphasis on the professional development of student affairs professionals builds on the work being done by faculty in graduate preparation programs. Since the late 1990s, faculty in student affairs have also begun considering how to include intentional coverage of spiritual development and creating campus communities that acknowledge and respect the role of spirituality, religion, faith, and life purpose in the lives of students and student affairs professionals (Rogers & Love, 2007). Professional associations have helped to promote this work by publishing such research and through faculty involvement in dialogue through ACPA's CSFRM and NASPA's SRHE KC. The impact of the exposure of graduate students in student affairs to spiritual development theories, issues of religious pluralism, and interfaith dialogue has been to heighten the sensitivity to these issues among these emerging professionals. Having been taught to ask these kinds of questions and consider these issues, these professionals will likely continue to ask these questions in their research and practice and be dissatisfied with the status quo that separates intellectual inquiry from the inner life and fails to challenge religious hegemony in institutional environments. However, the use of specific competencies to guide practice, such as those developed by Kocet and Stewart (2011), have yet to be consistently incorporated in graduate preparation program curricula.

National Advocacy Efforts

ACPA and NASPA have not kept their engagement in spirituality, religion, faith, and life purpose insulated to student affairs. However, efforts in national advocacy remain sparse and inconsistent and are not coordinated across the two organizations. Both associations have developed partnerships and collaborative programming with the Interfaith Youth Core (IFYC), which is an active participant and instigator of national dialogues about interfaith cooperation. Through IFYC's higher education advisory council,

ACPA and NASPA members to the council have been able to influence strategy and offer recommendations. These recommendations have included how IFYC can best address issues of religious privilege while maintaining its focus on interfaith cooperation and interpersonal relationships as well as how to draw student affairs professionals into their campus organizing efforts to reach a broader range of college students. These efforts are still relatively new, as IFYC created its higher education advisory council just in 2011; therefore, the long-term outcomes and effects of these collaborations are not yet known.

Neither ACPA nor NASPA has participated in legislative advocacy specifically related to spirituality, religion, faith, or life purpose in higher education. With so many other issues on the table related to higher education policy at the state and federal levels, these issues have not become critical foci in public policy. However, the dissemination of scholarship in professional journals has the potential to reach policy makers and legislative staffers. Moreover, ACPA and NASPA equipping their members to advocate for policies supportive of faith diversity and religious and secular pluralism through expanding their awareness, knowledge, and skills is an important facet in sustaining efforts to incorporate these issues into broader conversations about social justice.

RECOMMENDATIONS

Student affairs professional associations have made great strides in a relatively short period, just 15 years, in bringing meaning making to the foreground in student affairs research and practice. However, there are three gaps in particular that need further attention. Addressing these issues would make their work more complete and benefit the more thorough incorporation of spirituality, religion, faith, and life purpose into student affairs.

First, associations need to provide a space for professionals to focus on their own inner lives, as discussed by both Kocet and Stewart (2011) and Seifert and Holman-Harmon (2009). For student affairs professionals to effectively facilitate students' spiritual development, they must be in tune with their own spiritual development and aware of how it influences their work as student affairs professionals, both generally and in regard to life purpose. Moreover, in a field dedicated to helping others, it is important for student affairs professionals to remember to take care of themselves and continue their own development. The personal foundations core area in the

ACPA and NASPA (2010) professional competencies lays a suitable ground-work to encourage the exploration of student affairs professionals' inner lives.

Second, student affairs associations could more assertively influence the graduate preparation of new professionals. The field would benefit from greater advocacy on the part of these associations for the use of competencies related to discussing and facilitating spiritual growth, interfaith dialogue, and religious and secular pluralism. Precedent for this has been set by the publication of the professional competencies (ACPA & NASPA, 2010), which has already influenced and shaped master's level graduate preparation at institutions across the country. For example, Bowling Green State University's College Student Personnel Program has adopted these professional competencies as a tool for assessing students' knowledge and skills as a gradu-ation requirement. If new professionals have already been exposed to these considerations, they will be better prepared to continue their development in the field without having to start from scratch.

Third, it is necessary to establish collaborative partnerships across student affairs professional associations. ACPA's CSFRM and NASPA's SRHE KC have yet to engage each other collaboratively as partners to promote spiritual development and faith diversity in student affairs. Competition will ulti-mately hinder progress and threaten a sustainable and cohesive movement to advance conversations related to spirituality, religion, faith, and life purpose in the field. Fostering collaborative partnerships between ACPA and NASPA could be a way to amplify the work being done singularly and collectively.

CONCLUSION

The last 15 years have seen remarkable growth in the presence and visibility of topics related to spirituality, religion, faith, and life purpose in student affairs. This emergence is largely due to the efforts of the profession's two leading professional associations, ACPA and NASPA. Through their research and professional journals, professional development and graduate prepara-tion opportunities, and nascent engagement in national advocacy, ACPA and NASPA have answered the calls made by those earlier scholars to incor-porate spirituality as a substantive element in students' learning, growth, and development and to consider the place of religious pluralism in campus environments. With increasing national attention on issues of spirituality, faith, religion, and life purpose, student affairs professionals will continue to confront these issues on their campuses. ACPA and NASPA are poised to continue providing leadership to advance those conversations and positively affect growth and change in student affairs and higher education. In the next chapter of this book, Sharon Lobdell suggests some ways this growth may happen in the future.

REFERENCES

ACPA–College Student Educators International & NASPA–Student Affairs Administrators in Higher Education. (2010). *Professional competency areas for student affairs practitioners*. Washington, DC: Authors. Retrieved from http://www.naspa.org/programs/prodev/Professional_Competencies.pdf

American Council on Education. (1937). *The student personnel point of view*. Washington, DC: Author.

American Council on Education. (1949). *The student personnel point of view*. Washington, DC: Author.

Dungy, G., & Gordon, S. A. (2010). The development of student affairs. In J. H. Schuh, S. R. Jones, S. R. Harper & Associates (Eds.), *Student services: A handbook for the profession* (5th ed., pp. 61–79). San Francisco: Jossey-Bass.

Eck, D. L. (2001). *A new religious America: How a "Christian country" has now become the world's most religiously diverse nation*. San Francisco: HarperCollins.

Evans, N. J., & Reason, R. D. (2001). Guiding principles: A review and analysis of student affairs philosophical statements. *Journal of College Student Development, 42,* 359–377.

Fowler, J. W. (1981). *Stages of faith: The psychology of human development and the quest for meaning*. San Francisco: HarperCollins.

Jones, S. R., & Abes, E. S. (2010). The nature and uses of theory. In J. H. Schuh, S. R. Jones, S. R. Harper & Associates (Eds.), *Student services: A handbook for the profession* (5th ed., pp. 149–167). San Francisco: Jossey-Bass.

Jones, S. R., Torres, V., & Arminio, J. (2013). *Negotiating the complexities of qualitative research in higher education: Fundamental elements and issues* (2nd ed.). New York: Routledge.

Kocet, M. M., & Stewart, D. L. (2011). The role of student affairs in promoting religious and secular pluralism and interfaith cooperation. *Journal of College and Character, 12*(1). doi:10.2202/1940-7882.1762

Laurence, P. (1999). Can religion and spirituality find a place in higher education? *About Campus, 4*(5), 11–16.

Love, P., & Talbot, D. (1999). Defining spiritual development: A missing consideration for student affairs. *NASPA Journal, 37,* 361–376.

McDonough, P. (2013, July 14). How social conservatives won: Can progressives reverse the tide? *Salon.* Retrieved from http://www.salon.com/2013/07/14/how_social_conservatives_won_can_progressives_reverse_the_tide/

Nelson, J. (2010). The evolving place of research on religion in the American Educational Research Association. *Religion & Education, 37,* 60–86.

Nuss, E. M. (2003). The development of student affairs. In S. R. Komives & D. B. Woodard Jr. (Eds.), *Student services: A handbook for the profession* (4th ed., pp. 65–88). San Francisco: Jossey-Bass.

Rogers, J. L., & Love, P. (2007). Exploring the role of spirituality in the preparation of student affairs professionals: Faculty constructions. *Journal of College Student Development, 48,* 90–104.

Schafer, W. E. (1997). Religiosity, spirituality, and personal distress among college students. *Journal of College Student Development, 38,* 633–644.

Schafer, W. E., & King, M. (1990). Religiousness and stress among college students: A survey report. *Journal of College Student Development, 31,* 336–341.

Seifert, T. A., & Holman-Harmon, N. (2009). Practical implications for student affairs professionals' work in facilitating students' inner development. *New Directions for Student Services, 2009*(125), 13–21.

Stewart, D. L. (2002). The role of faith in the development of an integrated identity: A qualitative study of Black students at a White college. *Journal of College Student Development, 43,* 579–596.

Stewart, D. L. (2008). Being all of me: Black students' struggles with negotiating identity. *Journal of Higher Education, 79,* 183–207.

Stewart, D. L. (2009). Perceptions of multiple identities among Black college students. *Journal of College Student Development, 50,* 253–270.

Stewart, D. L., Kocet, M. M., & Lobdell, S. (2011). The multifaith campus: Transforming colleges and universities for spiritual engagement. *About Campus, 16*(1), 10–18.

Temkin, L., & Evans, N. (1998). Religion on campus: Suggestions for cooperation between student affairs and campus-based religious organizations. *NASPA Journal, 36,* 61–69.

6

Professional Associations as Collaborations and Support Networks for Student Affairs Professionals

Sharon A. Lobdell

AS STUDENT AFFAIRS PRACTITIONERS and faculty in graduate preparation programs, we spend a majority of our days working with and nurturing the students we serve. We help them shape their academic paths, and we provide them with guidance when issues affect their well-being. We apply the theories and concepts we learned in our graduate programs to help foster their identity development. We also work to help them learn to understand themselves as they undertake a journey of personal exploration.

There is an inherent problem, though, in that many professionals and faculty members do not engage in the same processes through which we guide our students. We have a protocol of what students should do and when and how they should do it, but because of reasons ranging from our own personal doubts to a lack of understanding or an unwelcoming campus climate, we don't always practice what we preach. For the seasoned practitioner, part of this is a result of the long work hours and the many professional commitments that must be honored (Craft & Hochella, 2010). Perhaps the larger issue, though, is that we don't know how to begin our own journeys. We don't hear the same songs we sing to our students. How can we as practitioners embrace the core values we stress to our students? What support networks do we have in place to help us accomplish this?

Chapter 5 examined professional organizations and the work they are currently doing regarding spirituality, religion, and meaning making. Their efforts are taking these issues and putting them into the spotlight through new programs and policies in higher education. This chapter continues to build on this by asking the following: How do these same organizations strengthen the professional development and growth of the practitioners? What kind of impact do they have on professionals' growth, as well as the growth of their institutions? And what does the future hold for these organizations and their role in shaping how spirituality, faith, religion, and life purpose influence higher education and its students? I also make the case that as more graduate programs include spirituality, faith, religion, and life purpose in their curricula, the new professionals who have matriculated through these programs are able to provide a greater level of support for the spiritual development of students they nurture at their employing institutions. The result is the creation of a virtuous cycle in which inclusion of this form of identity occurs more broadly throughout higher education.

BACKGROUND

As practitioners, it is vital for us to be exposed to other belief systems. This not only aids in how we understand our world but also helps us shape how we define our own spiritual journeys. The history of higher education in America is rooted in Christian doctrine, with the original student body being mostly White men (Thelin, 2011). Take a look at any college or university campus today, and you will see that has drastically changed. Our campuses today are a rich tapestry of races and spiritual identities. It is critical to understand this diversity as well as to open ourselves up to growth and exploration along the way. Where do we turn, though, if we don't have a support network on our campuses? If we do not feel safe or connected, it is hard for us to reveal our true selves (Moxley, 2000). As a result, we search for places where we find that connection and can safely explore and nurture our own beliefs and needs.

This is where professional organizations enter the equation. These groups can fill a personal and professional need for student affairs practitioners, in serving as a safe climate for dialogue and research and an open arena for the exchange of ideas and resources. My story is not unique for the most part, but it does serve as an example of how affiliation with the right group can enrich not only your mind but your being, as well.

I have worked in student affairs for over 15 years at the University of Michigan–Dearborn, located just outside Detroit. The student body is composed of many ethnic and religious groups, each with their own unique identities. Many of these groups are represented by student organizations that hold events to educate the campus community about their customs, origins, and other aspects of their identities. They understand their stories and wish to share them with others. Until four years ago, though, I had never stopped to consider my own story.

My spiritual development has been a rather convoluted journey. I wasn't exposed to any form of organized religion as a child, and I was left to explore options as I grew up. I have been a practicing Pagan for more than 30 years, but this identification was never something that I willingly shared, for fear of what the response would be. To be honest, as my professional career grew, my spiritual path was lost in the fog. It was more important to be a success and collect the accolades that went with it. I also never took the initiative to learn about the beliefs of those around me. I knew some of my friends and colleagues were Jewish and others Baptist or Catholic. But other than that, it didn't really matter to me how this shaped them as persons. I realize now, though, that I denied myself the opportunity to live fully in the light. Had I taken the time to make these connections and build these bridges, my spiritual journey would have been richer and more insightful. And this would have made me a stronger student affairs practitioner.

What was the turning point for me? In 2009, I received an e-mail about the formation of the ACPA–College Student Educators International Taskforce on Spirituality, Faith, and Religion. As I read, the e-mail awakened a feeling of need in me, especially when I read the line "we seek to become a community of practice for interfaith dialogue and religious pluralism." I responded to the message, asking the sender if a Pagan would be welcome on this journey. I wasn't sure what this experience was going to be, but I knew that I had to let myself be part of it.

I became part of the task force and then the Commission for Spirituality, Faith, Religion, and Meaning (CSFRM), at the same time starting to learn about my colleagues and about myself and my beliefs. It was extremely uncomfortable to disclose my beliefs to those in the commission, for fear that I would not be accepted. I soon found that I couldn't have been more wrong. My fear was replaced with a sense of acceptance that they embraced me for who I am, not what I am or what I practice. Without this group connection, I doubt that I would ever have openly acknowledged my beliefs and, in turn, begun my own journey.

THE JOURNEY

How many student affairs practitioners share this story? For some practitioners, expressing their spiritual/religious identities on their campuses is difficult or impossible. Their campus environments may be sectarian, and a deviation from what is seen to be the campus norm may create issues. Another possibility is that perhaps they are not ready or able to begin the journey. As a result, it can be difficult for them to be fully actualized practitioners, and, in turn, they are unable to serve the students they work with to the degree of passion and understanding that students want. Moran and Curtis (2004) suggested that safe environments need to be created to encourage dialogues between colleagues of different religious/spiritual/meaning-making backgrounds. Professional entities like those found in ACPA and NASPA–Student Affairs Administrators in Higher Education help to meet this need.

Institutions are also affected by the connection that practitioners have with professional organizations. At the core of all people's identities is their connection with the world. This spiritual dimension is the foundation on which existence is built. Our physical, emotional, psychological, social, environmental, and intellectual developments are tied to spiritual growth, for that is at the core of who we are. This development of "the habits of the heart" (Bellah, Madsen, Sullivan, Swindler, & Tipton, 1985, p. viii), a phrase borrowed from Alexis de Tocqueville's (1835/1981) *Democracy in America*, shapes individuals and the ways in which they connect to the world around them. It also shapes the institution, in that these same practitioners make up the heart of the organization. Practitioners who are in complete awareness and understanding of their beliefs will be more in tune with those around them. This creates a climate wherein fully actualized practitioners can allow their professional passions to come through in their daily work.

This same concept is at the core of why professional organizations can fill a critical void for student affairs practitioners. They allow professionals to continue to do interfaith work while engaging in intrapersonal work on the self. Allen and Kellom (2001) stated that spiritual principles develop from the belief that people have an interdependent relationship with each other and the world around them. If you add on the confines of their jobs, with the deadlines and protocols and long hours, many do not have time to embrace this connection. In turn, they slip further away from living in the present. Astin (2004) made the following argument:

Academia has for far too long encouraged us to lead fragmented and inauthentic lives, where we act either as if we are not spiritual beings, or as if our spiritual side is irrelevant to our vocation or work. Under these conditions, our work becomes divorced from our most deeply felt values and we hesitate to discuss issues of meaning, purpose, authenticity, wholeness, and fragmentation with our colleagues. At the same time, we likewise discourage our students from engaging these same issues among themselves and with us. (p. 6)

How do we as practitioners correct this? A great starting point is being exposed to a group of individuals that are on the same journey. This opportunity, not only to meet fellow practitioners that are on the spiritual journey, but also to actively engage in the journey with them, can be an adventure. Through the dialogues and collaborations that are nurtured we are given the chance to expand past the footprint of our institutions and see a more regional or even global perspective. We are challenged, questioned, and enlightened and in turn we grow and evolve along with our fellow travelers.

OVERVIEW OF PROFESSIONAL ASSOCIATIONS

Professional organizations that have an entity charged with addressing faith, spiritual, religious, or meaning-based concepts allow for the development of a network that encourages the discussion of these important topics. Part of the mission of these entities is to engage in dialogues to identify and shape professional competencies that are needed to engage issues of spirituality, faith, religion, and meaning by practitioners. As described in Chapter 5, the two major student affairs professional organizations that address issues of spiritual development are ACPA and NASPA.

According to the mission statement of ACPA's CSFRM, the commission will provide ACPA members an arena within which to conduct research and assessment, strengthen their professional competencies, and enrich their self-knowledge and professional knowledge about issues related to meaning-making, specifically spirituality, faith, religion, belief, and existentialism within the context of higher education. In addition, acting within the ACPA governance structure and with the ACPA International Office, CSFRM will assist in positioning ACPA to be an informed voice on existential pursuits of meaning-making, including spirituality, faith, religion, and belief as they relate to student development, the administration of student affairs, and the organization of governance structures within a college, community college, or university setting. These efforts will include examining various modes of pursuing meaning-making in the contextual experience of both the U.S. and the global higher education community. (ACPA–College Student Educators International, 2009, Mission section, para. 1)

NASPA addresses spiritual and religious work in higher education through its Spirituality and Religion in Higher Education knowledge community. Their mission is as follows:

> To enhance and contribute to the conversations about spirituality in higher education across all types of post-secondary institutions. This knowledge community welcomes practitioners, students and faculty members from the profession of student affairs as well as persons for whom spirituality and religion constitute a major element of their work in higher education. (NASPA–Student Affairs Administrators in Higher Education, 2009, About section, paras. 1–2)

These organizations have their own missions and memberships. But they do share the common goal of serving as a place for individuals seeking to look at spiritual development and how it impacts college students, institutions of higher learning, and student affairs practitioners. As more individuals seek a place to engage in open dialogues and to explore interfaith practices, they will become part of groups such as these or any other that might be created in the coming years. The world is rapidly changing, and U.S. institutions are becoming more of a microcosmic representation of the world. Practitioners will continue to search for havens where they can grow as professionals and also feel safe and nurtured as individuals. Another factor is that with funding to higher education becoming more of an issue, collaborations and affiliations can afford practitioners with resources and programming opportunities that they might not be able to find at their own institutions.

Affiliation with professional groups that have embraced the issue of meaning making allow practitioners exposure to colleagues that can serve as resources and sounding boards. According to Pavalko (1971) and Wilensky (1964), professional associations serve as a source of identity in that their meetings, procedures, and traditions encourage unity and collaboration. For some, this is the safe and inclusive environment that they do not have on their own campuses. Seifert and Holman-Harmon (2009) made the case that it will serve student affairs practitioners well to refocus on asking and struggling with their own Big Questions.

PROFESSIONAL AFFILIATION: A PLACE TO FOLLOW OUR HEARTS AND MINDS

What is the result for institutions of collaborations that are born from affiliations with organizations, such as ACPA and NASPA? As practitioners experience spiritual growth and become more productive, their institutions are enhanced, as well. The energy of the campus is stronger and more positive, and it is more attractive to students and others (Allen & Kellom, 2001). This upward trend benefits not only the practitioners but the institution and the students, as well. For example, if practitioners act with integrity and are authentic in their actions, this will influence others to do the same. As this energy grows, the energy of the campus is marked by authenticity, trust, and living in the moment.

Affiliation with a professional organization also encourages the enhanced exchange of ideas and is especially critical for new practitioners who have had limited exposure to such diversity in their graduate programs or entry-level positions. The membership body of a professional organization is a cross section of the profession in that it represents the newest professionals to the most seasoned professionals. Having the opportunity to be part of such a diverse collective allows new practitioners the opportunity to marry the knowledge mastered in their graduate programs with the tips, tactics, and best practices shared by colleagues who have already walked down this same path. As this exploration continues, practitioners further hone their skills and continue to evolve into stronger student affairs professionals on their campuses. For seasoned practitioners, as well, exposure to new ideas and practices can sometimes be the needed breath of fresh air that helps them begin to revitalize their approaches to the profession and their own searches for meaning in the world. They too continue to grow as practitioners and as spiritual beings.

Professional affiliations can sometimes lead to the development of specialists and scholars in the field. Collaborations, similar interests with colleagues and fellow group members, and research opportunities can shape the direction of personal journeys. Along the way, through research and dialogues, an understanding of the topic is developed. If it ignites people's passions, they want to learn more. So they dig deeper, talk to more individuals, and soon might be considered the people to speak to regarding the topic. *Making Meaning* is a good example of such an endeavor in that it represents a collaboration born of connections formed via membership in ACPA, and it focuses on a set of shared ideas and concepts, each told from the voice of a contributor.

Although the importance of spirituality, faith, religion, and life purpose within professional associations has expanded greatly in the past decade, there is still room for considerable growth. As the face of higher education continues to change, so will the collection of works that represents how student affairs practitioners interact with students and with themselves. U.S. campuses today are a slice of the global population. Therefore, student affairs practitioners must rethink how they interact not only with these students but also with the diverse group of professionals with whom they work. Suggestions as to how organizations can foster growth are examined later in this chapter.

GRADUATE PROGRAMS AND PROFESSIONAL ORGANIZATIONS

Graduate programs serve as a foundation for new practitioners, helping them to build the skill base they need to develop as professionals. Graduate students learn about student development, legal issues, diversity and inclusion, and other concepts critical to their profession. And some are exposed to the concept of spiritual or faith development of college students and how they as practitioners can guide students through the process of exploration. Graduate preparation programs address the issues of authenticity, connectedness, purpose, and transcendence, but the connection between these concepts and supporting the spiritual growth of students has at times not been clearly defined. Part of this disconnect could be a result of how spiritual growth has been overlooked in the grand scheme of student development. It is important for graduate students to understand these concepts so that they will possess the necessary knowledge as they move into the professional realm of student affairs (Rogers & Love, 2007).

The curriculum of student affairs preparation programs began to change in the late 1990s as more and more college students began to explore how spirituality and religion shaped their lives (Nash, 1999). Higher education professionals began to address this need, serving as catalysts for the spirituality movement exploding across our campuses over the next decade (Astin, 2004; Chickering, Dalton & Stamm, 2006). How has the curriculum for graduate programs in student affairs been affected by this exposure? Based on a study of nine southern student affairs graduate programs, Wiese and Cawthon (2009) indicated that there has not been enough improvement. They stated that they advocate

. . . an increased visibility of spirituality in student affairs graduate preparation programs. The findings of our study further this position. By utilizing the data pertaining to the current graduate student spirituality levels, researchers and faculty members can begin the process of altering the culture of spirituality within each institution. In doing so, preparation programs can counter the consistent findings that indicate a lack of this topic in the curriculum. In addition, since this study indicated no relationship between student spirituality levels and both the program of study and the institution, educational experiences developed and honed at one institution could be implemented by faculty at others with similar results. (p. 11)

Graduate programs include concepts such as authenticity, connectedness, and purpose in their coursework, but unless the connection to spirituality and meaning making is made clear, it may not prepare professionals for the diverse student bodies with whom they will work. The student affairs practitioner is ready to work with students after receiving a degree. But there is no one way to learn about spiritual development. There is no comprehensive text or standardized exam that assesses the level of understanding. Ideally, this growth should take place during the graduate program and continue to develop once the practitioner becomes part of a campus community. Perhaps the work of professional organizations will help shape graduate preparation programs in the coming years, in that they will be the entity producing the scholarly texts and articles, as well as the necessary competencies in this area.

Postgraduate support systems are needed to continue the development of the practitioner. It is critical for practitioners to understand their own spiritual identities before they can seek to encourage the students they work with to undertake this exploration. Being part of an organization can provide practitioners the first opportunity to better understand the connection of these concepts to the development of their own spiritual identities.

ISSUES WITH OUR HOME INSTITUTIONS

Having an affiliation with a professional organization provides practitioners with connections to a group of like-minded individuals, which is especially critical if this safe or open climate does not exist at their home institutions. Spiritual aims may not permeate the culture of colleges and universities, especially if the institution is religiously affiliated. According to Laurence (1999):

Even in schools still affiliated with a particular religious institution, educators struggle with the dilemma of how to support a suitable religious life for
populations in which in many cases almost half of the students come from
other traditions. (p. 13)

The challenge lies in finding balance between the religious doctrine of
the institution and the need to provide an inclusive and safe climate for its
students where they know that they are valued by the institution. Affiliation
with a professional organization could present a practitioner with access to
colleagues from across the country, or perhaps even the globe, that can serve
as the needed resources to help them and their institutions address this issue.

Another reason for a lack of safe space might be the campus population
viewing spirituality as being within the purview of the campus ministry or
off-campus religious groups. Many believe that issues of this matter should
be addressed by ministers, rabbis, or religious student organizations, as they
are perceived as not being integral to the daily operations of the campus.
This somewhat closed approach can be prohibitive in regard to the spiritual
development of the overall campus community, as it isolates and diminishes
a critical segment of student development. Taking a hands-off approach to
the subject of spirituality, religion, and meaning making will not make it go
away, nor should it be the charge of one or two individuals on the campus
to deal with it. This critical component of student development, and staff
development, as well, should be the concern of the entire institution. This
avoidance of spiritual issues has created a void that can be filled by bringing
together a coalition from religious groups and campus staff and administration to address how the campus culture can be changed by educating campus
personnel about the importance of this aspect of student development.

Chickering et al. (2006) discussed the fact that student affairs practitioners have not been influential in advocating for spirituality in higher education. Part of this is due to not understanding the connection between
individuals' spiritual cores and their identity development during their college careers. Practitioners, then, in an attempt to keep their distance, lose
the opportunity to tap into the core of their student's being. Seifert and
Holman-Harmon (2009) stated that "in order to be inclusive of all students,
student affairs practitioners from both ends of the spectrum (highly religious
to atheist) likely need to reconceptualize and reconcile how they support
students' inner development" (p. 17).

Because of these challenges, professional organizations such as ACPA and
NASPA provide a double service to higher education. For practitioners, they

provide a safe climate in which to continue their personal and professional development. For higher education, these organizations serve as a repository of research data, best practices, and collegial support. They also support collaborative efforts that bring together practitioners from the region or the globe. This collective support is critical to our institutions as they continue to navigate the changing face of higher education.

What do new professionals do if they find their campuses do not provide for them what they seek to enhance in their own identities, things that they were not taught in graduate school? Institutions that are religious based have an established doctrine that blankets the mission of the school. What if a practitioner is not part of this religious group? What if the campus treats religion, spirituality, and meaning making as something to be addressed by the ministry or as something not highly valued in the interactions with students? Institutions that take this stance do not embrace the total education of the student. Student affairs practitioners also are hindered in that they cannot be part of the holistic development of the students they serve.

Being affiliated with a professional organization can fill the void in several ways:

- Enhanced programming opportunities are made possible through exposure to the works being done on other campuses. A successful program at another university could easily be retooled for one's institution.
- Affiliation encourages collaborations between institutions and other entities that focus on spiritual development. In the four years that the CSFRM has existed, there have been several collaborations on webinars, writing projects, events, and sponsored programs at conventions. More important are the increased dialogues that have taken place between student affairs practitioners across the field. Being able to come together at the same table, both literally and figuratively, allows for the building of a community.
- Scholarly articles examining different aspects of spirituality, faith, religion, and life purpose can be born from graduate degree work. This early research, sometimes conducted with established faculty, can afford the developing practitioner the opportunity to nurture a concept that might grow from a paper to a dissertation to a published text.
- Greater opportunities for collaborative research are also born from affiliations within student affairs. The webinars and writing projects mentioned above were accomplished by practitioners from different

campuses and organizations from across the country, including Miami University, the University of Oregon, Boston College, Bowling Green State University, the University of Michigan–Dearborn, and Bridgewater State University. The list of those who participated in the webinars would be a sampling of practitioners of diverse backgrounds and levels of experience. The opportunity to work with or engage in dialogues with colleagues from other institutions truly expands the network of which practitioners are part.

◆ If the graduate program structure does not provide enough curricular support for students to evolve into competent supporters of spiritual development, professional associations can fill the resulting void. Having exposure to professional organizations during their studies allows graduate students to build their own skill bases as well as strong support/resource networks. There are opportunities to present papers, conduct research, and be exposed to a wide spectrum of practitioners who are already part of the profession. This exposure allows them to rethink how they approach their academic work as well as shapes the development of their professional identities.

ISSUES FACING PROFESSIONAL ORGANIZATIONS

What are some of the critical issues that professional organizations have to address going forward? Dalton (2006) presented a list of items critical to how these organizations see spirituality, faith, religion, and life purpose, and how they shape the holistic development of students. The items that can best be embraced by professional organizations include the following suggestions:

◆ Take a stronger role in advocating for the place of spirituality in the mission and culture of higher education and as an essential aspect of holistic student learning.

◆ Conduct more research on trends and patterns of contemporary college student spirituality.

◆ Clarify the meaning of spirituality for young adults' development in the higher education setting.

◆ Strengthen the education and training of professionals to work with college student spirituality and faith development. (A prime example here would be the competencies discussed in Chapter 5.)

- Integrate spirituality into current theories and research on college student development.
- Include spirituality as a component in staff development and training.

This list addresses the fundamental concepts that need to be considered when addressing spirituality in higher educational settings. Entities such as ACPA and NASPA are already exploring these issues through their research and collaborative efforts. In addition, the creation of a written doctrine for practitioners would serve to strengthen their professional development. The competencies by Kocet and Stewart (2011) presented in Chapter 5 of this book can serve as a framework for student affairs practitioners moving forward.

Strengthening the role of spirituality, religion, and meaning making in higher education will help institutions evolve into more inclusive and authentic places. Being concerned with students' development includes looking at what is at their core. It also means taking into consideration spirituality and religion when working with staff. If these individuals are not in touch with their beliefs, or if they do not feel safe or understood because of them, they will not thrive. And that will hurt not only their students but the campus as a whole.

COLLABORATIONS AND PARTNERSHIPS: LEVERAGING RESOURCES AND ACHIEVING CHANGE

Higher education is always changing and evolving. New research, diverse student bodies, and a global influence drive the need for collaboration. An awareness of spirituality, faith, religion, and life purpose can be fostered through collaborations with local, state, regional, or national entities that are currently engaged in projects that look at interfaith connections or the holistic development of the individual. These groups are not necessarily based within higher education, but they do realize the importance of having student affairs practitioners as partners in the process. Examples of a few important partners include Interfaith Youth Core (IFYC), the Michigan Roundtable for Diversity and Inclusion, and the National Campus Ministry Association (NCMA).

The mission of IFYC is to "build religious pluralism" (IFYC, n.d.). IFYC seeks to develop informed interfaith leaders on campus who will continue to shape and move discussions of interfaith cooperation. They have collaborated with the CSFRM on projects in the past and will partner again to work on potential webinars and publications. Through their work with strategic visioning and sustainability, they have created a series of reports and tools that campuses can use to increase involvement. Since 2002, IFYC has worked on more than 150 colleges and universities in their pursuit of interfaith cooperation (President's Advisory Council on Faith-Based and Neighborhood Partnerships, 2010, p. 84).

On the state level, the Michigan Roundtable for Diversity & Inclusion has partnered with universities and community groups over the years on projects ranging from inclusion issues to interfaith dialogues. Although not a professional organization along the lines of ACPA, they actively seek partnerships with corporations, higher education, and religious groups to ensure that the mission of the organization continues well into the future. That mission is as follows:

> Since 1941 The Michigan Roundtable for Diversity and Inclusion has been a not-for-profit civil rights organization located in Detroit working to overcome discrimination and racism by crossing racial, religious, ethnic and cultural boundaries. We bring together community leaders from government, law enforcement, education, faith, grass roots organizations and business to understand different points of view and then take action to overcome structural impediments to inclusion and equity. Our programs are recognized by national organizations for bringing about sustainable change. We work to address inequity throughout our region through a process of recognition, reconciliation/reorientation and renewal. We strive to build relationships that create social justice and build sustainable inclusive communities. (Michigan Roundtable for Diversity & Inclusion, n.d., Our Work section, para. 1)

The work of the roundtable makes it a valuable partner with higher education, in that it serves as a bridge between the communities and educational institutions. It strives, through the regional impact of its work, to improve the overall climate of the region.

The NCMA is a professional organization that focuses on the education and encouragement of practitioners working in campus ministry settings (National Campus Ministry Association, n.d.). Two of their areas of focus are maintaining a network for mutual support and resources as well as encouraging collegiate support and dialogue. They offer assistance for personal and professional growth to those engaged in campus ministry, full or part time, clergy or laity. This is a sectarian group, but their mission still affords those in campus ministry exposure to others in their field as well as a greater understanding of how spiritual identity is shaped. It is important to note that although this group is not directly connected to student affairs, they still represent the campus ministry component found on many campuses. Through their mission and goals, they offer support to individuals who might otherwise be disconnected from the campus.

NEW HORIZONS

One particularly exciting new venture promises to move student affairs' partnerships into the future. In March 2010, President Obama's first Advisory Council on Faith-Based and Neighborhood Partnerships released the Faith Council Report. This council was charged to focus its attention on making recommendations in the following areas:

- ◆ Economic recovery and domestic poverty
- ◆ Environment and climate change
- ◆ Fatherhood and healthy families
- ◆ Global poverty and development
- ◆ Interreligious cooperation
- ◆ Reform of the Office of Faith-Based and Neighborhood Partnerships (President's Advisory Council on Faith-Based and Neighborhood Partnerships, 2010)

For the purposes of this chapter only interreligious cooperation is examined as to how it applies to higher education. The White House has looked at higher education to be the leader in creating a new interfaith movement in our country. As student affairs practitioners, what will our role be in this process? How can our institutions be the foundation of a new approach to the interfaith conversation?

In terms of interreligious cooperation, the council has made three recommendations to be implemented on 500 U.S. college campuses (President's Advisory Council on Faith-Based and Neighborhood Partnerships, 2010, p. 81). The first is that funds should be allocated to provide financial incentives to stimulate campus/community partnerships that bring together people from different religious and secular lines. Second, senior university officials and members of the private/philanthropic sector should come together to commit to advance university/interfaith community service partnerships.

Third, a joint fund should be created that would allow for the implementation of student programming geared to developing service partnerships between faith-based and secular groups that have focused on service initiatives. This final recommendation holds the most promise in that student affairs practitioners can potentially work to implement the programming on their campuses. There is also the potential for groups such as ACPA and NASPA to be part of the process and create appropriate programming that could be done at multiple campuses.

Right now would be the perfect opportunity to implement programs that fall within the guidelines established by the President's Advisory Council. Graduate programs, external groups, professional organizations, and students could all come together with the final outcome being an enhanced level of interfaith cooperation. Student affairs will be changed as the students who are now exploring their own identities step into professional roles on campus. Roof (1999) stated that some Americans are exploring faiths and spiritual disciplines for the first time, whereas others are rediscovering their lost traditions. Others navigate to small groups and alternative communities to continue their journeys, or they create their own mix of values and metaphysical beliefs. Roof advocated a focus on the religious and spiritual narratives of individuals, to let their voices speak their stories. This allows the individual to fully understand how religion is shaped and how it shapes society.

FINAL THOUGHTS

As practitioners, our spiritual identities shape our daily interactions with students. Navigating our own professional journeys, we have undergone tremendous change and growth. We have collected degrees and the expertise that goes along with them. We have developed from children into adults. Perhaps we have started families or taken new jobs. Our journeys are diverse and ongoing. For some of us, spiritual identity was never in question. For others, though, the path has become unclear or even lost.

There are some practitioners who have difficulty working with students from diverse populations. This could be a result of personal issues. Or it could be a result of little or no exposure to students who do not share the same spiritual/religious identity. What if extremely religious practitioners are placed into the situation where they must work with atheist students? Do they need to put their own beliefs to the side to help these students? I personally believe that we all have to have a deep enough understanding of our own spiritual identities to put the needs of students first, for their development is the focal point.

As practitioners it is important for us to be in touch with our own spiritual development so that we are better equipped to deal with the personal and professional demands we face on a daily basis. Rogers and Dantley (2001) stated that "soul leaders" (p. 596) seek to comprehend the religious-spiritual dimension of others and that they develop open spaces where democratic, caring communities can be formed with others. The end result is the formation of a "holding environment" (p. 600) that encourages the inward journey. This is a perfect description for a professional entity focused on spirituality, faith, religion, and life purpose.

Affiliations with professional organizations offer practitioners the opportunity to interact with diverse professionals and to hopefully develop a better understanding as to how we can be inclusive of all faiths and practices. Through these affiliations, we can develop greater global understanding (Astin, Astin, & Lindholm, 2011), expanding our world beyond our campus boundaries and developing the skills needed to serve our diverse student bodies. In the process, we also benefit in that we gain an understanding that we are a small thread in a very large and vibrant tapestry.

The future of higher education is changing, almost on a daily basis. Growing focus is being placed on issues such as sustainability, veteran students, and inclusion. In the past decade, there has been an increased awareness of the importance of the spiritual identity of our students. Two hundred years ago, colleges and universities were White, male, Christianity-based entities. Today that is not the case. The rich diversity of our institutions is based in part on the tapestry of beliefs that comprise its communities. As professionals, we must understand ourselves and how we relate to the world around us if we fully wish to serve those students who look to us for support and guidance. Professional associations provide us with a venue in which to build this understanding. They afford us a new perspective that we can use to look at the world around us as well as exposure to other practitioners on the same journey. This is a critical piece of spiritual development in that it forces individuals to not only look around but also to look inside themselves. Our students see us as role models, so we must make sure that we do all that we can to be as fully actuated as possible.

REFERENCES

ACPA–College Student Educators International. (2009). *Task force for spirituality, faith, and religion*. Retrieved from http://www.myacpa.org/commsfrm

Allen, K. E., & Kellom, G. E. (2001). The role of spirituality in student affairs and staff development. *New Directions for Student Services, 2001*(95), 47–55.

Astin, A. W. (2004). Why spirituality deserves a central place in higher education. *Spirituality in Higher Education Newsletter, 1*(1), 1–12.

Astin, A. W., Astin, H. S., & Lindholm, J. A. (2011). *Cultivating the spirit: How college can enhance students' inner lives*. San Francisco: Jossey-Bass.

Bellah, R. N., Madsen, R., Sullivan, W., Swindler, A., & Tipton, S. M. (1985). *Habits of the heart: Individualism and commitment in American life*. Berkeley: University of California Press.

Chickering, A. W., Dalton, J. C., & Stamm, L. (2006). *Encouraging authenticity and spirituality in higher education*. San Francisco: Jossey-Bass.

Craft, C. M., & Hochella, R. (2010). Essential responsibilities of student affairs administrators: Identifying a purpose in life and helping students do the same. *Journal of College and Character, 11*(4). doi:10.2202/1940-1639.1744

Dalton, J. C. (2006). The place of spirituality in the mission and work of college student affairs. In A. W. Chickering, J. C. Dalton, & L. Stamm (Eds.), *Encouraging authenticity and spirituality in higher education* (pp. 145–164). San Francisco: Jossey-Bass.

de Tocqueville, A. (1981). *Democracy in America* (T. Bender, Ed.). New York: Modern Library. (Original work published 1835)

Interfaith Youth Core. (n.d.). *About the movement*. Retrieved from http://www.ifyc.org/about

Kocet, M. M., & Stewart, D. L. (2011). The role of student affairs in promoting religious and secular pluralism and interfaith cooperation. *Journal of College and Character, 12*(1). doi:10.2202/1940-7882.1762

Laurence, P. (1999). Can religion and spirituality find a place in higher education? *About Campus, 4*(5), 11–16.

Michigan Roundtable for Diversity & Inclusion. (n.d.). *Our work*. Retrieved from http://www.miroundtable.org/ourwork.htm

Moran, C. D., & Curtis, G. D. (2004). Blending two worlds: Religio-spirituality in the professional lives of student affairs administrators. *NASPA Journal, 41*(4), 631–646.

Moxley, R. S. (2000). *Leadership and spirit: Breathing new vitality and energy into individuals and organizations*. San Francisco: Jossey-Bass.

Nash, R. J. (1999). *Faith, hype and clarity: Teaching about religion in American schools and colleges.* New York: Teachers College Press.

NASPA–Student Affairs Administrators in Higher Education. (2009). *Spirituality and religion in higher education.* Retrieved from http://www.naspa.org/ constituent-groups/kcs/spirituality-and-religion-in-higher-education/history

National Campus Ministry Foundation. (n.d.). *Our mission & purpose.* Retrieved from http://www.campusministry.net/purpose/

Pavalko, R. M. (1971). *Sociology of occupations and professions.* Itasca, IL: F. E. Peacock.

President's Advisory Council on Faith-Based and Neighborhood Partnerships. (2010). *A new era of partnerships: Report of recommendations to the President.* Washington, DC: Author.

Rogers, J. L., & Dantley, M. E. (2001). Invoking the spiritual in campus life and leadership. *Journal of College Student Development, 42*(6), 589–603.

Rogers, J. L., & Love, P. (2007). Exploring the role of spirituality in the preparation of student affairs professionals: Faculty constructions. *Journal of College Student Development, 48*(1), 90–104.

Roof, W. C. (1999). *Spiritual marketplace: Baby boomers and the remaking of American religion.* Princeton, NJ: Princeton University Press.

Seifert, T. A., & Holman-Harmon, N. (2009). Practical implications for student affairs professionals' work in facilitating students' inner development. *New Directions for Student Services, 2009*(125), 13–21.

Thelin, J. R. (2011). *A history of American higher education* (2nd ed.). Baltimore, MD: Johns Hopkins University Press.

Wiese, D., & Cawthon, T. W. (2009). The uniformity of spiritual culture in nine southern student affairs graduate preparation programs. *Journal of College and Character, 10*(7). doi:10.2202/1940-1639.1441

Wilensky, H. L. (1964). The professionalization of everyone? *American Journal of Sociology, 70*(2), 137–158.

Part Three

Practice

7

Campus Practice in Support of Spirituality, Faith, Religion, and Life Purpose

What Has Been Accomplished and Where Do We Go Next?

Kathleen M. Goodman, Katie Wilson, and Z Nicolazzo

A MERE 13 YEARS AGO, WHILE introducing an issue of *New Directions for Student Services* on the topic of student spirituality, Jablonski (2001) stated that the reason for publishing the issue was that "student affairs and student affairs preparation programs have been reluctant to address spirituality" (p. 1). In fact, from the 1990s through the turn of the century, it was quite common for student affairs educators to lament that a focus on spirituality and spiritual development was lacking in undergraduate education (Laurence, 1999; Love & Talbot, 1999).

This book is evidence that a great deal has changed in a short time. The topic of spirituality has become ubiquitous in student affairs and higher education, as demonstrated by numerous articles for student affairs practitioners appearing in *Liberal Education* (for example, Adler, 2007), *About Campus* (for example, Subbiondo, 2011), and the *Journal of Student Affairs Research and Practice* (for example, Park & Millora, 2010). Books have been written on the topic (for example, Astin, Astin, & Lindholm, 2011), and the theme has been approached in student affairs preparation programs (Rogers &

118

Love, 2007). Campus practice in support of spirituality, faith, religion, and life purpose has become quite common, but little has been written about why it has rapidly assumed a place in higher education and student affairs. It is likely that large cultural shifts have played a role in this growth. Globalization and the effects of September 11, 2001, made it clear that religious diversity must be engaged (Patel, 2012). Furthermore, "the rise of post-modern, post-positivist, feminist, and minority-group scholarship has called into question the ideals of objectivity and value-free scholarship" (Mahoney, Schmalzbauer, & Younis, 2001, p. 40), making it easier for discussion of spirituality and religion to find a place in college education. It is also likely that at least four pragmatic/material changes have contributed to increased awareness of spirituality in higher education: leadership of professional organizations, increased grant funding designed to support spirituality, production of highly visible research, and the personal interests of campus administrators and faculty.

Leadership of Professional Organizations

ACPA–College Student Educators International and NASPA–Student Affairs Administrators in Higher Education are the two primary professional organizations for student affairs educators. Both organizations have hosted conferences focused on spirituality in higher education. Each has also developed a formal structure for guiding spirituality work. The influences of NASPA's Spirituality and Religion in Higher Education knowledge community and ACPA's Commission for Spirituality, Faith, Religion, and Meaning (CSFRM) are discussed in Chapters 5 and 6 of this volume.

Increased Grant Funding

A large influx of grant money supporting campus projects related to spirituality, faith, religion, and life purpose has contributed to campus practice. The Templeton Foundation (John Templeton Foundation, 2010; Johnson-Mondragon, 2005) and the Lilly Foundation (Lilly Endowment, 2013; Sterk, 2002) have invested millions of dollars to invigorate the topic of spirituality and religion in higher education. Mahoney et al. (2001) described the phenomenon in the Association of American Colleges & Universities' *Liberal Education* journal:

> In the 1990s religion in the academy found a powerful ally in philanthropy, with Lilly Endowment, the Pew Charitable Trusts, the John Templeton

Foundation and other charitable groups spending tens of millions shoring up Christian higher education and fostering religious scholarship. A red-hot stock market created new wealth that helped underwrite the revitalization of religion on campus, as donors and foundations funded research, faculty development, student programs, centers, institutes, and new universities, all with an eye toward strengthening religion's place in the academy. (p. 40)

This funding has been responsible for much of the research that has been published since 2004.

Production of Highly Visible Research

In 2004, the Higher Education Research Institute (HERI) at the University of California–Los Angeles began a national longitudinal study of spirituality and college students, using the systems, relationships, and knowledge base that the institute had developed during decades of conducting Cooperative Institutional Research Program studies of college students. As addressed in other chapters, this research led to several research reports (for example, HERI, 2005), books (Astin et al., 2011; Bryant Rockenbach & Mayhew, 2013), and journal articles (for example, Park & Millora, 2010). The research demonstrates the positive benefits (intellectual and personal) of spiritual development and articulates the practices that can lead to spiritual development. This provides powerful evidence for any campus practitioner who wants to justify adding or maintaining practices related to spirituality, faith, religion, and life purpose. This is especially important given that many of the spirituality efforts on campuses tend to be based on personal interests rather than organizational structure.

Personal Interests of Campus Administrators and Faculty

Mahoney et al. (2001) referred to the revitalization of spirituality on campus as a "grassroots" movement (p. 40) because the proliferation of courses and programs has relied on the support and interest of individual administrators and faculty members. In our experience, this is true. Many of the programs we see on campuses exist because of someone's personal interest rather than as an assigned job. The great number of programs and initiatives that exist is a testament to the many people working on college campuses who value spirituality, faith, religion, and life purpose as part of the educational experience.

THE RISE OF PRACTICES RELATED TO SPIRITUALITY, FAITH, RELIGION, AND LIFE PURPOSE

The four mechanisms for change that we have described (leadership from professional organizations, increased grant funding, highly visible research, and personal interest in spirituality work) often work in unison. For example, the highly visible research conducted by HERI was largely funded by the Templeton Foundation. The research was done by individuals with a personal interest in spirituality. Many programs developed by campus practitioners who have personal interests in spirituality use the HERI research to justify their work and get ideas for practice through networks of people connected through ACPA and NASPA.

Miami University is an example of how these factors coalesce. The university was given a financial gift to support spirituality, faith, religion, and life purpose. Katie Wilson took on the work related to the grant, in part because it related to her position in student activities but in large part because of her personal interest. Katie has used the findings from the HERI study, referred to articles and books on best practices, and counted on ACPA and NASPA for professional support. Katie's story of the spirituality, faith, religion, and life purpose programming at Miami University is detailed in the following section.

Miami University: A Case Study

Soon after beginning a job as senior director for student engagement in 2009, I (Katie Wilson) was given stewardship of a new gift to the university designed to encourage programs and initiatives around "spirituality, meaning, and purpose." This gift provides funding for programs that develop and support students who are searching for more meaning in their lives, regardless of whether that is through religion, higher education, nature, music, and so on. The donors specifically cited the desire to create programs for faculty and staff to develop their ability to facilitate deeper dialogue around issues related to spirituality and discussions that invoke religious beliefs. They also encouraged the implementation of cocurricular programming around meaning making and spirituality. Finally, a stipulation of the gift was that Miami University create a second-year living–learning community where students could examine issues of religion, purpose, difference, and personal meaning. The living–learning community will provide opportunities for students to explore topics such as how to live lives of integrity, engaging in meaningful civic engagement, finding personal meaning in careers, and creating a life that is personally rewarding.

Opportunities and Challenges at Miami University   As I (Katie Wilson) began to present programming about spirituality, purpose, and meaning designed for Miami students, I received positive feedback from students and fellow student affairs staff yearning to have conversations about what they believe and why they believe it. Some of these conversations were specifically about religion rather than the broader concept of spirituality. Others related to an even broader sense of students trying to discern their own voices from the many other influences in their lives. In contrast, I also had experiences that highlighted the challenges of programming in this area. Although I have been blessed with amazing, resourceful, and insightful faculty partners, I have also faced skepticism by faculty and staff who may not see spiritual development as a legitimate goal of education at a public university.

At secular institutions like Miami University, spirituality remains an often overlooked dimension of student affairs programs and services. This may be rooted in fear of overstepping the boundaries of the public institution or may reflect the concern that it could be viewed as promoting religion and evangelism. An observation made during a webinar stuck with me. During the informal discussion near the conclusion, someone pointed out that, in some ways, a secular institution adhering to a doctrine of not holding any religious perspective above any other has a greater opportunity to make the link between pluralism, interfaith work, and meaning making than a faith-based institution does. Rather than considering the secular nature of the university as a limitation, it can actually provide abundant opportunity. Rather than seeing the secular nature of the institution as a barrier to campus practices related to spirituality, faith, religion, and life purpose, I needed to focus on the possibilities.

For example, the Religious Community Advisors (RCAs) at Miami University are an independent group of individuals representing community organizations of many faith traditions that have Miami students as congregation members and affiliated members of student organizations. These advisers frequently invite university staff in as guests to their monthly meetings. As a result, RCAs and Miami staff members have become partners in providing holistic support to students. We keep one another up-to-date on current campus issues and available resources. Invited guests to the RCA meetings have discussed everything from alcohol abuse to supporting students who are struggling academically. This partnership allows us to work together for the holistic well-being of students.

Another partnership developed in the spring of 2012, when I was approached by the director of the Campus Ministry Center (an off-campus organization) and the executive director of Hillel at Miami University about initiating a program to bring filmmaker Nathan Lang and the "God in the Box" project to Miami's campus (Lang, 2012). Lang traveled around the country filming people's answers to the questions, "What does God look like to you?" and "What does God mean to you?" Lang created an award-winning documentary that interwove footage from people in the box, his personal meaning-making journey, and the insights of a variety of leaders from many faith backgrounds. As I discussed the idea with students and other staff, I found a great deal of enthusiasm for this program, the creativity of this approach as an educational program, and the potential for engaging students in self-reflection and dialogue.

We worked with student organizations to build a 4-foot-square, 8-foot-high box to replicate Lang's approach and used our footage to create a 5-minute Miami video clip. As I stood alongside students from both faith-based and secular student organizations in a prominent campus location and asked people if they wanted to participate, we received curious questions and polite rejections from most of the people who walked by. No students were rude or dismissive.

Ultimately, more than 200 people participated in some organized aspect of the program, and it generated insightful dialogue all over campus. The students involved in the project represented both faith-based organizations and secular students at Miami. All of them reported having meaningful conversations with their friends about the project. The discussion after the film was robust and authentic. Some students shared comments that underscored their confidence in their beliefs, and others shared their uncertainty and commitment to a journey of determining their beliefs. More than anything else, though, the overriding theme from the students was gratitude for the opportunity to talk about what is on their minds and the importance of these conversations to their college experience.

A final example of partnership demonstrates how we were able to collaborate creatively with existing campus experts to provide spiritual development opportunities that are wholly secular. We were able to use some of our endowment gift to support the launch of the "Breathe Campaign," initiated by the Student Counseling Center and Student Wellness offices. The campaign promotes mindfulness as a way of relieving anxiety and preparing students to respond to stressful situations with greater ease. "Mindfulness helps students by teaching them to be fully present and aware of each experience; to quiet negative self-talk; to live a deeper, richer and more fulfilling life; and to optimize their health physically, emotionally and spiritually" (R. Baudry & K. Alishio, personal communication, July 19, 2012). In addition to mindfulness training, students can participate in guided imagery, pet therapy, yoga, and relaxation programs.

What's Been Accomplished at Miami University? In the first three years of developing programming focused on spirituality, meaning, and purpose, we have had some great successes. By capitalizing on partnership opportunities such as those discussed above, Miami has begun to address the goal of supporting students' search for meaning and purpose. Furthermore, we have focused on programs for faculty and staff, developed cocurricular programming for students, and created a living–learning community, as specified by our endowment gift.

The campus community was fortunate to have His Holiness the Dalai Lama visit in the fall of 2010. His visit was a catalyst for partnering with a group of faculty and staff, including the university's Performing Arts Series, the Art Museum, the Comparative Religion Department, and the Center for American and World Cultures, to present the Mystical Arts of Tibet's Sand Mandala and Sacred Music Sacred Dance for World Healing programs. These programs combined art, music, and lectures during a weeklong visit of monks from the Drepung Loseling Monastery in Atlanta. Nearly 4,000 students, faculty, and staff participated in events related to the monks' visit on campus. In the spring, we again collaborated with our Performing Arts Series to provide educational programming related to Ragamala Dance from Minneapolis. Their presentation combined dance, visual arts, and music. The evening before the event, we invited the artists to share their stories about the symbolism behind the art forms and the meaning making they derive from these practices.

In addition to larger formal programming, the spirituality, meaning, and purpose initiative has also begun to provide funding for student organization initiatives that are consistent with the objectives of the gift. We were able to support student travel to the Interfaith Youth Core (IFYC) conference, a student traveling on an interfaith program to Palestine and Israel, and an interfaith alternative spring break to Arizona to experience multiple perspectives regarding border issues and immigration. We have also worked with student organizations to replicate Baylor's "Blinded" program and implement Hillel's "Ask Big Questions" program.

As student-oriented programming has emerged as a regular fixture on campus, faculty and staff have also approached me with great ideas for their own personal and professional development related to spirituality. We participated in an ACPA webinar that focused on the role of student affairs in promoting religious/secular pluralism and suggested student affairs competencies for addressing spirituality, secularism, religious pluralism, and interfaith cooperation (Kocet & Stewart, 2011). We also began a lunch series, "Mid-Day Meaning Making," which provides opportunities for faculty, staff, and graduate students to come together to talk about how we make meaning in our work. In one of our first activities, we mapped out our personal journeys in the context of spirituality, faith, religion, and life purpose, and we reflected as a group on the complexity of factors that influence this journey. We discussed the implications of this complexity related to our practice of supporting students and promoting student development.

We have also used Astin et al.'s (2011) five dimensions of spiritual development as a prompt for discussion about how our spiritual, faith, and religious perspectives inform our work. This led to a fascinating conversation about the challenges of facilitating discussions on these topics given the levels of conviction and range of perspectives among those participating. In 2011, we brought in Whittney Barth, a Miami University alumna and assistant director of the Pluralism Project at Harvard University, as a consultant and speaker for moving our initiatives forward. She met with students, faculty, staff, and our off-campus partners from the local ministries. Her knowledge about creating an infrastructure for interfaith initiatives, combined with reflections on her own interfaith work as a student at Miami, provided great insight for developing programs and initiatives, particularly our evolving living–learning community.

In the fall of 2013, a new sophomore living–learning community, "Meaning and Purpose (MAP)," opened at Miami University. The goal of this community is to:

> . . . encourage the development of a broad and pragmatic spiritual literacy that helps students articulate spiritual questions in their own lives and understand the variety of ways others respond to them, especially as they relate to dimensions of self-identity (e.g., What makes me a worthy human being?); relationship to others (e.g., What does it mean to be faithful?); and purpose and direction (e.g., What am I called to do in life?). (T. Barlage & M. O'Neal, personal communication, April 5, 2012)

We currently serve 13 students in this living–learning community. In addition, a steering committee of faculty and staff will help develop intentional experiences to promote the mission and learning outcomes of the living–learning community experience.

Finally, in January 2014, Miami University's new student center opened with a signature space devoted to providing a quiet area for meditation and reflection. The meditation and reflection room is an open and bright space with a flexible format that can accommodate many types of prayer, reflection, and mindfulness activities. There are restrooms on either side of the entrance that have amenities to accommodate the Muslim foot-washing ritual. The room demonstrates Miami's commitment to supporting the development of spirituality, faith, religion, and life purpose among all students, regardless of their faith orientation.

AN OVERVIEW OF CAMPUS PRACTICES

The successes at Miami University mirror what is happening on campuses across the United States. As a result of increased funding, personal interest, high-profile research, and the leadership of professional associations, campus practices dedicated to spirituality, faith, religion, and life purpose have increased dramatically in the past several years. Like Miami, many institutions have developed new courses and pedagogy, cocurricular programming (including living–learning communities), and initiatives focused on the intersection between spirituality and health. Many campuses are working on developing interfaith activities and are struggling to find a location in the organizational structure to house efforts focused on spirituality, faith, religion, and life purpose. In the following section, we provide a brief overview of campus practices, drawing on our professional experiences, connections throughout the field, and a review of the literature.

Courses and Pedagogy

Courses connected to spirituality, faith, religion, and life purpose are common. From Brown University offering a concentration in contemplative studies to Mount Aloysius College providing a course titled "The Self and Beyond: Psychology and Spirituality" and to classes on comparative religions and spiritualities taught at multiple colleges and universities, there is a diversity of opportunities for students to explore spirituality, faith, religion, and life purpose through the curriculum. Whittier College offers a "Buddhism class that is taught in a classroom setting during the semester and at a local monastery during an intensive winter session" (Lindholm, Millora, Schwartz, & Spinosa, 2011, p. 30), coupling intellectual and experiential dimensions of learning to create a holistic experience for enrolled students. Many campuses have also developed majors, minors, and/or concentrations for students wanting to explore these issues through curricular avenues.

Several scholars have developed spirituality-based pedagogical practices, including Pigza and Welch's (2010) spiritually engaged pedagogy, which they define as "a pedagogical framework that focuses on intentional practices that support both spiritual development and social justice education" (p. 5). Additionally, Nash's (2009) crossover pedagogy, a method in which educators use knowledge and skills from an array of disciplines (e.g., constructivist philosophy, storytelling, developmental theory) to encourage students to make meaning of their lives, engages students in the process of exploring their life purposes in the classroom. Many campuses have also begun to incorporate moments of silence (e.g., Alvernia University) and "technology-free periods," or class periods when students are not permitted to use technology (e.g., laptops at Monmouth College) in classroom pedagogy (Lindholm et al., 2011, p. 30). These types of activities allow students to step back from their busy lives to be more reflective and contemplative.

Cocurricular Practices

There are abundant opportunities for students to connect with spiritual development through cocurricular programming. Cocurricular programming can range from awareness weeks (e.g., Franklin College's Religious Emphasis Week) to onetime events (e.g., alternative spring break programs, faith-based speakers, and discussion groups; see Lindholm et al., 2011). Educational and diversity programming in the form of speakers and dialogue can provide a forum for students to clarify what they believe, why they believe it, and how they came to hold their beliefs. Many campuses participate in Hillel's "Ask Big Questions" program (Hillel: The Foundation for Jewish Campus Life, n.d.). Initiated by students and the Hillel director at Northwestern University in 2005, this program expanded nationwide in 2008 and provides resource guides for questions such as "For whom are you responsible?" and "Are you free?" From our colleagues, we know that similar programs have emerged on other campuses such as Bowling Green State University and Carnegie Mellon University.

Other programs integrate questions of religious and spiritual beliefs as part of broader diversity programming. One such example is "Blinded," hosted by the student government at Baylor University (Baylor Student Government, n.d.), where students are blindfolded and asked to participate in small group discussions on questions of race, religion, sexual orientation, and socioeconomic status. At Montclair State University, a variety of groups work collaboratively to address such issues throughout the year, including the celebrating of a U.S. Constitution Day that recognizes freedom of speech and religious expression; groups focused on the intersections of sexual orientation, gender identity, and faith communities; a Jesus Awareness Day led by Muslim students; and Jewish-feminist Seder dinners to celebrate Passover (Lindholm et al., 2011).

As living–learning communities continue to dominate the residence life landscape as a good practice for maximizing the learning that can occur in the residence hall setting, it is not surprising that spirituality has begun to emerge as a focus in this area, as well. These broad-based and inclusive programs are often intentional in their efforts to ensure that participating students fully understand that it is a diverse community designed for people to learn from one another's divergent viewpoints. Residence life staff members often partner with faculty in religious studies or comparative religion and present programming in wellness, diversity, and critical thinking. For example, the SEARCH Residential Living Community at Bowling Green State University is facilitated by professor of higher education and student affairs Dr. Carney Strange. Each year it serves more than 40 students, representing many majors and belief systems, who come together to investigate "the big questions of life as part of a diverse community of learners" (Bowling Green State University, n.d., para. 1).

Spirituality and Health Initiatives

Meditation and reflection programming focused on practices of healthy minds provide tools for students to connect and develop their inner selves. Counseling and student wellness offices have begun to create small-group interventions and proactive programming integrating practices such as yoga and meditation into their offerings. Likewise, creating quiet spaces on campus has become common. For example, if there is chapel on campus, it is often open all day. The Interfaith Prayer and Reflection Room in the Ohio

Union at the Ohio State University, the Quiet Prayer and Meditation Lounge at Portland State University (Samuelson, 2013), and the Serenity Room at the University of South Florida are three examples of quiet spaces that meet needs related to spirituality, faith, religion, and life purpose for a wide array of students from different traditions.

The Center for Spirituality and Health at the University of Florida, which opened in 1998 as a way to connect conversations regarding spirituality with academic discourse in the health sciences, is a broad-based initiative that spans academic and cocurricular boundaries. It started with an interdisciplinary board of 10 faculty members; the group "quickly grew to about 25 by adding faculty, a few graduate students, and interested members of the community" (Neims, Ardelt, Isenberg, & Ritz, 2008, p. 2). The expansion of the advisory board also led to an expansion in the scope and reach of the Center, which "sponsors various programs that fall into five overlapping categories: 1) A speaker series; 2) retreats and workshops; 3) communal self-care; 4) academic courses offered to undergraduate, graduate, and professional students, and 5) research" (Neims et al., 2008, p. 3). Although not directly stated, it is clear that the center, which started with a primarily academic orientation, has shifted to offering cocurricular involvement opportunities for students, faculty, staff, and outside community members.

Interfaith Initiatives

Interfaith initiatives focused on increasing student connections across faith backgrounds exist on many campuses (e.g., Giess & Patel, 2010; McLennan, 2010; Stewart, Kocet, & Lobdell, 2011; Watt, Fairchild, & Goodman, 2009). Interfaith initiatives often lead to collaborative programming on the campus communities where they exist. Moreover, these initiatives create rich environments for interfaith dialogues, which are themselves an important intervention related to spirituality, faith, religion, and life purpose. Developed in the 1980s, the framework of intergroup dialogue is critical–dialogic (Nagda & Maxwell, 2011), as that the intent is that the experience "focuses on storytelling and sharing one's experiential knowledge (dialogic) and understanding systems of power, privilege, and inequities that marginalize some while advantaging others (critical)" (Quaye, 2012, p. 102). Whereas intergroup dialogue has traditionally focused on race, interfaith dialogues provide an opportunity to discuss faith beliefs in an effort "to go beyond tolerance and mere coexistence . . . to respect the identities of faith communities and individual believers in the process" (Larson & Shady, 2012, p. 7).

Eboo Patel's IFYC provides one example of such interfaith dialogue that many campuses are using to engage students in conversations across multiple axes of faith differences (Giess & Patel, 2010; Larson & Shady, 2012).

Interfaith initiatives provide an opportunity to focus on charitable involvement and ecumenical worldview, which Astin et al. (2011) identified as dimensions of spiritual development. These dimensions highlight the opportunity for community service and social justice programming to tap into broader meaning-making opportunities. For example, in 2011–2012, 273 campuses participated in the President's Interfaith and Community Service Campus Challenge (Office of Faith-Based and Neighborhood Partnerships, n.d.). This program harnessed existing energy related to civic engagement and interfaith work. Participating institutions committed to a year focused on developing interfaith and community service programming. Infusing reflection and discussion with community service can transform the experience from one of civic engagement to an experience that provides powerful lessons in spirituality, as well.

Partnerships

Generally, the position of campus minister does not exist at public institutions. However, there is often a group of ministers who define their role as community advisers who work with recognized campus student organizations and, therefore, are loosely affiliated with the university. Organizations of these ministers either exist outside the university administration or exist in partnership with someone at the university. An illustrative example is the Religious Advisors Association at Oregon State University. In 2002, the university and the advisors outlined their "cooperative and mutually supportive relationship" (Oregon State University, 2002, para. 1). This agreement defined the relationship between the university and advisers who are recognized by student organizations designated in the religious, spiritual, and philosophical category. The agreement provided a public statement that the university values the role that spiritual growth can play in a community and in the development of students. It also created an avenue for individuals who are supporting students in their personal lives to connect to campus crisis services. Finally, by affiliating with advisers chosen by students to counsel their student organizations, the university maintains a position that does not "promote religion per se or favor one particular faith over another" (Oregon State University, 2002, para. A). In recent years, the Religious Advisors Association has become more integrated with other student affairs work around student and spiritual development. The group has organized to participate in new student orientation and has hosted a spiritual awareness week, thus demonstrating the effectiveness of their partnership.

ROOM FOR IMPROVEMENT

Our case study and this brief overview of campus practices demonstrate that many people within the student affairs profession have attempted to craft practices to support the development of spirituality, faith, religion, and life purpose among college students. These practices include any number of cocurricular activities; interfaith dialogues; pedagogical innovations; spirituality and health initiatives; partnerships between student affairs staff and campus ministries; living–learning communities; and spaces for contemplation, meditation, or prayer. Yet a close reading suggests that there is room for improvement in the way members of the profession approach these topics.

Even with the existence of these practices on many campuses throughout the country, the student affairs profession lacks a widespread commitment to supporting the development of spirituality, faith, religion, and life purpose. As we have pointed out, many of the practices are developed because of the interests of a particular individual rather than from organizational commitment. The fact that universities often leave the spirituality work to their off-campus partners and do not have staff positions dedicated to this aspect of student development and identity also demonstrates a lack of widespread commitment. As a result, many faculty and administrators scoff at spirituality practices, especially at public institutions where it is easy for individuals to cite separation of church and state as a reason to not engage in practices related to spirituality, faith, religion, and life purpose. (As we discuss below, this is faulty logic.) Another sign that the profession as a whole has not committed to spirituality work is the lack of training related to the topic. Professional organizations such as ACPA and NASPA provide some resources, but, overall, those entering student affairs jobs receive little or no guidance in learning how to do spirituality work. Even in the literature, we found a lack of guidance to help faculty and staff create a shared vision for engaging students in practices related to spirituality, faith, religion, and life purpose (Lindholm et al., 2011). Without methods to enhance educators' ability to infuse these issues throughout the curriculum and cocurricular activities, the development of innovative approaches will stagnate.

Finally, our experiences and review of the literature demonstrate that although many practices related to spirituality, faith, religion, and life purpose have developed over the past decade, there are certain groups who have been left out. For example, campus groups, curricular interventions, and programmatic efforts geared toward students who identify as atheist, agnostic, and/or humanist are rare. This absence mirrors the invisibility of the atheist college student discussed by Goodman and Mueller (2009). It demonstrates a need for educators to focus on those who disavow traditional mono- and polytheistic religious associations, and sometimes even the term *spirituality*, because they base their life purposes on science, reason, humanity, or other sources.

WHERE DO WE GO NEXT? POSSIBILITIES AND PROVOCATIONS FOR STUDENT AFFAIRS

It is clear that within student affairs in the past decade or so many practices have been implemented to address the spiritual development of college students. It is also clear that there is still room for improvement in this area. In the remainder of this chapter, we provide four suggestions for improving and institutionalizing student affairs practices related to spirituality, faith, religion, and life purpose.

Stop Using the Public Institution Defense

It is quite common for faculty and administrators to claim that there is no place for spirituality at a public institution (Glanzer, 2011; Magolda, 2010). Some may suggest that it is not relevant to the mission of public institutions, whereas others suggest that to address anything faith related would be unconstitutional. We disagree with both of these premises.

A primary tenet of the student affairs profession is to attend to the holistic development of students, including their religious and spiritual growth (Keeling, 2004). Furthermore, many public institutions are committed to liberal arts education, which entails both personal development and intellectual growth. For example, Miami University's vision statement begins with the sentence, "Miami University is a scholarly community whose members believe that a liberal education is grounded in *qualities of character* [emphasis added] as well as of intellect" (Miami University, 2002). As for the legal argument that public institutions cannot engage students in spiritual and religious initiatives, several articles document the limitations and cautions that must be adhered to but conclude that there is no legal reason student affairs professionals cannot attend to the spiritual and religious needs of the students they serve, as long as they are providing equal opportunity for all religious groups rather than promoting a single perspective (Clark, 2001; Glanzer, 2011).

Given these realities, it seems that the public institution defense may be more of an excuse than a true obstacle. The vast majority of U.S. college students (approximately 80%) attend public institutions (Heller, 2011). Those in student affairs committed to supporting the development of spirituality, faith, religion, and life purpose among college students must find ways to enact their commitment within the legal boundaries, rather than letting their work be quashed because of fears over what one cannot do at a public institution. Vital to enacting that commitment is to enhance education and training for student affairs professionals, faculty, and students.

Enhance Education and Training

As discussed earlier in this chapter, current literature provides little guidance for educators who wish to engage students in practices related to spirituality, faith, religion, and life purpose. One of our (Kathy Goodman's) own experiences teaching master's degree students illustrates this need for guidance and training. The 17 students in Kathy's spirituality in higher education course expressed a strong interest in working with undergraduate students on issues related to spirituality but bemoaned the fact that they had few role models and no experience having spirituality-related conversations outside this one elective course. The guest speakers invited to the class represented many areas within student affairs, and they were each committed to doing spirituality-related work, yet they shared that they had had no training or experience to prepare them to do it, even within their student affairs master's degree programs.

As far back as 1999, Love and Talbot pointed out that spirituality and spiritual development "have been conspicuously absent from student development theories and ignored by many student affairs professionals" (p. 361). Lack of preparation, contextualization, knowledge, and skill development may be behind the skepticism demonstrated by those who may not believe spirituality work has a place on campus. Furthermore, lack of education and discomfort with entering unchartered territory may be part of the reason that so many faculty and staff are quick to use the public institution excuse not to engage in spirituality-related work. Until the student affairs profession moves from talking about the importance of spirituality-related work to talking about *how* to do spirituality-related work, it seems unlikely that we will improve and institutionalize student affairs practices related to spirituality, faith, religion, and life purpose.

Recently, ACPA's CSFRM proposed competencies for the student affairs profession related to addressing spirituality, secularism, religious pluralism, and interfaith cooperation (Kocet & Stewart, 2011). The authors of the proposal stated that student affairs professionals must have the requisite training, education, and competencies to work effectively with students, faculty, staff, and other campus constituents, but "there has been a gap regarding the application of multiculturally competent practice when it comes to student affairs professionals' awareness, knowledge, and skills regarding world religion, spirituality, and secular or humanistic perspectives within a cultural diversity context" (Kocet & Stewart, 2011, p. 4). Although the competencies they propose are a step toward closing that gap, training and education are necessary to help student affairs professionals learn how to do this work. Learning the facilitation and communication skills to talk about the many ways individuals approach the spiritual, religious, and secular paths to finding purpose and meaning in their lives is vital.

Kathy's student affairs master's degree students openly acknowledged their fear of saying "the wrong thing," or offending others by what they said. Within the class, we often had to remind ourselves of one of the ground rules we set at the beginning of the semester: "We are here to learn, not to believe." In other words, there is no reason to be offended when someone expresses a belief that is counter to your own, because the goal is to learn and understand what others believe, not to accept those beliefs as your own. Talking about spirituality-related matters is scary and difficult, yet if students do not engage in these conversations during their graduate studies, it seems unlikely that we will be able to engage in them with undergraduate students. Thus, training and education for student affairs faculty and administrators, both within professional preparation programs and in the profession at large, are integral to this work.

Broaden the Notion of Spirituality in Order to Be More Inclusive

An inevitable part of diving into the messy and scary conversations about spirituality and religion is addressing privilege. I (Kathy) have found that the student affairs master's degree students I teach have not deeply considered

Christian privilege. And I often hear people in student affairs say, "I know Christian privilege exists, but . . ." The profession needs to move beyond ignoring or minimizing Christian privilege, because it is nearly impossible to address the topic of spirituality without wandering into the topic of religion. This also says nothing about theist privilege, which privileges belief in God over atheist or agnostic beliefs. We need to broaden the notion of spirituality to be more inclusive.

It is our experience that the use of the word *spirituality* in student affairs is meant to be inclusive. The problem is, as educators, we cannot proscribe for others their inclusion within certain categories. We need to talk about things in ways that allow people to see *themselves* as included. For example, I once saw an atheist student say to a speaker that he didn't see how he (the atheist) fit into the conversation about spirituality in higher education. The well-intentioned speaker responded that he meant *spirituality* in the broadest sense possible, which included atheism. This was an unsatisfactory answer to the atheist, who asked the question and who clearly did not define himself as spiritual, even if the speaker did. It seems it would have been better to acknowledge the student's identity as atheist and that he did not consider himself spiritual. Then the speaker, or others in the audience, could have engaged the student in conversation about what he does believe, what gives his life purpose, what guides his values, and so on. This would have affirmed the student rather than minimizing his perspective.

Therefore, we believe that the student affairs profession should be focusing on the ways that bring purpose and meaning to one's life and not defining that as spirituality. If we start from the broad topic of meaning and purpose, we allow students to position themselves in the conversation in ways that apply to them. For some students, that will include talking about the influence of religion in their lives; for others, it will entail spirituality; and still others will identify reason, science, or humanism as their source of purpose and meaning. We visualize this as different pathways that lead to meaning and purpose (Figure 7.1); those pathways can be distinct or overlapping. We suggest that educators let the students identify their pathways, and we use more inclusive terminology (for example, *purpose and meaning*, or *religious, spiritual, and secular traditions*) to frame the conversations. Ironically, by broadening the definition in this way, we open up the conversation to be more precise (e.g., students can identify the specific influences in their life, such as Catholicism or Buddhism, rather than trying to use generic language such as *spirituality*). In other words, we can move away from the fruitless attempt to make *spirituality* mean the same thing for everyone.

Figure 7.1 Multiple Pathways to Meaning and Life Purpose

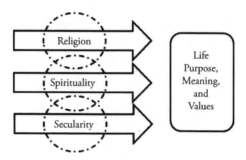

Create New Institutional Structures and Partnerships

Our final recommendation for improving and institutionalizing student affairs practices related to spirituality, faith, religion, and life purpose is to create a structural home for it within student affairs divisions. If student affairs professionals are serious about working with students as they develop their spirituality and life purpose, then that function should be funded by the division and assigned to an individual or office to show it is valued. Responsibility for this area of student life could be joined with other diversity-oriented programs and services, given that the spiritual, religious, and secular ways that students use to find purpose and meaning in their lives are aspects of diversity.

Creating a structural home for practices related to spirituality, faith, religion, and life purpose could make it easier to create partnerships such as those discussed in the Miami University case study. There may be off-campus ministers, religious studies faculty, or student affairs educators who have great ideas for programming and events but do not know to whom to turn with their ideas. Assigning this work to a specific position ensures that programming related to life purpose and meaning will become a permanent part of the institution and individuals interested in contributing to that work will know whom to partner with to bring their ideas to fruition.

CONCLUDING THOUGHTS

In this chapter we have illustrated, through a literature review and personal experiences, that many practices related to spirituality, faith, religion, and life purpose exist on campuses. These practices have been implemented over the past 15 or so years because professional organizations such as ACPA and NASPA have provided support, increased grant funding designed to support spirituality has been available, highly visible research has been published, and individual administrators and faculty have taken personal interest in the topic. We believe this shows that many educators are committed to the holistic development of students. However, we also believe that the practices can be improved and institutionalized if educators heed our four suggestions. First, stop using the public institution defense as an excuse for not doing work related to spirituality, faith, religion, and life purpose. Second, enhance education and training to help educators learn how to do this type of work. Third, broaden the notion of spirituality by using the language *purpose and meaning* in order to be more inclusive. Finally, create new institutional structures that provide a permanent home for doing work related to purpose and meaning. Although our profession has done a great deal to meet the spiritual, religious, and life purpose needs of students, there is a long way to go to make this work a more permanent and central part of student affairs. We believe that the four recommendations we have provided are the necessary steps to institutionalize services related to life purpose and meaning.

REFERENCES

Adler, N. (2007). Faith and reason on campus. *Liberal Education, 93*(2), 20–27.

Astin, A. W., Astin, H. S., & Lindholm, J. A. (2011). *Cultivating the spirit: How college can enhance students' inner lives.* San Francisco: Jossey-Bass.

Baylor Student Government. (n.d.). *Blinded.* Retrieved from http://www.baylor .edu/sg/index.php?id=63719

Bowling Green State University. (n.d.). *SEARCH.* Retrieved from http://www.bgsu .edu/offices/sa/reslife/communities/page86032.html

Bryant Rockenbach, A., & Mayhew, M. J. (Eds.). (2013). *Spirituality in college students' lives: Translating research into practice.* New York: Routledge.

Clark, R. T. (2001). The law and spirituality: How the law supports and limits expression of spirituality on the college campus. *New Directions for Student Services, 2001*(95), 37–46.

Giess, M. E., & Patel, E. (2010). Building a campus movement of interfaith cooperation: Interfaith Youth Core in action. *Spirituality in Higher Education Newsletter, 5*(5). Retrieved from http://spirituality.ucla.edu/publications/newsletters/

Glanzer, P. L. (2011). Peter Magolda's proposal for an unholy alliance: Cautions and considerations regarding collaboration between student affairs and faith-based student organizations. *Journal of College and Character, 12*(3). doi:10.2202/1940-1639.1779

Goodman, K. M., & Mueller, J. A. (2009). Invisible, marginalized, and stigmatized: Understanding and addressing the needs of atheist students. *New Directions for Student Services, 2009*(125), 55–63.

Heller, D. E. (Ed.). (2011). *The states and public higher education policy: Affordability, access, and accountability* (2nd ed.). Baltimore, MD: Johns Hopkins University Press.

Higher Education Research Institute. (2005). *The spiritual life of college students: A national study of college students' search for meaning and purpose.* Los Angeles: University of California, Higher Education Research Institute.

Hillel: The Foundation for Jewish Campus Life. (n.d.). *Ask big questions.* Retrieved from http://askbigquestions.org/

Jablonski, M. A. (Ed.). (2001). Editor's notes. *New Directions for Student Services, 2001*(95), 1–5.

John Templeton Foundation. (2010). *Mission.* Retrieved from http://www.templeton .org/who-we-are/about-the-foundation/mission

Johnson-Mondragon, K. (2005). *Youth ministry and the socioreligious lives of Hispanic and White Catholic teens in the U.S.* Stockton, CA: Instituto Fe y Vida Research and Resource Center.

Keeling, R. P. (2004). *Learning reconsidered: A campus-wide focus on the student experience.* Washington, DC: NASPA & ACPA.

Kocet, M. M., & Stewart, D. L. (2011). The role of student affairs in promoting religious and secular pluralism and interfaith cooperation. *Journal of College and Character, 12*(1). doi:10.2202/1940-7882.1762

Lang, N. (Director). (2012). *God in the box: A documentary film* [Motion picture]. Retrieved from http://www.godinthebox.com

Larson, M. H., & Shady, S. L. (2012). Confronting the complexities of Christian privilege through interfaith dialogue. *Journal of College and Character, 13*(2). doi:10.1515/jcc-2012-1824

Laurence, P. (1999). Can religion and spirituality find a place in higher education? *About Campus, 4*(5), 11–16.

Lilly Endowment. (2013). *The endowment.* Retrieved from http://www.lillyendowment .org/theendowment.html

Lindholm, J. A., Millora, M. L., Schwartz, L. M., & Spinosa, H. S. (2011). *A guidebook of promising practices: Facilitating college students' spiritual development.* Los Angeles: Regents of the University of California.

Love, P., & Talbot, D. (1999). Defining spiritual development: A missing consideration for student affairs. *NASPA Journal, 37,* 361–376.

Magolda, P. M. (2010). An unholy alliance: Rethinking collaboration involving student affairs and faith-based student organizations. *Journal of College and Character, 11*(4). doi: 10.2202/1940-1639.1734

Mahoney, K. A., Schmalzbauer, J., & Younis, J. (2001). Religion: A comeback on campus. *Liberal Education, 87*(4), 36–41.

McLennan, S. (2010). Interfaith interaction on campus. *Journal of College and Character, 11*(2). doi:10.2202/1940-1639.1265

Miami University. (2002). *Values statement.* Retrieved from http://www.miamioh .edu/about-miami/office-of-the-president/values-statement.html

Nagda, B. A., & Maxwell, K. E. (2011). Deepening the layers of understanding and connection: A critical-dialogic approach to facilitating intergroup dialogues. In K. E. Maxwell, B. A. Nagda, & M. C. Thompson (Eds.), *Facilitating intergroup dialogues: Bridging differences, catalyzing change* (pp. 1–22). Sterling, VA: Stylus.

Nash, R. J. (2009). Crossover pedagogy: The collaborative search for meaning. *About Campus, 14*(1), 2–9.

Neims, A. H., Ardelt, M., Isenberg, S. R., & Ritz, L. A. (2008). The Center for Spirituality and Health at the University of Florida. *Spirituality in Higher Education Newsletter, 4*(2). Retrieved from http://spirituality.ucla.edu/docs/newsletters/4/ Neims_Final.pdf

Office of Faith-Based and Neighborhood Partnerships. (n.d.). *The president's interfaith and community service campus challenge.* Retrieved from http://www .whitehouse.gov/administration/eop/ofbnp/interfaithservice

Oregon State University. (2002). *Statement of relationship between OSU Religious Advisors Association and Oregon State University.* Retrieved from http://regonstate. edu/deanofstudents/hci/spirituallife

Park, J. J., & Millora, M. (2010). Psychological well-being for White, Black, Latino/a, and Asian American Students: Considering spirituality and religion. *Journal of Student Affairs Research and Practice, 47*, 439–455. doi: 410.2202/1949-6605.6143

Patel, E. (2012). *Sacred ground: Pluralism, prejudice, and the promise of America.* Boston: Beacon Press.

Pigza, J. M., & Welch, M. J. (2010). Spiritually engaged pedagogy: The possibilities of spiritual development through social justice education. *Spirituality in Higher Education Newsletter, 5*(4). Retrieved from http://spirituality.ucla.edu/ publications/newsletters/5/4/welch.php

Quaye, S. J. (2012). White educators facilitating discussions about racial realities. *Equity & Excellence in Education, 45*, 100–119.

Rogers, J. L., & Love, P. (2007). Exploring the role of spirituality in the preparation of student affairs professionals: Faculty constructions. *Journal of College Student Development, 48*, 90–104.

Samuelson, R. (2013). Fostering spiritual development through prayer and meditation spaces. *Bulletin, 81*(3). Retrieved from https://www.acui.org/publications/
bulletin/article.aspx?issue=41797&id=21026

Sterk, A. (Ed.). (2002). *Religion, scholarship, & higher education: Perspectives, models,
and future prospects.* Notre Dame, IN: University of Notre Dame Press.

Stewart, D. L., Kocet, M. M., & Lobdell, S. (2011). The multifaith campus: Transforming colleges and universities for spiritual engagement. *About Campus, 16*(1),
10–18.

Subbiondo, J. L. (2011). Spirituality on campus: The emergence of a postsecular age
in American higher education. *About Campus, 16*(5), 30–32.

Watt, S. K., Fairchild, E. E., & Goodman, K. M. (Eds.). (2009). Intersections of
religious privilege: Difficult dialogues and student affairs practice [Special issue].
New Directions for Student Services, 2009(125).

8

Personal Exploration and National Trends

The Future for Students of All Faith Backgrounds

Frank Shushok Jr. and Patricia A. Perillo

THE CAMPUS CONTEXT—NEW OPENNESS
FOR SPIRITUAL LEARNING

As we began our exploration of spiritual life on campus, we were reminded of the momentous societal changes that underscore the context for colleges and universities, including substantial shifts in views about religion and spirituality. To set the stage, it is important to note that about a third of the American population, depending on the poll we consulted, define themselves as spiritual but not religious. According to a Pew Forum on Religion & Public Life survey (2009), additional findings further defined the fluidity in religious practices, including that 44% of Americans have left the faith or the denomination in which they were raised, 25% of people 18–29 years old do not affiliate with any particular religion, and men are much more likely than women to claim no religious tradition at all (p. 8).

On college and university campuses of every type, there is new energy surrounding age-old matters of faith, religion, spirituality, and meaning making—an expansive category we call "spiritual life." Given that most private institutions in American higher education emerged with a formal connection to religious traditions, it makes sense that institutional structures that

141

highlight spiritual life are embedded in campus architecture, services, and culture, even after denominational ties were severed and a history of seculari- zation unfolded. At many private nonsectarian institutions today, chaplains, chapels, and support services maintain a prominent presence. Even so, many private institutions aim to strengthen efforts to engage students around mat- ters of spirituality, as evidenced by new facilities, personnel, and programs. In 2013, for example, Elon University opened its first multifaith center for reli- gious and spiritual life "to encourage students to honor the spiritual dimen- sion of life [and] to be vitally connected to a faith tradition" (Elon University, n.d., para. 1). Support for students exploring their spiritual lives is conveyed also by emerging efforts to acknowledge a broadened definition of *spiritual life*, even if that means a belief in the absence of God. In 2012, for example, Stanford University made news when it appointed its first chaplain for athe- ists. Atheist chaplain John Figdor responded this way: "Atheist, agnostic and humanist students suffer the same problems as religious students—deaths, or illness in the family, questions about the meaning of life—and would like a sympathetic nontheist to talk to" (Asimov, 2012, para. 4).

Perhaps the most notable shift in the expanding comfort with spiritual and religious life is displayed in the growing propensity of public colleges and uni- versities to include matters of faith, religion, and spirituality in campus life by promoting a more robust dialogue around such topics. Moreover, an increas- ing number of public institutions have taken this advocacy further by provid- ing institutional infrastructure signaling a substantive shift in openness to the spiritual lives of students. Although some colleagues at public universities dis- miss the word *spiritual* as something outside the mission of their institutions, one of us (Frank) has pointed out, "It is important to remember that spiritual- ity, as broadly defined in higher education, represents the pursuit of life's big questions, meaning, purpose, and moral development in such a way that the human spirit is altered, reshaped, and transformed" (Shushok, 2011, p. 5). In fact, we agree with Astin, Astin, and Lindholm (2011) when they argue, "In many respects, the secular institution is the ideal place for students to explore their spiritual side because, unlike many sectarian institutions, there is no offi- cial perspective or dogma when it comes to spiritual values and beliefs" (p. 6).

Many public institutions are taking the shift in environment to heart. In 2010, for example, the University of Massachusetts–Amherst established the Office of Religious and Spiritual Life to do the following:

> Foster mutual understanding and respect among students of all religious back- grounds (whether religiously observant or not); to promote dialogue; and to

provide appropriate support for and heighten awareness of the diverse religious and spiritual traditions which are present on our campus. (University of Massachusetts–Amherst, 2011, para. 3)

In 2009, Florida State University launched its Spiritual Life Project to gather together religious leaders, faculty, staff, and students around discussions to strengthen spiritual programming, increase the number of spiritual spaces on campus, and explore future institutional direction around the topic (Florida State University, 2012).

What is driving this renaissance in spiritual and religious life on American college and university campuses? What are the sociological conditions moving religion and spiritual life from the margins back to an accepted position in higher education? One common assumption is that college-age people are more spiritual than previous generations were. Smith and Snell (2009), however, believed these claims are frequently exaggerated and misunderstood, especially because being spiritual is often used synonymously with being religious. In their comprehensive study of the sociological evidence, college-age people (whom Smith and Snell referred to as "emerging adults"), "are the least religious adults in the United States today" (p. 102). Although 60% of emerging adults identify as religious, Smith and Snell found "the importance and practice of religion generally declines between the ages of 13–17 and 18–23" (p. 142). Still, there is broad variance depending on subpopulations, and those with backgrounds of Latter-day Saints, conservative Protestant, and Black Protestant remain steadily involved religiously. Acknowledging research on college students reporting high levels of interest in spirituality and frequent claims characterizing young people as more spiritual than religious, Smith and Snell emphasized there remains a solid majority of emerging adults not interested in matters religious or spiritual. Smith and Snell contended the reason many survey instruments find higher levels of interest in spirituality is that "the surveys themselves are constructed in a way that leaves the language of 'spirituality' as the only way for respondents to register any kind of religious or nonatheistic interest" (p. 296).

Whether the increased acceptance of spiritual life on college and university campuses is compelled by real or perceived increases in student interest may be neither here nor there. What is important is that there are many students for whom spiritual exploration is an important aspect of the educational journey. And most compelling are the convincing data that convey that such exploration leads to all sorts of positive outcomes. Smith and Snell (2009) summarized the findings in this way: "Whatever its depth, character, and substance, [such exploration] correlates significantly with, and we think actually often acts as a causal influence producing, what most consider to be more positive outcomes in life for emerging adults" (p. 297). Colleges and universities have recognized as much and made movement to fill the gap by opening a dialogue that conveys spiritual life, or as commonly characterized, the search for meaning and purpose, a legitimate topic for consideration. Sharon Daloz Parks (2000) also noted:

> The promise and vulnerability of young adulthood lies in the experience of the birth of critical awareness and the dissolution and re-composition of the meaning of self, other, world, and "God." This work has enormous consequences that follow in adulthood. (p. 5)

Similarly, there is a large group of students for whom such exploration will be of little interest. This perspective must not be pushed to the margin, either. However, the invitation to delve into the important questions can be extended through an open and inclusive campus environment.

There is hope that the openness, dialogue, and support for those students across religious traditions and spiritual or nonspiritual dispositions is laying the groundwork for greater sensitivity, compassion, and understanding for those from diverse backgrounds and perspectives. Moreover, there is increasing evidence that addressing the spiritual and meaning-making dimensions of development during college is especially important to retention and success of particular subpopulations, especially those identifying as African American (Paredes-Collins, 2012).

In a recent *Chronicle of Higher Education* essay, Minasian (2010) cheered rich religious diversity that is in fact even richer than one might suspect. The "big five" religions—Hinduism, Buddhism, Judaism, Christianity, and Islam—are just the start of the conversation. Minasian wrote, "Nuances in the theological continuum become more evident when you actually talk with students about spirituality, religion, and faith" (para. 1). Minasian, a university chaplain at Franklin and Marshall College, sought to nurture a campus culture where students engaged around the subject. With regard to interest in these matters, she wrote, "In the midst of being committed, hostile, curious, and even indifferent, they also seemed to be hungry to share, discuss, and consider different voices" (para. 2). Minasian, like so many educators on college campuses, found religious and spiritual dialogues are providing an important tool for many of the learning aims so coveted in higher education.

According to Jacobsen and Jacobsen (2012), the flourishing openness about faith, religion, and spirituality on college and university campuses is bolstered by its grassroots origin, a profound change from past history when religion was imposed on students from positions of power and authority. In contrast to the 19th and 20th centuries, current interest appears to be emerging from the bottom up as a sizable constituency of students view spirituality as a personal journey into meaning and purpose, sometimes informed by religion—sometimes not.

STUDENTS' MEANING MAKING IN PRACTICE

Whether the emergence of a stronger interest in issues of spirituality or meaning making is university led or student inspired, what we know for sure is that students will learn as they engage with and across religious difference. In Light's (2001) influential work, *Making the Most of College: Students Speak Their Minds*, ways in which issues of religious difference contribute to the development of college students are clearly articulated. Light's study informs the reader that "most students feel very positive about the impact of cultural, racial, and, especially, religious diversity on college campuses" (Cowling, 2002, para. 12). These students also found value in going out of their way to meet people who disagree with their core values, particularly those with religious difference. Students indicated that although disagreement is common, dialogue around difference helped them come to know why they believed what they believed. And students reported that encounters with others of different religions could be simultaneously the most challenging and most enlightening of all the experiences with a diverse student body.

In addition to knowing that students learn when engaging within and across religious diversity, we also know that many students come to college seeking opportunities to learn about their faith, religion, or sense of spirituality; we did ourselves. I, Patty, went to a faith-based high school and considered following suit for college. But as a first-generation college student struggling with separation from and commitment to my family, I went to the state public university just 25 minutes away from my home. My mother was Methodist and my father was Catholic, so I learned early in life that for me denomination did not matter as much as theology and community. I grew up next to a cloister convent and spent considerable hours, over many years, with these cloistered sisters. Also, being one of eight Catholic children who went to Catholic grade school, I spent much time in the church for special ceremonies and rituals. Even as a little girl, I thought about ministry work.

When I went to college my first-year resident assistant (RA) was an older student, obtaining her master's degree, and also on the journey to becoming a nun in a progressive order. I spent much time with my RA, as we became fast friends, and we talked a lot about issues of faith. My college roommates were identical twins who were Jewish. I would go home with them during academic breaks and experience the traditions and holidays of Judaism, and they deepened my understanding of and commitment to my own faith and inspired a deepened curiosity to learn about other faith traditions. I do not recall ever discussing faith or religion in the classroom, nor do I remember conversations after my time with my RA. However, I do remember that my interest in my faith grew exponentially given social interactions, yet I did not engage any religious affiliation during my undergraduate years.

Upon reflection, it is clear to me that I did not engage any church-relatedness because I was struggling with my sexuality, and I knew my Christian brothers and sisters would not welcome such questioning. My own faith development accelerated when my younger brother died tragically; it was also strengthened when my grandparents, parents, life partner, mother-in-law, and older sister passed in subsequent years. I am a faith-filled Christian woman who continues to cocreate campus cultures to welcome and affirm the mind, body, and spirit connection of the whole person.

I, Frank, remember having what I now call a "spiritual sense" as a child. Wondering about spiritual matters was a natural inclination. Even though my family was involved in the Episcopal tradition in a cursory way, I was frequently maneuvering ways to be involved in church without feeling uncomfortable that the rest of my family were not regular attendees. As a middle-school student, I volunteered to teach Sunday school and record worship services—anything that allowed me to be in church but not feel awkward that I was there alone. The Episcopal tradition offered me what I now know as a "big tent" (all are welcome under the tent) way to explore my understanding of God. In short, it was a world of questions and very few answers. Yet, there was enormous reverence for a Creator and a symbolically rich environment full of stories, art, and compassionate people. As a child and teenager, I also learned from a gay music minister and a female priest and director of Christian education. This was a welcoming world for me.

I elected to attend a private faith-based college in the Protestant tradition. In many ways, it was the seriousness with which I pursued spiritual matters that drew me to a place where faith was fully integrated into the academic experience. Every student at my college was required to take two semesters of religion courses, and other courses did not shy away from theological and spiritual questions, especially in the sciences. My in-class experiences were safe venues to explore questions, but the out-of-classroom environment seemed to provide answers rather than entertain questions. The social culture also emphasized particular political narratives, moral codes, and religious rules. In retrospect, this was dizzying. On the one hand, I celebrated that matters of faith were part of the curriculum. On the other hand, the narrowing of God's identity and activity in the world was constraining. Despite what I believe was a nonsupportive culture for broad theological exploration, I am grateful for the kind of education I received. In 1987 when I entered college, I suspect the incorporation of this important aspect of my life and learning may have been even more marginalized had I attended my second college choice—a public institution down the road.

In fact, perhaps it is precisely this sort of scenario that has given rise to greater openness of spiritual life in the public domain. As educators, we know well that students learn in holistic ways. Simply put, to lop off as irrelevant a potentially foundational aspect of a student's worldview does not convey a commitment to sound pedagogy.

The ways in which institutions of higher learning respond to the quest for faith, religion, and spirituality has significant impact on faith development of college students. According to Light (2001), campus leaders "should make a thoughtful, evidence-based, purposeful effort to get *in* each student's way; in fact, shaping a certain kind of campus culture may be the biggest contribution campus leaders can make" (p. 209). Light went on to say:

> A critical role for campus leaders is to "get in the way" of each student, to help the young adult evaluate and re-evaluate his or her choices, always in the spirit of trying to do it better the next time. (p. 210)

Students in Light's (2001) study were quick to point out that only when certain preconditions exist does "the good stuff" actually happen. They indicated that campus leaders can impact the environment in important ways so that diversity strengthens learning (p. 10).

We wanted to learn more about whether or not college "got in the way" of our Virginia Tech students and staff members' faith development. We reached out to colleagues and recent graduates and told them we were writing a book chapter that focused on personal spiritual exploration of students during the college years. We informed them that we were interested in understanding the stories of a few individuals who had traversed a spiritual journey during their college years. We asked them to respond to five questions, only offering as much or as little as desired; much was learned by their personal reflections. Several individuals gladly participated and offered permission to have their stories published. However, we changed participants' names to ensure a level of privacy.

Lauren was born and raised Baptist, and she admitted that she attended church in college because "it was a social scene" and she did not "want to be left out." She also shared that she had "too many questions to fully believe, but was afraid to not believe." Although she had many questions, her church did not welcome her inquisitive exploration nor did she have any "disbelieving role models." Before attending college, Lauren's religion taught her that "everyone who was not a Christian was going to hell." Reflecting on life before college, she felt that she "was deprived of the right to even explore other religions." As Lauren learned more via reading, observing, and asking questions, it became difficult for her to believe the things she had grown up hearing about God and religion. She developed a "new philosophy of a loving God that allowed for more than one path to heaven." She would go to church and try to "twist and mold what was being said into what was learned from books and others." For Lauren, it became harder and harder, so she "quit trying." Lauren still believed in God but did not believe that she needed to go to church to have a relationship with God. As the dissonance between what she was taught and what she was learning grew wider, Lauren decided not to believe in God as she was taught. Today, she does not define herself as religious or spiritual nor does she identify as atheist or agnostic. She believes that it is her "responsibility to treat everyone well" and that she "must do something good while here." She has "faith in people, science, nature, and community."

Like Lauren, Kelly's faith journey prior to attending college was not "very individualized to a personal experience." She used "a lot of 'Christian speak' without thinking about the depth of the meaning." Kelly was a self-identified "black-and-white thinker when it came to faith and spirituality" as it "was more defined within a box of Christian church culture." But opportunities to engage in higher learning were shaping her, especially as her faculty asked challenging questions and she learned that it was "okay to not have the 'right' answer." She was majoring in business but loathed accounting and found herself really enjoying a literature course on the Bible. Her faculty provided a classroom environment where curiosity was welcomed. This rocked her Sunday school upbringing, "where it was best to have the 'right' answers" and "where when you didn't know, you just needed to trust your faith, and not research further." This unique freedom to learn and the fear she would not get this opportunity again inspired her to change her major from business to religion.

In one class, "a most pivotal academic experience," Kelly was told that the goal of the class was to strip away all of what she believed before, then build back her personalized theological system or belief. She acknowledged "writing papers for this class was the most mentally and emotionally challenging task of my collegiate work." This freedom to learn, deconstruct, and reconstruct provided her with "a total reframe to view God as someone who was not just reverent, but relatable." Although Kelly had a new and solid theological framework, it was mightily challenged her senior year when one of her best friends was killed in a car accident. Once again, faculty encouraged her to think deeply about the dissonance. As such, Kelly wrote her capstone paper on the paradox of faith and doubt, which served as a "reflective and healing assignment." Kelly reflected that her spirituality moved from a "black-and-white dualistic perspective to a dynamic of thinking in both/ and/or ways." Her spirituality grew to accommodate her "desire to combine faith with intellect."

For Taylor the term *spirituality* was troubling. Although he believes that one can have a relationship with a spiritual being absent of the institution of religion, he believes "the overwhelming majority of people who say this . . . are at a crossroads where they're finding it hard to have a faith for whatever reason, but aren't strong enough to admit they don't believe." Taylor came to college "with every intention of finding a religious or spiritual group to be a part of." He said, "At that time in my life I was frankly grasping for anything that would convince me my faith was real." He described his spirituality at the beginning of college as "shaky and unstable at best." His faith came from a place of "absolute strength" supported by every member of his family and all of his friends. He said that "it was only because I had begun to think about it and do some homework and analyze, and, yes, judge, those that I was associating with in these spiritual circles that it began to unravel." Taylor was strongly encouraged to find a faith group at college, but he did not find one. He said that he saw "two kinds of people in these groups: either kids with everything going for them or kids with nearly nothing who came from hardship." For Taylor, "being real average" meant he "didn't fit."

Then the April 16, 2007, massacre at Virginia Tech happened, and Taylor began to think more and more objectively about all of it. He then "stumbled across a video and it sort of made sense after that." Taylor said that the turning point for him was "wanting to make faith work." Taylor acknowledged that there was quite a bit of anger that emerged for him when discussing issues of spirituality. He was clear, however, that he was not "angry about my journey and the result but rather angry about the rest of the followers who are in it blindly and using it as excuses for things they don't understand."

Lauren, Kelly, and Taylor have compelling stories about their meaning-making journeys precollege and how they came to the university actively seeking opportunities to affirm or denounce what they believed; they also had major life events happen while in college, which they sought to better understand on a spiritual level. They, like other students, will become ever more sophisticated, committed, and deeply questioning as they are supported by campus professionals.

For those of us working with students such as Lauren, Kelly, and Taylor, one appropriate question is, "What are some of the ways that campus leaders have gotten 'in the way' of students?" Another is, "What conditions are necessary in order for 'the good stuff' to emerge?" I (Frank) wrote that "students appear especially open to big questions and life learning in the midst of tragedy, and when these moments occur, making space to engage is important" (Shushok, 2010, p. 19); this is a time when the good stuff can emerge. I explored the ways unfortunate times can impact student learning. I said:

> Tragedy is a special, unique and powerful time to invite students to learn about some of the most important questions related to living: Who are we? Why are we here? How can we make the world more humane and just? (2010, p. 20)

Virginia Tech got in the way after the April 16, 2007, tragedy, the very one that clearly impacted Taylor's spiritual journey. I (Shushok, 2010) recollected a brief encounter with another student that caught my attention when the student said:

> The whole thing made me question the purpose of my life. . . . Thank goodness that I had good friends and faculty to help think through these things with me. I changed my major, changed my relationships, changed my priorities, and I started taking the Virginia Tech mission, "that I may serve," to heart. (p. 19)

This Virginia Tech experience clearly brought about a national review of safety and risk management policies and, as important, the community allowed for the bigger questions of life to take hold.

Campus response encouraged growth and learning in a variety of ways. The community got in the way by holding a candlelight vigil to reflect, pray, meditate, and seek solidarity. Virginia Tech also responded by placing a permanent memorial in a prominent place on campus; it is a place where people can visit to pay respects, pray, reflect, and offer remembrances for those deceased and for those who survived. A student in the honors program was killed in the massacre, and this loss was enormous. Students retreated to their honors community, where "mentors in the honors house facilitated meaningful dialogue, afforded uncanny care, and perhaps unwittingly, took advantage of the learning window afforded by unfortunate times" (Shushok, 2010, p. 21). Other students started Activelycaring4people.org as a way to elevate acts of kindness and care, to live out the university motto of *Ut Prosim* (That I may serve). When a community member is witnessed performing a humane act, he or she is offered a green wristband as a way to show gratitude for this kindness. The recipient is asked to "pay it forward" by offering this wristband to the next person he or she experiences as kind. And still the campus got in the way via a service-learning experience where community members volunteered their time for "32 for 32," 32 hours of community service in memory of the 32 victims of the April 16 tragedy. This "32 for 32" was a foundational program that ultimately helped give birth to Virginia Tech's VT Engage: The Community Learning Collaborative office. Today, this office continues to help Virginia Tech get in the way of students' meaning making.

Goals of VT Engage are to "foster authentic civic partnerships by connecting the human and intellectual capital of Virginia Tech with local and global publics" and to "cultivate social and ethical responsibility through engaged learning and reflection" (Virginia Polytechnic Institute and State University, 2014, paras. 1–2). Although this office hosts many service immersion programs, staff decided to facilitate a particular experience in the Dominican Republic with a focus on learning about education and training for at-risk youth as an international social issue and fostering inclusive, interfaith dialogue and reflection around service and social justice. In January 2013, 19 students and faculty embarked on an interfaith service-learning experience with intentionally structured, facilitated conversations on issues of faith and meaning making. Participants of the Christian, Jewish, and Muslim faiths were represented.

An article in the *Virginia Tech News* described the trip:

> The Virginia Tech delegation designed and carried out daily computer and leadership workshops. They also performed manual labor at a ranch in

the Dominican Republic to prepare a new softball field for the youth . . . Evenings were dedicated to group discussion and reflection on topics such as social justice, poverty, faith, and moral responsibility. (Doss, 2013, paras. 11, 16)

Jake Grohs, associate director of student engagement, said:

We took great care to make this trip as inclusive and meaningful as possible . . . Our core principle when we developed it was that each individual's unique story and perspective holds inspiration and insight for others and that by honoring both our commonalities and our differences, we can embrace the beauty of what it is to be human. (Doss, 2013, para. 20)

Students were impacted deeply by this experience because Virginia Tech decided to get in the way and fostered an opportunity for transformative learning to happen. Light (2001) recommended specific ways that campuses can get in students' way. He stated:

In our interviews, student after student has shared stories that cumulatively illustrate an overarching theme, and I want to stress it. The theme is the interplay, the complex interaction, among different parts of campus life. Learning can be enhanced, sometimes dramatically, by activities outside of classes. (p. 210)

Light (2001) went on to state that religious diversity is different than other forms of diversity, given the personal nature of religion and that students learn about religious diversity as they engage this difference outside the classroom more than they do in class discussions. Integrative learning—learning that "engages the students in the systematic exploration of the relationship between their studies of the objective world and the purpose, meaning, limits, and aspirations of their lives" (Palmer, Zajonc, & Scribner, 2010, p. 10)—is a pedagogical approach that gets in the way. Critics of such movements as integrative education (e.g., Fish, 2008) would say that providing conditions for students to seek meaning and purpose in their lives is not the job of universities. However, Palmer et al. (2010) responded to such criticism by saying that the need is so critical, so vital to the future of our world (p. vii), that its realization cannot be "left to chance" (p. 56). We agree.

ENCOURAGING SPIRITUAL EXPLORATION ON CAMPUS—THREE GOOD FIRST STEPS

In Chapter 7 of this volume, Goodman, Wilson, and Nicolazzo suggest several methods for improving and institutionalizing student affairs practices related to spirituality, faith, religion, and life purpose. One of those suggestions, creating new institutional structures and partnerships, may be actualized by following three first steps.

Space and Place

Those who have been afforded the opportunity to study student development theory have likely encountered the depth of scholarship that emphasizes the influence of the physical environment on human behavior. Person–environment theories have long posited that human behavior is a function of the interaction between the person and the environment. Campus ecology approaches to student development emerged from a more general movement called social ecology (Banning & Kaiser, 1974; Moos, 1986; Strange & Banning, 2001). In short, these theories of interactionism suggest that both positive and dysfunctional student behavior, and thus learning, are best understood when the environment is included in the equation. These theories, therefore, emphasize creating campus environments that recognize and support students as physical, mental, social, and spiritual beings.

Perhaps Chapman (2006) captured this sentiment best when he wrote, "The campus is a tapestry of sensory, cognitive, and intellectual experiences that are meaningful in and of themselves, and that can profoundly reinforce one another" (p. xxiv). Every university has a story to tell about itself, and, whether knowingly or unknowingly, the architecture and artifacts speak loudly into the experiences each student creates for themselves. Strange and Banning (2001), who have thoughtfully summarized the research about the impact of the physical environment, poignantly wrote, "Whether we want them to or not, or whether we understand them or not, educational environments do exert an impact on students" (p. 4). If welcoming exploration of spirituality, faith, religion, and life purpose is an aim of a campus community, the environment is the best place to begin offering signals that this aspect of student life is welcome.

In a culture where the pace of student life and the influence of technology are overwhelming, offering places for reflection, prayer, and interfaith dialogue is a reasonable first step toward inviting students to listen to their lives in new ways. For some campuses, few designated spaces are intentionally designed as sacred or reserved places for quiet moments. Providing opportunities in the physical environment to invite engagement in spiritual life sends an almost audible voice welcoming students to explore this dimension. Spiritually laden architecture, for example, is readily apparent when touring the residential colleges of Oxford and Cambridge, including space for meditation, reflection, and prayer. Even amid an English higher education culture that is fundamentally secular, contemporary residential colleges at Oxford and Cambridge preserve chapels and other environmental details related to spiritual growth. More recently, the University at Albany opened Chapel House, an "interfaith meditation and prayer room available to all students, faculty and staff on campus for a tranquil setting to pray and meditate" (www.albanyinterfaithcenter. org). The room is available for people of all religions and also for those without a practiced religion. The meditation room has sacred texts and objects from the five major world religions: Buddhism, Christianity, Hinduism, Islam, and Judaism. The Addir Interfaith Program at Massachusetts Institute of Technology and the Pasquerilla Spiritual Center at Pennsylvania State University (http://studentaffairs.psu.edu/spiritual) provide additional examples of institutions making strong commitments to student spiritual life.

On some campuses, movement away from a particular religious tradition has provided an opportunity to broaden the mission of the space. At Mount Holyoke College, Abbey Sanctuary (www.mtholyoke.edu/religiouslife /interfaith_sanctuary) was once a small Christian prayer chapel, for which students, staff, and faculty implemented a two-year, community-wide plan and converted the structure to serve a more inclusive future. The following regarding Abbey Interfaith Sanctuary can be found on its website:

> Open to students of all faith backgrounds (and no faith as well) for reflection, journal writing, meditation, and walking the sacred labyrinth . . . Abbey Interfaith Sanctuary holds sacred objects and texts from the different faith groups represented on campus. Each week, Abbey Interfaith Sanctuary is filled with the words, songs, and shared silence of the Mindfulness Meditation, the Unitarian Universalists service and many informal visits by individuals and groups in search of a peaceful moment away from the busyness of everyday life. (Mount Holyoke College, 2014, para. 1)

If the mission of an institution is to educate "the whole student" (NASPA & ACPA, 2004, p. 3), including spiritual life, opportunities to create spaces that represent such priorities should become as readily apparent as spaces that celebrate the intellectual and physical lives of students. Given that students spend most of their time outside the classroom, faculty and staff members face the inevitable question, "In what spaces, other than formal chapels or sanctuaries, can we meet students where they are, with convenient locations for reflection and quiet?"

Certainly the residence hall presents options for on-campus residents, who most often share living and study space with others, sometimes in a noisy environment full of bustle and interpersonal activity. A quiet reflection lounge area in a more isolated area of a residence hall or community can provide students such a place to center their thinking without leaving the vicinity of their rooms—important for self-imposed time-outs from stress, interpersonal tensions, or loss of focus as well as deeper inquiry. These spaces can be designed during new construction or incorporated into renovations in the planning stages.

Student centers, traditionally centers of recreation, art, and study, can also include quiet non-study-lounge spaces for reflection and renewal. Whereas on-campus students can at least retreat to their rooms as a base of operations, off-campus residents often use the student center as their base for refreshments, study breaks, and group projects between classes, and having a quiet zone set aside in the floor plan can provide sanctuary for introspection, with unscheduled time for spontaneous visits or programmed opportunities for group discussions around issues of the spirit and meaning making.

Finally, the outdoor environment can and should complement inside sacred places, with gardens, trees, shrubs, and flowers; benches and tables; low walls for seating; and walking paths strategically designed to provide way stations in the thoroughfares of sidewalks traveled by students and staff between classes and appointments. While working at Davidson College, I (Patty) supported the construction of a labyrinth: "an archetype, a divine imprint, found in most religious traditions in various forms around the world" (Artress, n.d., p. 3). It was placed on campus as a way to encourage meditative walking, quiet space, and a deeper connection. Nature can provide the backdrop for an individual's search for serenity or a quiet place for groups to meet, talk, or even listen to music designed to decompress tension and promote reflection.

It should be noted here that a strongly emerging focus of student affairs professionals across all types of institutions is the integration of learning opportunities into the physical spaces as well as the curricula and programming for students outside the classroom or lab. This trend emphasizes collaboration between academic and student affairs educators as they establish geographical locations, curricula, and programming opportunities for the education of the whole person. In this case, locales and intentional opportunities for students' discovery and deep reflection, discussions, and civilized debates in the area of spiritual exploration and development are as critical as other elements of student development and are best expressed in collaboratively designed and implemented spaces that directly address these needs.

People and Roles

Physical space, of course, is but one element of the campus ecology formula for creating dynamic learning environments. The people and the roles they play also interact intricately in the equation. At Virginia Tech, student affairs staff realized that one of the most underutilized resources was the committed and diverse cadre of campus ministers and spiritual leaders working with students; people in these roles had not been fully invited into the infrastructure of university life. By inviting these professionals to serve on student affairs committees, attend university-wide celebrations and events, and collaborate in the collective work of caring for students, Virginia Tech bolstered a sense of commitment to student spiritual life. The most important outcome, however, was the recognition by students of this increased interaction. Students discerned this increase in collaboration and many of them expressed their appreciation that these efforts conveyed a belief that the university respects, appreciates, and celebrates spiritual life. The Virginia Tech Dean of Students Office also regularly convenes an interfaith council to strengthen relationships among clergy and university faculty and staff.

Whereas many private institutions have been more likely to hire a range of personnel to serve students in chaplaincy, ranging from religious traditions to Stanford's newly hired humanist chaplain, public institutions have been more reserved in this practice. Still, there are examples of public institutions like the University of Maryland–College Park, which provides physical space for chaplains in the interfaith Memorial Chapel (http://thestamp .umd.edu/engagement/memorial_chapel). "The chaplains, supported by and representing their faith communities, serve their faith traditions while demonstrating a unity that contributes to the rich diversity and quality of life at the University and in the community" (University of Maryland, n.d., para. 1), modeling the type of peaceful acceptance and respect that is possible among faith traditions. Similarly, while working at the University of Maryland–Baltimore County, a university without a campus chapel or faith centers adjacent to campus, I (Patty) worked to create an Interfaith Center on campus (http://osl.umbc.edu/diversity/interfaith/). Using a vacated space in the heart of the campus, a community space with offices and open areas for gathering and meeting was opened for faith leaders and students. The next step may be for public institutions to create and maintain a permanently staffed position that serves as a coordinating entity for spiritual life. Using the word *spiritual* in the title again serves as an outward symbol of an inherent value for spiritual lives of students.

In addition to serving the day-to-day spiritual needs of students and creating a continuity of available services, the value of such unified efforts truly shines forth in the times that crises strike campuses, whether the community is hit by violence, accident, or natural disasters. The fact that the university is already positioned for discussion and support for students' (and staff members') spiritual well-being provides a strong infrastructure through which to react to the event and begin the process of healing and returning to a sense of normalcy, safety, and pursuit of mission.

Conversation and Community

Once educators in an institution have made a commitment to bring the concepts of spirituality, faith, religion, and life purpose forward into full view and have considered physical spaces and staffing levels that are available and appropriate to the effort as discussed above, what does the end product look like to students, parents, and the public? How does an institution present this often-sensitive subject so that the real intent of the effort is clear and is perceived as proper vis-à-vis the mission of the university? How are students alerted that these issues are relevant to them? It is certain that these issues cannot be satisfactorily addressed unless they are effectively positioned in the unique context in which each institution operates.

Although it seems simplistic, the educators collaborating toward the outcomes must understand the specific outcomes and have a common language in which these outcomes can be discussed. For example, the division of student affairs, academic colleagues, and participating students at Virginia Tech developed five specific student learning outcomes—goals that each student should have reached as a result of their college experience. These goals, not directly reflected by a university degree, address the need for lifelong curiosity and learning, the development of self-understanding and integrity, the practice of civility, the need for a life of courageous leadership, and dedication to a life of service to others. These goals are not meant to replace the university mission, but to "flesh it out," to put it in terms with which anyone can participate. These Aspirations for Student Learning are widely disseminated on the division's web page, in brochures provided to incoming students, and in the materials used in daily operations across the division. Campus ministers and clergy have embraced the aspirations. They have become integral to discussions of resource allocation, program development, and student interventions. It is not unusual to hear the question, "How does this (idea, proposal, asset) fit within the Aspirations for Student Learning?" Certainly, aspects of spiritual development fit well into all these goals and complement the outcomes, but spiritual development alone was not the sole intent for developing these aspirations. The intent was, in common terms, the true education of the whole person.

Each university will have its own mission and guiding principles, but academic and student affairs colleagues in that institution should strive to develop a language through which they can help students make it their own, by defining the intent of these discussions of and about the spirit and meaning making. Students want to know why a subject is relevant to them directly, and they want to know before they get involved that there will be benefits from participating in the work involved in understanding the subject. For secular institutions not pursuing a particular religious agenda or platform, a presentation of clear language and intent in written and verbal information becomes even more important. Once students begin to spend time reflecting, journaling, and participating in quality informal and intentionally designed discussions of spiritual issues and they can report positive experiences, other students will be encouraged to join the discussion. To confirm this, we need only look at the most popular classes taught by professors at our own institutions; often these classes are standing room only and include students from many different majors. The classes may be history, philosophy, ecology, or ethics, but some inherent value of what the instructor has to say has reached through the words of the course descriptions and found students where they live.

The concept of marketing also fits within the context of the discussion of spiritual and meaning-making pursuits. Although the term *marketing* may not seem congruent with the subject matter, communication of the intent (such as the Aspirations for Student Learning), as well as the who-what-when-where-why-how for specific opportunities such as panel discussions, roundtables, exercises, speakers, and so on, must be communicated. Social networking is a valuable tool; although more open invitations might be issued earlier in the academic year, later electronic communications might be more limited to those who opt in to distribution lists. The same channels of communication that work for programs on other topics such as study skills or yoga are valid; programs concerning spiritual issues should be listed along with all other programming as an option.

Certainly, some guidelines emerge from the examples and discussions above. Colleagues must work as a team, with the highest dedication to keeping the benefit of individual students and the student body in mind. The personal context for each student must be respected as they balance academics and perhaps work, student organization involvement, and service-learning with their attempts to integrate and understand their personal history, family, faith background, and core belief system. They must not face condemnation, even when their deliberations lead them to face doubts or disillusionment or euphoria that has not yet been challenged. They must be encouraged to talk about these phases of the self-discovery and development process, so that those who are truly facing significant crises at some point in their college careers can seek aid and receive guidance as appropriate or necessary.

Another aspect of meeting the spiritual needs of the community of students is the feeling of inclusion among all students in the process. This is easier on the surface in the residence hall environment than it is for off-campus students, but even in the confines of the residence halls, some students intentionally or unintentionally become isolated. One of the observations of educators over the last two decades is that isolation and lack of feeling connected, spiritually as well as emotionally or interpersonally, can have negative outcomes in terms of campus violence, harm to oneself, and academic failure (Shushok, 2008). Although we strive to use the same language to describe our mission to integrate spiritual awareness and growth among students, there are many different ways to reach students. The most effective way to reach out and include students who might otherwise be isolated are repeated invitations by other students, or faculty and staff mentors, to be a part of the hall or learning community.

Of course, although it is vital that every member of the community has the opportunity to be involved in any type of student learning, we must recognize and respect that a significant number of students will opt out of these efforts for many different reasons. Some students may start out participating and change their minds, or never engage to begin with, and that is the student's absolute right. Particularly in public institutions, the academic mission and the general success of students in terms of finding employment, recruitment and retention, research, and identification as alumni are of public interest. Just as students pursue many different interests in college—intra-murals, leadership opportunities, undergraduate or graduate research—they are also at different stages of personal development. Exploration of the spiritual domain is part of critical holistic development and should be a choice we all make (both students and educators), if together we understand our greatest mission to be the utmost development of human potential.

REFERENCES

Artress, L. (n.d.). *Lauren Artress: Speaker, author, spiritual director.* Retrieved from http://www.laurenartress.com/wp-content/uploads/2011/04/speakers_packet_LAnewcnsV2.pdf

Asimov, N. (2012, December 22). Stanford gets a chaplain for atheists. *San Francisco Chronicle.* Retrieved from http://www.sfgate.com/news/article/Stanford-gets-a-chaplain-for-atheists-4139991.php

Astin, A. W., Astin, H. S., & Lindholm, J. A. (2011). *Cultivating the spirit: How college can enhance students' inner lives.* San Francisco: Jossey-Bass.

Banning, J. H., & Kaiser, L. (1974). An ecological perspective and model for campus design. *Personnel and Guidance Journal, 52,* 370–375.

Chapman, P. M. (2006). *American places: In search of the twenty-first century campus.* Westport, CT: Praeger.

Cowling, T. K. (2002). *How to make the most of your college experience.* Retrieved from http://www.familytlc.net/college_experience.html

Doss, C. (2013, March 22). Students explore faith, service, learning in international immersion experience. *Virginia Tech News.* Retrieved from http://vtnews.vt.edu/articles/2013/03/032213-outreach-interfaith.html

Elon University. (n.d.). *Truitt Center for Religious and Spiritual Life.* Retrieved from http://www.elon.edu/e-web/students/religious_life/

Fish, S. (2008). *Save the world on your own time.* New York: Oxford University Press.

Florida State University. (2012). *Spiritual life project at The Florida State University.* Retrieved from http://slp.fsu.edu/

Jacobsen, D., & Jacobsen, R. H. (2012). *No longer invisible: Religion in university education.* Oxford: Oxford University Press.

Light, R. J. (2001). *Making the most of college: Students speak their minds.* Cambridge, MA: Harvard University Press.

Minasian, S. A. (2010, November 14). Spiritual life on campus: Agreeing to disagree. *Chronicle of Higher Education.* Retrieved from http://chronicle.com/article/Spiritual-Life-on-Campus-/125328/

Moos, R. H. (1986). *The human context: Environmental determinants of behavior.* Malabar, FL: Krieger.

Mount Holyoke College. (2014). *Abbey Interfaith Sanctuary.* Retrieved from https://www.mtholyoke.edu/religiouslife/interfaith_sanctuary

National Association of Student Personnel Administrators & American College Personnel Association. (2004). *Learning reconsidered.* Washington, DC: Authors.

Palmer, P. J., Zajonc, A., & Scribner, M. (2010). *The heart of higher education: A call to renewal.* San Francisco: Jossey-Bass.

Paredes-Collins, K. (2012). Thriving in students of color on predominantly white campuses: A divergent path? In L. A. Schreiner, M. C. Lewis, & D. D. Nelson (Eds.), *Thriving in transitions: A research-based approach to college success* (pp. 65–85). Columbia, SC: National Resource Center for the First-Year Experience.

Parks, S. D. (2000). *Big questions, worthy dreams: Mentoring young adults in their search for meaning, purpose and faith.* San Francisco: Jossey-Bass.

Pew Forum on Religion & Public Life. (2009). *U.S. religious landscape survey.* Washington, DC: Author.

Shushok, F., Jr. (2008). Learning friendship: The indispensable basis of a good society. *About Campus, 13*(3), 19–26.

Shushok, F., Jr. (2010). When good people happen to bad things: Student learning in unfortunate times. *About Campus, 15*(1), 18–23.

Shushok, F., Jr. (2011). Spiritual and moral friendships: How campuses can encourage a search for meaning and purpose. *Journal of College and Character, 12*(4). doi: 10.2202/1940-1639.1822

Smith, C., & Snell, P. (2009). *Souls in transition: The religious & spiritual lives of emerging young adults.* New York: Oxford University Press.

Strange, C. C., & Banning, J. H. (2001). *Educating by design: Creating campus learning environments that work.* San Francisco: Jossey-Bass.

University of Maryland. (n.d.). *Chaplains.* Retrieved from http://thestamp.umd.edu/engagement/memorial_chapel/chaplains

University of Massachusetts–Amherst. (2011). *Religious and spiritual life.* Retrieved from http://www.umass.edu/religious_affairs/

Virginia Polytechnic Institute and State University. (2014). *Mission & core values.* Retrieved from http://www.engage.vt.edu/mission/

9

Conclusions

Jenny L. Small

I N THE INTRODUCTION TO this book, I raised the following questions: (a) what has enabled the topic of spirituality, faith, religion, and life purpose to reach a "tipping point" (Gladwell, 2000) in student affairs research and practice, so that it has become an acceptable, even integral, aspect of the field; and (b) how scholars and practitioners can build on this success for the future. Throughout the subsequent chapters, faculty members, practitioners, graduate students, and leaders in professional associations have contributed to answering these questions. I have encouraged the authors to speculate, given that they are experts in this area of research and practice. In this conclusion, I synthesize their arguments and share both a collective hypothesis and a way forward in our work in the field of higher education student affairs. As with the overall organization of the book, I examine three broad categories of influence: research, professional associations, and practice. I also consider which events were intentionally caused and which were external, even uncontrollable. And although this book has touched on areas of higher education that fall outside the purview of student affairs, such as curriculum and hiring practices, student affairs remains the focus of this chapter's analysis.

A TIMELINE OF CHANGE

I have chosen to frame this final analysis around a timeline of key events, divided into three time periods: (a) a period of initial exploration, from 1997

162

to 2001; (b) a period of heightened, urgent focus, from 2002 to 2007; and (c) a period of sustained and expanded interest, from 2008 through the preparation of this book in 2013. Within each period fall the three major areas of internal influence (research, professional associations, and practice), as well as the external. Two notes of caution: First, changes in on-campus practice are difficult to measure. Resources such as Lindholm, Millora, Schwartz, and Spinosa's (2011) guidebook of practices, although useful, have not tended to trace the development of these practices over time. Second, this timeline should not imply that there was no interest in the topic before 1997. For example, Parks (1986) published her first major book over a decade prior, and Florida State University began hosting the Institute on College Student Values in 1991 (Florida State University, 2012). However, change began to become nationally visible with the publications of the late 1990s.

Initial Exploration: 1997–2001

The period of initial exploration, beginning slightly more than a decade and a half ago, saw the awakening (or reawakening) of student affairs professionals' interest in matters of spirituality, faith, religion, and life purpose. As discussed throughout this book, three publications during this time were critical in kick-starting the conversation about meaning making as a valid topics in student affairs, those by Schafer (1997), Temkin and Evans (1998), and Love and Talbot (1999). Parks's (2000) highly influential second book was released shortly afterward, and it still remains a rallying point for student affairs work around spirituality, faith, religion, and life purpose. This period of initial exploration also saw some of the early calls for religious pluralism to be seen as an educational imperative. Works by Kazanjian and Lawrence (2000), Nash (2001), and Jablonski (2001), to name a few, remain touchstones in the conversation.

The content of scholarship changed, as well. In their major review of the research between the years of 1989 and 2002, Pascarella and Terenzini (2005) noted that research in this area had begun to become more targeted in its approach, pointing toward "increases or refinements in students' religious values during college" (p. 335). Although the authors cautioned that studies during this time period were able to do little more than suggest this finding, it represented a major contradiction from previous assumptions that students' religiosity in fact declined during the college years. This abrupt change in scholars' understanding of college student religiosity undoubtedly opened the doors to others' interest in studying this topic.

On the other hand, during these early years of exploration, the major student affairs professional associations were fairly quiet, with little coordinated organization around topics of meaning making. Others, however, were already taking action, forming what would later become key partners for student affairs practitioners. The fledgling Interfaith Youth Core (IFYC) was established in 1999 (Patel, 2007). The Secular Student Alliance was founded in 2000 (Secular Student Alliance, 2006). Elsewhere in education, the Spirituality and Education Special Interest Group was founded within the American Educational Research Association in 2001 (Nelson, 2010). And Jacobsen and Jacobsen (2012) identified the 1998 "Education as Transformation: Religious Pluralism, Spirituality, and Higher Education" conference at Wellesley College as the signal of "a sea change" (p. 6). Despite all the positive developments led by student affairs associations in the years following (many of which have been noted throughout this book), properly speaking, these organizations were comparatively late to the game.

Urgent Focus: 2002–2007

The world was changed by the terrorist attacks of September 11, 2001. This major historical event impacted colleges and universities to a great degree, including the ways college and university students, staff, and faculty members addressed issues of religious and secular diversity. This marked a period of urgent focus starting in 2002 just after the attacks, when considering these topics no longer seemed tangential or secondary.

The most influential body of research on the topic during this time period—and continuing to the present—was the Higher Education in Research Institute's (HERI) major Spirituality in Higher Education study (HERI, 2005). Directed by Alexander Astin, Helen Astin, and Jennifer Lindholm, highly regarded leaders in the field, this study took a national data set and examined it in new ways: through a variety of spirituality and religion measures and across many religious affiliations, states of nonaffiliation, and specific denominations. This took the research well beyond universal theories of faith development, emphasizing the particularities inherent in divergent belief systems. The data set also enabled new kinds of studies, such as an examination of nonmajority worldviews that did not compare the students against a Christian majority sample (Bryant, 2006).

The HERI study was not the only national study on religion and spirituality in young people to appear during this time period. The National Study of Youth and Religion (NSYR) released its first volume of results in 2005

(Smith & Denton, 2005), using a sociological lens to trace teenagers' understandings of religion and spirituality. Although not as frequently discussed in *Making Meaning*, the NSYR is a longitudinal study that continues to this day, offering rich findings about these teens as they have become college students and young adults. It introduced the critical concept of *moralistic therapeutic deism*, which Smith and Denton indicated "appears to have established a significant foothold among very many contemporary U.S. teenagers" (p. 262). It is defined as including these beliefs:

1. A God exists who created and orders the world and watches over human life on earth.
2. God wants people to be good, nice, and fair to each other, as taught in the Bible and by most world religions.
3. The central goal of life is to be happy and to feel good about oneself.
4. God does not need to be particularly involved in one's life except when God is needed to resolve a problem.
5. Good people go to heaven when they die. (Smith & Denton, 2005, pp. 162–163)

Moralistic therapeutic deism is also "alive and well among 18- to 23-year-old American youth" (Smith & Snell, 2009, p. 155). It is an idea that continues to be discussed both within academia and in popular media.

As Goodman, Wilson, and Nicolazzo point out in Chapter 7, it is apparent that foundations were highly impactful during this time period. Two in particular had strong roles in supporting these major research studies. The NSYR was funded by the Lilly Endowment (NSYR, n.d.). The Spirituality in Higher Education project was funded by the John Templeton Foundation (HERI, n.d.). National research projects are expensive. At funding amounts of $4 million for just the first four years of the NSYR (Lilly Endowment, 2002, p. 46) and more than $2 million for the HERI study (John Templeton Foundation, 2010), those who sought funding needed to be quite persuasive and also able to find a receptive audience. The Lilly Endowment and the John Templeton Foundation both deserve credit for furthering this work.

As Siner discussed in Chapter 2, research during this time period also began to push against the notion of one universal, Christian path for spiritual development, with notable publications on atheists' (Nash, 2003) and Muslims' worldviews (Peek, 2005). This research represents a major shift away from the dominant theories of faith development, those of Fowler (1981) and Parks (1986, 2000). Additionally, the notion of Christian privilege in higher education became mainstream, with Schlosser's (2003) highly influential publication on the topic further underscoring the notion that students of different religious and nonreligious backgrounds do not all experience the world in the same way. Early studies of intersectionalities (e.g., Watt, 2003) between elements of identity began to delve further into developmental complexities. Finally (although I have chosen to identify this period of urgent focus as beginning in 2002, just after the September 2001 historical events), Stewart's analysis in Chapter 5 clearly shows a more than tripling in the total number of research articles published in student affairs journals about these topics between 2004 and 2008, as compared with 1997 to 2003. Nelson (2010) noted a similar trend in related papers presented at the annual conference of the American Educational Research Association, rising from 17 in 2001 to 74 in 2007 (p. 67).

Beyond the upward publication trend, two critical advances occurred during this time period within student affairs professional associations. NASPA's Spirituality and Religion in Higher Education knowledge community was founded in 2003, and an ACPA conference on spirituality, held in 2006 at the University of Vermont, was a critical precursor to a similar group being formed within this association.

Expanded Interest: 2008–2013

Seven years after religious and secular diversity became a crucial topic of consideration on college campuses, the immediate urgency had faded. Taking the place of that urgency was a sense of deliberate, intentional commitment, one not necessarily sparked by dramatic world events but instead sustained by the deep dedication of students, practitioners, and scholars. One outcome of this dedication was the formation of ACPA's Commission for Spirituality, Faith, Religion, and Meaning (CSFRM) in 2009. Among the CSFRM's first major undertakings was to address the lack of comprehensive competencies for student affairs faculty and practitioners interested in addressing meaning making needs in the field. The resulting document, "The Role of Student Affairs in Promoting Religious and Secular Pluralism and Interfaith Cooperation," containing a description of "The Proposed Student Affairs Competency Model for Addressing Spirituality, Secularism, Religious Pluralism, and Interfaith Cooperation" (Kocet & Stewart, 2011), paved the way for best practices throughout student affairs.

As thoroughly recounted in Chapters 7 and 8, campus-based approaches to meaning making have expanded at a rapid pace during the past five years.

The programs described in these chapters have almost entirely been developed during this time period. At least 10 articles since 2011 have described how individual institutions have created multifaith spaces on their campuses and/or have offered advice to others on how to do so (e.g., Chambers, 2011; Johnson & Laurence, 2012; Karlin-Neumann & Sanders, 2013; Sapp, 2013), establishing a clear publication niche. Practice in the field is also now expanding beyond notions of Christian privilege to consider the broader notion of spiritual privilege, in which those who identify spiritually receive advantages over the nonspiritual and those who identify as secular and/or atheist. In the practice arena, this has resulted in a few institutions hiring chaplains for atheist students (Asimov, 2012). Authors are also offering advice for practitioners working with religious minority students, such as Hindus (Chander, 2013), who have received little attention in the literature.

Critically, 2011 saw the publication of the final results of HERI's Spirituality in Higher Education study (Astin, Astin, & Lindholm, 2011). According to Google Scholar, the book had already been cited in 83 other publications by the time *Making Meaning* was in preparation. After these leaders came their first followers, many of whom have contributed to *Making Meaning*. With pardon for inadvertently labeling anyone a "nut," the *first follower* concept is described in this way:

> It was the first follower that transformed a lone nut into a leader. There is no movement without the first follower. We're told we all need to be leaders, but that would be really ineffective. The best way to make a movement, if you really care, is to courageously follow and show others how to follow. (Sivers, 2010, paras. 14–17)

Fortunately for the work at hand, there have been people willing to courageously follow, despite the fact that meaning making has not been the most acceptable topic of study within higher education. Many scholars, including new faculty members and graduate students, received grants from HERI in 2009 to analyze the Spirituality in Higher Education project data. This funding was not large, but it was enough to launch or (re)direct many research agendas. It resulted in the culminating volume edited by Bryant Rockenbach and Mayhew (2013). Several of these and other first followers of Astin, Astin, and Lindholm's work became influential players themselves, continuing to do much of the heavy lifting of moving forward this research agenda. Some have contributed to this book. Others appear on the editorial board lists of the *Journal of College and Character* and *Religion & Education*.

Perhaps it is the presence of all these visible names and faces that makes the topics of spirituality, faith, religion, and life purpose feel safe for others to explore. That visibility offers implicit support to those younger faculty who:

> Often seem more attuned to the pluriform religious realities of today and to the need for colleges and universities to pay attention to those realities, but they also feel caught between the demands of "making it" in their disciplines (i.e., satisfying the expectations of older faculty) and "being themselves." (Jacobsen & Jacobsen, 2012, p. 33)

In addition, research since 2008 has expanded both in depth and breadth. The depth saw researchers digging into the components that make up spiritual and religious identities, such as ecumenical worldview (Mayhew, 2012), and differentiating between the worldviews of students from varied religious and secular backgrounds (Small, 2011). The breadth saw researchers including consideration of intersectionalities of religion and spirituality with both sexual identity (Rahman, 2010) and racial identity (Stewart & Lozano, 2009).

COMMON THEMES

In reflecting on this timeline, it strikes me that the events of the last decade and a half can seem almost inevitable. Higher education professionals inhabit a middle ground between the sectarian and the secular, aiming to come to nuanced understandings of individuals' identities and their existences within their environment. More broadly, the American people live in a postmodern age, reclaiming the narratives of ourselves and our communities (Mahoney, Schmalzbauer, & Youniss, 2000). This is the pendulum theory Seifert discussed in Chapter 4.

One could look at events like the conference in Vermont in 2006 or the gathering of researchers at UCLA as a series of unrelated points in time or perhaps individual efforts to make change happen, but one could also look at these things as a sort of a web that is being woven together. Over the years, with more events, more gatherings of researchers, more funding, more colleagues to support this kind of research, professional practice, and association work, everything becomes more tightly woven, with practitioners and researchers having more support and more contributory colleagues. It becomes truly a close network of support and of change, with people who want to do this work and make it happen in higher education.

Yet, this network also did not develop by following a master plan. In analyzing how it came together, I have identified certain themes that transcend the three core areas of research, practice, and professional associations discussed above, themes that grew in their own impact over the last decade and a half.

Virtuous Cycles

It is unquestionable that higher education faculty paved the way for these conversations and that, without their passion and commitment, the road would have been much bumpier. Alexander and Helen Astin, Robert Nash, Carney Strange, Patrick Love, Donna Talbot, Nancy Evans, Arthur Chickering, Jon Dalton—these were some of the people who made the early calls to start the lines of research inquiry, who cultivated new scholars, who convened symposia and conferences, and who participated in the founding of affinity groups within associations. As time passes, additional faculty members (such as Dafina-Lazarus Stewart, Nicholas Bowman, Kathleen Goodman, and Tricia Seifert, all of whom contributed to this volume) who are known for doing this kind of research attract potential graduate students who share similar interests, through their demonstrations that these are permissible research topics.

It is not just well-known faculty who can influence those who come after them. Anyone involved in research and practice or the preparation of new faculty and practitioners can contribute. For example, when I was a doctoral student at the University of Michigan, religion and spirituality were not topics of expertise among my faculty, but to their credit, they supported and encouraged me. I knew of two students before me who had studied this topic, which made it feel safer for me, and I have had many students following me who have reached out to ask about my experience, perhaps feeling safer themselves because of my successful example.

This is the virtuous cycle Lobdell discussed in Chapter 6 that includes graduate preparation programs, new professionals impacting their home campuses, students passing through these more accepting institutions, and professional associations giving their support to the field. It works similarly in training programs for new faculty. All these components yield a more inclusive field of student affairs, broadly speaking. As early as 2001, voice was given to this idea that student affairs preparation programs should attend more closely to graduate students' "periods of transition in life when fundamentals of self identity, relationship with others, and ultimate direction are open to examination and reformation" (Strange, 2001, p. 58). Yet the most recent articles to discuss these trends (e.g., Rogers & Love, 2007; Wiese & Cawthon, 2009) suggest that there is still much work to be done in this area.

Undergraduate students have a particularly important role in these cycles, as research clearly shows their interest in discussing topics related to meaning making (HERI, 2005). As much as faculty members may drive the conversation down through the ranks in their professional preparation classrooms, students impact the conversation up from the other end of the spectrum. There is no research, teaching, or practice on the religious, spiritual, and secular development of college students without the participation of the students themselves.

Inclusion of Diverse Voices

One of the most critical changes in the field has been the growing acceptance of diverse voices in the conversation, both from those of minority religious backgrounds and from those who identify as atheist and/or secular. This includes both the subjects of the research (students) and those conducting the research: faculty members and scholar–practitioners. *Making Meaning* itself is an example of this, with authors' personal stories including backgrounds in Judaism, Paganism, Protestantism, and Catholicism—and those were only the authors who chose to discuss their own narratives within this text. In keeping with the pendulum shift away from the strictly scientific, reason-based view of the world, research on meaning making does not currently require a total separation of the researcher from the subject matter, often intentionally invoking the deeply personal nature of the questions.

The literature body has gained much from this openness. With so many types of students and aspects of their experiences lacking full analysis and description, authors looking to expand their research or discover a new topic to elucidate have plenty of options from which to choose. Journal articles, conference presentations, dissertations: With a research area still continuing to grow, these are open outlets in which graduate students and new scholars could make their mark. With several graduate students and new professionals contributing to *Making Meaning*, this volume demonstrates the openness of the topic.

As well, undergraduate students from religious minority, nonreligious, and atheist backgrounds have also benefited greatly from the desires of practitioners and scholars to create inclusive campus environments (Mayhew & Bryant Rockenbach, 2013). The most substantial change is arguably in the amount of support given to atheist and other secular students, which has grown since

Nash's (2003) critical call for their inclusion over 12 years ago. Continuing to involve atheists and nonreligious people in interfaith dialogues, and expanding their involvement whenever possible, will greatly benefit this population (Stedman, 2012). Their inclusion also benefits students who do identify as religious and/or spiritual, as the intentional language of inclusivity respects all individuals' paths toward inner development (Goodman & Teraguchi, 2008).

None of this is to say that the growth of openness toward atheist and agnostic students has been completely smooth. Certainly it is work that is not yet complete (Soria, Lepkowski, & Weiner, 2013). But the progress thus far does invoke developmental changes within the field of student affairs. Growing pains identified earlier in this book, such as Seifert's (2007) *About Campus* article and Siner's ACPA and NASPA conference presentations, were necessary steps for scholars in the field to go through. Undoubtedly, the pushback received by both of these contributors to make their scholarship more inclusive of atheist voices has had a positive impact. That dialogue helps everyone in the field as we struggle to move forward respectfully and with minds open to learning.

Historical Shifts

Finally, one has to consider the significant impact of historical events on the values held by students, faculty, and staff in higher education. Some of these events, such as the September 11, 2001, attacks and the campus shooting at Virginia Tech discussed in Chapter 8, were abrupt, shocking, and traumatic. They spurred people to immediate changes in thought and action. Attention from the government, such as through the President's Advisory Council on Faith-Based and Neighborhood Partnerships (2010), helps bring positive outcomes out of difficult situations. Other historical shifts, such as the diminishment of the centrality of Christianity at many nonsectarian colleges and universities discussed in Chapter 3, have been gradual but as equally impactful as the abrupt changes. This decentralization of Christianity, happening over a long period of time, in a sense left higher education poised for the dramatic changes ushered in by the occurrences of the 2000s. After this convergence, higher education administrators, faculty, and students can no longer behave as though there is one unified religious voice on their campuses. Citizens at all levels of these institutions know this to be true and desire the means to live authentically within this changed reality.

Interestingly, these historical shifts have helped the field of student affairs to return to its foundations, as when individuals reconsider documents such as the *Student Personnel Point of View* (American Council on Education, 1937, 1949) and its inclusion of the religious, spiritual, and ethical meanings of students' lives. In this regard, student affairs has come full circle, yet arriving in a place it could not have reached without having experienced these historical growing pains.

MOVING FORWARD

As I laid out in the introduction of *Making Meaning*, one of my goals was to offer instruction to others within student affairs wishing to move a topic from the fringes of research and practice to the mainstream. What do the conclusions of this book have to offer? With spirituality, faith, religion, and life purpose, we seem to be very much in an "all of the above" situation. In other words, it was not one or two or even five factors that drove this evolution, but rather the confluence of outside events, people, and funding, snowballing bigger and bigger—all in all, not something that is easily replicable.

But certain noteworthy items stand out, and some of the lessons uncovered by the contributors to this book are transferrable in a variety of situations. Virtuous cycles that include faculty members, graduate students, practitioners, and undergraduates can be cultivated if the committed few are willing to teach the subjects of their passions and promote safe spaces for learning about contested or seemingly less significant ideas. First followers must visibly attach themselves to those leaders others may see as "nuts" (Sivers, 2010), thereby demonstrating that, actually, theirs is an idea worth pursuing. After the first followers, the circle must be dramatically widened to include all diverse voices, even and especially those who push back and demand modifications to fully represent their needs in the conversation. These voices must be heard both on their own merits and within dialogues with those who oppose or merely fail to understand them. Finally, all participants must be willing to capitalize on moments of historical significance. Of course, one would not hope for another event with the impact of September 11 to be required to continue to promote change. But again, not all events are so dramatic or traumatic, and even gradual shifts can be seized on as productive tools.

What is the future of research and practice in student affairs around spirituality, faith, religion, and life purpose? If anything is possible, what outcomes should we reach for? The following represents a sort of wish list of the authors in this volume, consolidated to address research, practice, or student affairs professional associations.

Research Topics

◆ Intersections of religious, spiritual, and secular identities with race, culture, sexual orientation, and other identities
◆ The developmental experiences of students of each religious and secular group, particularly religious minorities and the nonreligious
◆ The developmental experiences of students from different denominations within each religion
◆ How diverse students at varied institutional types experience meaning-making identity development
◆ Empirical validation of as yet only conceptual theories
◆ The impact of participation in programs such as the IFYC on students' identity development

Advances in Practice

◆ Support for professionals' own identity development around meaning making
◆ The end of the public institution defense (see Chapter 7)
◆ The end of privileging spirituality over other forms of meaning making
◆ The creation of structural homes for spirituality, faith, religion, and life purpose within student affairs divisions, including but not limited to official interactions between campus ministers and student affairs staff
◆ The establishment of places for reflection, prayer, and interfaith dialogue on college and university campuses
◆ A common language in which these outcomes can be discussed, perhaps borrowing from the "Proposed Student Affairs Competency Model for Addressing Spirituality, Secularism, Religious Pluralism, and Interfaith Cooperation" (Kocet & Stewart, 2011)

Contributions From Professional Associations

◆ Additional space for professionals to focus on their own inner lives
◆ Assertive influence over the contents of graduate preparation programs
◆ Collaborative partnerships across student affairs professional associations and with other educational associations;
◆ Training and education for student affairs faculty and administrators

CONCLUSION

Personally, I take from all of these recommendations the understanding that there is much important work yet to be done for student affairs to fully embrace spirituality, faith, religion, and life purpose as an integral element of the field. But as Kazanjian (2013) has said, "the discourse about these topics has become an important part of the conversation about education and not just about religion" (p. 103). We have made great progress. As well, none of these recommendations represent a wild or insurmountable leap forward from our current position. Instead they seem to request that faculty, practitioners, and students collectively take the next logical steps, perhaps ushering in a fourth phase of the timeline, which we could label with the hopeful description of *transformation*. We arrived at this moment through a confluence of unplanned outside forces with intentional, driven, internal purposes. We utilized our passions, courage, and leadership skills to capitalize on those moments of opportunity. Many of us acted despite fear of professional criticism or alienation. And higher education is all the better for it. The title of this book served a dual purpose: making meaning (or understanding) of how student affairs enables meaning making among students, faculty, and staff. I believe we now have a greater appreciation of the answers to this question, one that will lead us further along that path to transformation.

REFERENCES

American Council on Education. (1937). *The student personnel point of view.* Washington, DC: Author.

American Council on Education. (1949). *The student personnel point of view.* Washington, DC: Author.

Asimov, N. (2012, December 22). Stanford gets a chaplain for atheists. *San Francisco Chronicle.* Retrieved from http://www.sfgate.com/news/article/Stanford-gets-a-chaplain-for-atheists-4139991.php

Astin, A. W., Astin, H. S., & Lindholm, J. A. (2011). *Cultivating the spirit: How college can enhance students' inner lives.* San Francisco: Jossey-Bass.

Bryant, A. N. (2006). Exploring religious pluralism in higher education: Nonmajority religious perspectives among entering first-year college students. *Religion & Education, 33*(1), 1–25.

Bryant Rockenbach, A., & Mayhew, M. J. (Eds.). (2013). *Spirituality in college students' lives: Translating research into practice.* New York: Routledge.

Chambers, R. (2011). Putting theory to practice at the University of Toronto Multi-Faith Centre. *Developments, 9*(2). Retrieved from http://www.myacpa. org/developments

Chander, V. (2013). A room with a view: Accommodating Hindu religious practice on a college campus. *Journal of College and Character, 14*(2), 105–115. doi:110.1515/jcc-2013-0015

Florida State University. (2012). *Jon C. Dalton Institute on College Student Values: History*. Retrieved from http://studentvalues.fsu.edu/History

Fowler, J. W. (1981). *Stages of faith: The psychology of human development and the quest for meaning.* San Francisco: HarperCollins.

Gladwell, M. (2000). *The tipping point: How little things can make a big difference.* New York: Little, Brown.

Goodman, K. M., & Teraguchi, D. H. (2008). Beyond spirituality: A new framework for educators. *Diversity & Democracy, 11*(1), 10–11.

Higher Education Research Institute. (2005). *The spiritual life of college students: A national study of college students' search for meaning and purpose.* Los Angeles: University of California, Higher Education Research Institute.

Higher Education Research Institute. (n.d.). *Project funding*. Retrieved from http:// www.spirituality.ucla.edu/about/project-funding/

Jablonski, M. A. (Ed.). (2001). The implications of student spirituality for student affairs practice [Special issue]. *New Directions for Student Services, 2001*(95).

Jacobsen, D., & Jacobsen, R. H. (2012). *No longer invisible: Religion in university education.* Oxford: Oxford University Press.

John Templeton Foundation. (2010). *Spirituality in higher education: A national study of college students' search for meaning and purpose*. Retrieved from http:// www.templeton.org/what-we-fund/grants/spirituality-in-higher-education-a-national-study-of-college-students%E2%80%99-search-fo

Johnson, K., & Laurence, P. (2012). Multi-faith religious spaces on college and university campuses. *Religion & Education, 39,* 48–63.

Karlin-Neumann, P., & Sanders, J. (2013). Bringing faith to campus: Religious and spiritual space, time, and practice at Stanford University. *Journal of College and Character, 14*(2), 125–132. doi:110.1515/jcc-2013-0017

Kazanjian, V. (2013). Spiritual practices on college and university campuses: Understanding the concepts—broadening the context. *Journal of College and Character, 14*(2), 97–103. doi:110.1515/jcc-2013-0014

Kazanjian, V. H., & Lawrence, P. L. (Eds.). (2000). *Education as transformation: Religious pluralism, spirituality and a new vision for higher education in America.* New York: Peter Lang.

Kocet, M. M., & Stewart, D. L. (2011). The role of student affairs in promoting religious and secular pluralism and interfaith cooperation. *Journal of College and Character, 12*(1). doi:10.2202/1940-7882.1762

Lilly Endowment. (2002). *Annual report 2002.* Indianapolis, IN: Author.

Lindholm, J. A., Millora, M. L., Schwartz, L. M., & Spinosa, H. S. (2011). *A guidebook of promising practices: Facilitating college students' spiritual development.* Los Angeles: Regents of the University of California.

Love, P., & Talbot, D. (1999). Defining spiritual development: A missing consideration for student affairs. *NASPA Journal, 37,* 361–376.

Mahoney, K. A., Schmalzbauer, J., & Youniss, J. (2000). *Revitalizing religion in the academy: Summary of the evaluation of Lilly Endowment's Initiative on Religion & Higher Education.* Chestnut Hill, MA: Lilly Endowment.

Mayhew, M. J. (2012). A multi-level examination of college and its influence on ecumenical worldview development. *Research in Higher Education, 53,* 282–310.

Mayhew, M. J., & Bryant Rockenbach, A. N. (2013). Achievement or arrest? The influence of campus religious and spiritual climate on students' worldview commitment. *Research in Higher Education, 54,* 63–84.

Nash, R. J. (2001). *Religious pluralism in the academy: Opening the dialogue.* New York: Peter Lang.

Nash, R. J. (2003). Inviting atheists to the table: A modest proposal for higher education. *Religion & Education, 30*(1), 1–23.

National Study of Youth and Religion. (n.d.). *National study of youth and religion.* Retrieved from http://www.youthandreligion.org/

Nelson, J. (2010). The evolving place of research on religion in the American Educational Research Association. *Religion & Education, 37,* 60–86.

Parks, S. D. (1986). *The critical years: The young adult search for a faith to live by.* New York: Harper & Row.

Parks, S. D. (2000). *Big questions, worthy dreams: Mentoring young adults in their search for meaning, purpose and faith.* San Francisco: Jossey-Bass.

Pascarella, E. T., & Terenzini, P. T. (Eds.). (2005). *How college affects students, volume 2: A third decade of research.* San Francisco: Jossey-Bass.

Patel, E. (2007). *Acts of faith: The story of an American Muslim, the struggle for the soul of a generation.* Boston: Beacon Press.

Peek, L. (2005). Becoming Muslim: The development of a religious identity. *Sociology of Religion, 66,* 215–242.

President's Advisory Council on Faith-Based and Neighborhood Partnerships. (2010). *A new era of partnerships: Report of recommendations to the President.* Washington, DC: Author.

Rahman, M. (2010). Queer as intersectionality: Theorizing gay and Muslim identities. *Sociology, 44,* 944–961.

Rogers, J. L., & Love, P. (2007). Exploring the role of spirituality in the preparation of student affairs professionals: Faculty constructions. *Journal of College Student Development, 48,* 90–104.

Sapp, C. L. (2013). A great and towering compromise: Religious practice and space at Duke University. *Journal of College and Character, 14*(2), 117–124. doi:110.1515/jcc-2013-0016

Schafer, W. E. (1997). Religiosity, spirituality, and personal distress among college students. *Journal of College Student Development, 38,* 633–644.

Schlosser, L. Z. (2003). Christian privilege: Breaking a sacred taboo. *Journal of Multicultural Counseling and Development, 31,* 44–51.

Secular Student Alliance. (2006). *A brief history of the Secular Student Alliance.* Retrieved April 7, 2010, from http://www.secularstudents.org/node/154

Seifert, T. (2007). Understanding Christian privilege: Managing the tensions of spiritual plurality. *About Campus, 12*(2), 10–17.

Sivers, D. (2010). *Leadership lessons from dancing guy.* Retrieved from http://sivers.org/ff

Small, J. L. (2011). *Understanding college students' spiritual identities: Different faiths, varied worldviews.* Cresskill, NJ: Hampton Press.

Smith, C., & Denton, M. L. (2005). *Soul searching: The religious and spiritual lives of American teenagers.* New York: Oxford University Press.

Smith, C., & Snell, P. (2009). *Souls in transition: The religious & spiritual lives of emerging young adults.* New York: Oxford University Press.

Soria, K. M., Lepkowski, C. C., & Weiner, B. (2013). Living in the margins: Examining the experiences of atheist undergraduates on campus. *Developments, 11*(2). Retrieved from http://www.myacpa.org/developments

Stedman, C. (2012). *Faitheist: How an atheist found common ground with the religious.* Boston: Beacon Press.

Stewart, D. L., & Lozano, A. (2009). Difficult dialogues at the intersections of race, culture, and religion. *New Directions for Student Services, 2009*(125), 23–31.

Strange, C. C. (2001). Spiritual dimensions of graduate preparation in student affairs. *New Directions for Student Services, 2001*(95), 57–67.

Temkin, L., & Evans, N. (1998). Religion on campus: Suggestions for cooperation between student affairs and campus-based religious organizations. *NASPA Journal, 36,* 61–69.

Watt, S. K. (2003). Come to the river: Using spirituality to cope, resist, and develop identity. *New directions for student services, 2003*(104), 29–40.

Wiese, D., & Cawthon, T. W. (2009). The uniformity of spiritual culture in nine southern student affairs graduate preparation programs. *Journal of College and Character, 10*(7). doi:10.2202/1940-1639.1441

About the Editor and Contributors

EDITOR

JENNY L. SMALL was most recently the research coordinator for the Roche Center for Catholic Education at Boston College. Dr. Small holds a PhD from the Center for the Study of Higher and Postsecondary Education at the University of Michigan, an MA from Teachers College, Columbia University, and a BA from Brandeis University. Her research has focused on the spiritual lives of religiously diverse college students and how students use language to define their identities. Her first book, entitled *Understanding College Students' Spiritual Identities: Different Faiths, Varied Worldviews* (2011), is available from Hampton Press. Dr. Small's work is also available in *Research in Higher Education, Journal of College Student Development, Journal for the Scientific Study of Religion, About Campus,* and *Religion & Education,* and in chapters in edited volumes. She currently serves as the chair of the ACPA Commission for Spirituality, Faith, Religion, and Meaning and as an associate editor of *Journal of College and Character.*

CONTRIBUTORS

NICHOLAS A. BOWMAN is an assistant professor of higher education and student affairs at Bowling Green State University. He has had peer-reviewed articles published in journals such as *Review of Educational Research, Educational Researcher, Personality and Social Psychology Bulletin,* and *Journal for the Scientific Study of Religion.* His research interests include college diversity experiences, religion/worldview on college campuses, assessment of student outcomes, and college student success.

VIVIENNE FELIX, an Education Pioneers Fellow, is a doctoral candidate in the Higher Education Administration program at Bowling Green State University. Felix received her BA in international affairs and English from Lafayette

College, an MS in management from Friends University, and an MA in education from the University of Connecticut. Her research interests include comparative and international education, and access and equity in higher education. She is currently a member of ACPA–College Student Educators International and NASPA–Student Affairs Administrators in Higher Education.

KATHLEEN M. GOODMAN is assistant professor of student affairs in higher education at Miami University (OH). She earned her PhD at the University of Iowa in May 2011. While at Iowa, she was a research assistant at the Center for Research on Undergraduate Education. Prior to that, she held an administrative position at the Association of American Colleges and Universities. Kathy's research and teaching interests include the impact of college experiences on student development; diversity and equity in higher education; spirituality, life purpose, and atheist college students; and incorporating critical perspectives into quantitative research.

SHARON A. LOBDELL is an academic adviser and tutoring services coordinator at the University of Michigan–Dearborn. She received her BA degrees (1996) in psychology and art history from the University of Michigan–Dearborn and her MA degree (1999) in educational leadership from Eastern Michigan University. Her professional interests include working with adult learners and academic support programs. Lobdell is a past chair of the ACPA Commission for Spirituality, Faith, Religion, and Meaning, and she has also served on the Michigan College Association Equity and Inclusion Summit Team. She is a member of ACPA–College Student Educators International, NASPA–Student Affairs Administrators in Higher Education, and the College Reading and Learning Association.

Z NICOLAZZO is a doctoral candidate in the Student Affairs in Higher Education Program at Miami University (OH). Z received hir BA in philosophy from Roger Williams University and an MS in college student personnel from Western Illinois University. Z was a past chair of the ACPA Standing Committee on Men and Masculinities and currently serves as a member of the ACPA *Developments* editorial board. Hir research interests include trans* college students and activism in higher education as well as alternative epistemologies, methodologies, and representations of knowledge.

PATRICIA (PATTY) A. PERILLO serves as the vice president for student affairs and assistant professor of higher education at Virginia Tech. Dr. Perillo provides leadership and oversight for 24 departments and 3,600 employees in the Division of Student Affairs. Prior to her work at Virginia Tech, Patty served as the associate dean of students at Davidson College and the assistant vice president for student affairs at the University of Maryland–Baltimore County. Additional professional experiences include work at the University of Maryland–College Park; State University of New York at the Plattsburgh and Albany campuses; and the University of Delaware. Patty served as the 69th president of ACPA–College Student Educators International. She has received many awards over the years, most notably the ACPA Esther Lloyd-Jones Professional Service Award and the ACPA Diamond Honoree Award for Service to Higher Education. She has been inducted into Phi Kappa Phi, Omicron Delta Kappa, and Phi Alpha Epsilon. Patty holds a doctoral degree from the University of Maryland and her master's and bachelor's degrees from the University of Delaware.

TRICIA A. SEIFERT is assistant professor in the adult and higher education program at Montana State University and is an affiliate faculty member in the higher education program at the Ontario Institute for Studies in Education at the University of Toronto. Her current research examines how postsecondary institutions organize to support student success. She is also interested in how postsecondary experiences assist students in their journeys toward developing a sense of life purpose. Dr. Seifert teaches graduate courses on quantitative research methods and student services in postsecondary institutions.

FRANK SHUSHOK JR. serves as senior associate vice president for student affairs and associate professor of higher education at Virginia Tech, a role he has held since 2009. Frank's writing and research interests focus on student learning and engagement, positive psychology and its influence on student growth and development, honors programs, residential colleges, and approaches to reorganizing colleges and universities to bolster student engagement and learning. He is a frequent contributor to higher education literature. In 2013, Frank was selected to be the fifth executive editor of *About Campus*, a bimonthly magazine dedicated to educators who want to thoughtfully examine the issues, policies, and practices that influence the learning experiences of college students. Previously, Frank served as associate editor for the *Journal of College and University Student Housing* and on the editorial board of the *Journal of Student Affairs Research and Practice*. In 2014, Frank was recognized by ACPA–College Student Educators International as a Diamond Honoree for outstanding and sustained contributions to higher education and to student affairs. In this same year, the Virginia Tech Class of 2015 selected Frank as its sponsor and honoree.

SAM SINER is a residence hall coordinator at the University of Texas at Austin. Sam earned his master's degree in higher education and student affairs from Indiana University–Bloomington, where he published a theory of atheist student identity development that he presented as a sponsored program at ACPA and NASPA. He attended the University of Illinois at Urbana-Champaign and Harvard University. His research interests include spiritual identity development, first-generation college students, honors students, living–learning communities, and student employment learning outcomes.

DAFINA-LAZARUS STEWART is associate professor of higher education and student affairs at Bowling Green State University. Her research, teaching, and professional service, generally focused on issues of diversity and social justice for higher education students and institutions, have included under that umbrella a focus on spiritual development, professional competencies for effectively engaging religious and secular pluralism, and transforming campus climates to be more inclusive and reflective of faith diversity. Dr. Stewart also helped to establish and served as the first chair of the ACPA Commission for Spirituality, Faith, Religion, and Meaning.

KATIE WILSON is the director of the Armstrong Student Center at Miami University (OH), where she also has responsibility for implementing initiatives that support students and faculty in increasing understanding of how to support the development of spirituality, meaning, and purpose, both in and out of the classroom. Dr. Wilson has worked in a wide range of student affairs areas, including student unions, student activities, fraternity and sorority life, leadership programs, community service, multicultural initiatives, and residence life. Katie earned her doctorate degree in educational leadership at the University of Oregon, her master's degree at Miami University, and her bachelor's degree from the University of Virginia.

Index

(Continued from the following page)

Why Aren't We There Yet?

Taking Personal Responsibility for Creating an Inclusive Campus

Edited by Jan Arminio, Vasti Torres, and Raechele L. Pope

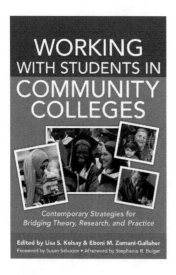

Working With Students in Community Colleges

Contemporary Strategies for Bridging Theory, Research, and Practice

Edited by Lisa S. Kelsay and Eboni M. Zamani-Gallaher

Foreword by Susan Salvador

Afterword by Stephanie R. Bulger

22883 Quicksilver Drive
Sterling, VA 20166-2102

Subscribe to our e-mail alerts: www.Styluspub.com

(Continued from the following page)

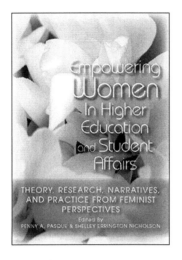

Empowering Women in Higher Education and Student Affairs

Theory, Research, Narratives, and Practice from Feminist Perspectives

Edited by Penny A. Pasque and Shelley Errington Nicholson

Foreword by Linda J. Sax

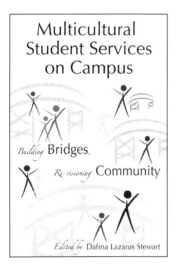

Multicultural Student Services on Campus

Building Bridges, Re-visioning Community

Edited by Dafina Lazarus Stewart

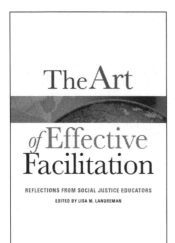
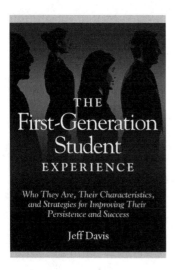